The Democratic Unionist Party

The Democratic Unionist Party

From Protest to Power

Jonathan Tonge, Máire Braniff, Thomas Hennessey,
James W. McAuley, and Sophie A. Whiting

OXFORD
UNIVERSITY PRESS

Great Clarendon Street, Oxford, OX2 6DP,
United Kingdom

Oxford University Press is a department of the University of Oxford.
It furthers the University's objective of excellence in research, scholarship,
and education by publishing worldwide. Oxford is a registered trade mark of
Oxford University Press in the UK and in certain other countries

First Edition published in 2014

Impression: 2

Published in the United States of America by Oxford University Press
198 Madison Avenue, New York, NY 10016, United States of America

British Library Cataloguing in Publication Data
Data available

Library of Congress Control Number: 2014932446

ISBN 978–0–19–870577–2

Printed and bound by
Clays Ltd, St Ives plc

Acknowledgements

The project would not have been possible without the very generous funding offered by the Leverhulme Trust (Research Grant RPG-2012-4033), for which we are extremely grateful. We are also very grateful to all the DUP MPs, MLAs, councillors, and ordinary members (well over one hundred in total) who generously gave their time to be interviewed or participate in focus groups. We especially thank the Rt Hon. Peter Robinson MLA, Richard Bullick, Philip Weir, Councillor Lee Reynolds, and the DUP HQ staff at Dundela Avenue, who all facilitated access to the party in various ways. They may agree or disagree with our conclusions, but without access from the party to its members, those verdicts would have been impossible to draw.

Dr Raul Gomez Martinez proved to be a brilliant research assistant on the project from the outset and we are indebted for his input. The librarians in the Northern Ireland Political Collection in the Linen Hall Library in Belfast were outstanding, as ever. We are also indebted to our own university librarians for their excellent assistance. Dominic Byatt at Oxford University Press has been very supportive.

We are very grateful to our families for their forbearance during long absences in Northern Ireland (and when back home...) in conducting the research and writing up of the project.

Finally, as tends to still be the case in Northern Ireland, the background of the authors may be checked out to see if potential bias can somehow be found. For the record, we contain a mixture of Protestant, Catholic, and Dissenter, proof that all can get along (usually). We won't say which one is which.

Contents

List of Tables

List of Figures

List of Abbreviations

APNI	Alliance Party of Northern Ireland
DUP	Democratic Unionist Party
IRA	Irish Republican Army
LAW	Loyalist Association of Workers
NIWC	Northern Ireland Women's Coalition
PIRA	Provisional Irish Republican Army
PSNI	Police Service of Northern Ireland
PUP	Progressive Unionist Party
RUC	Royal Ulster Constabulary
SDLP	Social Democratic and Labour Party
SF	Sinn Féin
TUV	Traditional Unionist Voice
UDA	Ulster Defence Association
UUP	Ulster Unionist Party
UUUC	United Ulster Unionist Council
UVF	Ulster Volunteer Force

Introduction

Despite the voluminous academic literature on Northern Ireland, there is remarkably little written about the party which has become its most popular political force—the Democratic Unionist Party (DUP). For more than forty years following the party's formation in 1971, it was led by a fundamentalist Protestant preacher, the Reverend Ian Paisley, who opposed all compromises with Irish Catholic nationalists and republicans in his stout defence of Northern Ireland's position within the UK. Yet in 2006, Paisley amazed many by concluding the St Andrews Agreement with the historic republican enemy, agreeing to share power with Sinn Féin at the head of Northern Ireland's government. The DUP had already become the largest party in Northern Ireland and asserted itself as the embodiment of unionism. Now it moved decisively from being a party of protest to one of power, to the astonishment and concern of some, not least many members of the party.

Obvious questions begged are why was the deal done by Paisley and the DUP? Who orchestrated the agreement and, above all, how was it sold to a hitherto unyieldingly religious, conservative, and unionist membership? Who are those members anyway? To what extent is that membership changing? Can the DUP still be described as a religious-based party? This book aims to answer all those questions. Drawing upon the first-ever membership survey of the DUP, funded by the Leverhulme Trust and facilitated by the party from the First Minster of Northern Ireland and party leader, Peter Robinson, downwards, this volume offers a unique quantitative study of the demographic basis and attitudes of the DUP's membership, accompanied by the most extensive range of qualitative interviews of party members yet undertaken. Detailed data on the demography and attitudes of the DUP membership have finally been obtained via this project. A total of 900 party members, from a random sample of 75 per cent of DUP branches across Northern Ireland, plus a similar percentage of individual members, were mailed a detailed questionnaire (sent from the DUP head office) in 2012. It contained over eighty questions on a wide range of issues and elicited demographic data on the membership. A total of 474 replies, a response rate of 52 per cent, were received. 107 semi-structured interviews were conducted in 2012 and 2013 with a wide range of party members, including the party leader and deputy leader, seven of the party's eight MPs, all thirty-eight DUP members of the Northern Ireland Assembly, and over fifty councillors. These interviews were complemented by several focus group discussions, comprising ordinary party members, conducted across Northern Ireland. The tables throughout the book are constructed from the sample number of 474.

The Aims of the Book

The book will explain how a fundamentalist ethno-religious party seemingly destined to oppose political deals (such as the 1973 Sunningdale and 1998 Good Friday agreements) finally offered compromise and sold a deal to a disbelieving electorate, surely one of the most remarkable political pacts accompanying any peace process. Already the most popular unionist party at the time of the St Andrews deal, the DUP has consolidated its position and is the seemingly unchallenged dominant force within unionism.

Yet academic literature on the DUP is far from huge. The only academic to be granted regular access to the DUP has been Steve Bruce, who produced two important volumes. *God Save Ulster! The Religion and Politics of Paisleyism* in 1986 was followed by his equally excellent *Paisley: Religion and Politics*.[1] Quite reasonably, both concentrate particularly on religious aspects of Paisleyism and, equally understandably, focus especially upon the Reverend Ian Paisley. Those books also provide useful data on the extent of Free Presbyterian Church membership amongst the party's elected representatives and offer judicious considerations of the extent of influence—and the clear limits of overlap—wielded by Free Presbyterian thinking upon the DUP. The journalist Ed Moloney has written interesting and fairly well-informed books on Paisley.[2] In both his co-written account (with Andy Pollak) and single-authored follow-up, he is frank, however, in acknowledging the denial of access to senior layers of the party and did not study the DUP's ordinary members in any depth, the focus (understandably) being on the seemingly all-dominant leader of the time. There are other biographies of Paisley, offered by Clifford Smyth and by Dennis Cooke, again reflecting the focus not upon the DUP as an entity, but upon its leader for thirty-seven years.[3] Brian Rowan's *Paisley and the Provos* offers a detailed analysis from a leading journalist of pre-St Andrews shenanigans as the DUP prepared to do a deal.[4] David Gordon has provided an entertaining and insightful account of the political changes in the DUP and some of the political and more personal difficulties encountered following the St Andrews Agreement.[5]

Beyond these, coverage of the DUP is confined to broader books on Northern Ireland or unionist politics generally, chapters, or journal articles. Some of these are highly useful, such as Ganiel's sophisticated analysis of DUP discourses during the peace process[6] and Southern's nuanced treatment of the role of evangelical Protestantism within the party[7]. What remains striking is the lack of dedicated book treatment, compared to the existence of volumes on Northern Ireland's three other sizeable (historically or currently) political forces, the Ulster Unionist Party, Sinn Féin, and the SDLP.[8]

This volume is broader ranging in scope and research methodology than the limited existing works on the DUP. No book has ever offered a full membership survey of the entire DUP, nor has a title offered an analysis of the post-Paisley DUP across a broad range of analyses: political, religious, class, attitudinal, and social. It assesses why individuals joined the DUP in different eras; charts the changing demography of the party; explores issues of identity; and analyses in detail how and why an extraordinary political compromise was reached between the DUP and Sinn Féin leaderships. By allowing the members their voice, the book attempts to capture the modern essence of what motivates what remains one of the most faith-influenced parties found in a western democracy. The book analyses how a faith-derived party can nonetheless appeal to those of strong Protestant faith and none.

The book thus attempts to answer a wide range of questions of contemporary salience. Who belongs to the DUP? Why did they join? What are their beliefs? How strong is the Free Presbyterian wing, or does Protestant denomination no longer matter? Have any Roman Catholics joined? How strong is Orange membership within the DUP? Are there many women within the party—and what are their roles? Beyond the demography, the book assesses the political questions which concern the membership. What are their views on power-sharing with Sinn Féin? How was that deal done? How do they see the future of Northern Ireland and of their party? Would they ever consider voting across the sectarian divide? What are their views on Roman Catholics? How would they approach the integration of Northern Irish society and tackle key issues of division?

In order to answer these questions, the book undertakes a variety of tasks. It analyses the primary political, religious, and social motivations and inspirations that lead to unionists joining the DUP, seeking office within the party, and/or seeking to become elected representatives within the party. The volume explores the relationships between the leaders and the led within the party. Is that relationship essentially 'top down', or is it indeed a 'Democratic' Unionist Party, in which members are satisfied with internal party communications, tested most strongly at the time of the St Andrews Agreement?

The book examines the perceptions of party members and leaders concerning the extent, rationale, and desirability of the political changes undertaken by the DUP during the peace and political processes, including sharing power with Sinn Féin. In so doing, the volume addresses what constitutes the DUP core. It assesses the fundamental bases and repositories of unionism and loyalism within the party; what, for DUP members, provides the contemporary unionist core: Britishness, Ulster identity, Protestantism, Free Presbyterianism, Orangeism, or opposition to republicanism?

As the DUP assumes a hegemonic position within unionism, the book also analyses the views of DUP party members and leaders regarding prospects for unionist bloc unity: should unionist parties unite politically or electorally and on what basis? Beyond the constitutional question, do members perceive that there are common social and political agendas, or are there strong right versus left rivalries? The book also assesses what are the most important future items for DUP members. Are they still conflict-related, based around issues of victims, truth, parades, policing, and concerns over republican 'dissidents', or are they socio-economic and if so, which issues, such as employment or housing, dominate?

These questions are all cogent in assessing political, religious, and social change in a region dogged for years by conflict, yet at present we have virtually no information on the composition and roles of members of Northern Ireland's most sizeable political force, one that has moved from hardline bystander to major governing force. This book will analyse the demographic and attitudinal bases of the party and tell the reader what the party is about, who joins it, how religious a party it is, and where it is going.

The Plan of the Book

The opening chapter analyses the transformation of the DUP from a 'No' to 'Yes' party. In the three decades before devolution, the public face of the DUP remained remarkably consistent, manifest in expressions of dissatisfaction with the direction and policies of the British government, notably at the time of the 1973 Sunningdale Agreement and the 1985 Anglo-Irish Agreement. This excoriation was extended at the time of the Belfast Agreement to the policies of the Ulster Unionist Party (UUP). The DUP declared that political agreement involving republicanism marked further calibration along the path to a united Ireland. This stance rested on three core DUP discourses: first, that the UUP had been ineffectual in its tactics and commitment to the defence of unionism; second, that the UUP remained distant from the 'ordinary' unionist people, whom the DUP claimed to represent. Underpinning this was the third key strand of DUP thinking, that the UK government's intentions were to eventually abandon Northern Ireland and that the Belfast Agreement involved a sacrifice of British identity in Northern Ireland to meet the demands of republicans. For the DUP, during the post-Belfast Agreement and pre-St Andrews Agreement period, the deeds of transfer of Northern Ireland out of the Union had been signed and whilst expulsion was not imminent, defeat in an ongoing cultural war, amid a hollowing out of the Britishness of the region, was close to reality. This opening section assesses the party's apparent lack of development from the 1970s until the early 2000s under Ian Paisley, outlining the intellectual and political bases of its hardline unionism, seemingly grounded in permanent opposition and negativity.

The second chapter reveals, through detailed interviews with those involved, how the DUP clinched what, at the time, appeared an utterly star-tling deal at St Andrews in 2006. In addition to detailing the mechanics of change, the chapter assesses the politics of the DUP's shift from consistent opposition to what it perceived as unjustified republican (and Irish govern-ment) involvement in the political process towards an agreement justified by Ian Paisley as indicative that Sinn Féin had accepted 'the right of Britain to govern' Northern Ireland. This chapter tests the extent of support for the options taken by the DUP, representing movement from opposition to (*a*) power-sharing, (*b*) accepting republicans in government, and (*c*) endorsing an Irish dimension to political arrangements. It examines membership views on these issues, revealing support for the principles of power-sharing, but indi-cating continuing antipathy towards (i) the 1998 Good Friday Agreement, (ii) Sinn Féin's automatic place in government, and (iii) some of the principles of mandatory coalition. As such, the St Andrews Agreement was very much a 'top–down' deal constructed by the party leadership, with the base expected to fall in line. Since then, the DUP, with Sinn Féin, has been the dominant strand of government. How cordial or hostile are relations with Sinn Féin and is there much common ground with republicans?

Drawing upon extensive interviews with DUP ministers, the chapter exam-ines the divisions between those in the party who have struck up reason-able working relationships across the sectarian chasm and those for whom hostility remains largely insurmountable. The chapter assesses how the DUP intends to move beyond the rigid consociational power-sharing of the cur-rent arrangements towards a more normal system of government and opposi-tion. The chapter examines the extent to which party members see devolved power-sharing as the key to local control. Has sufficient confidence devel-oped regarding power-sharing with nationalists and republicans to persuade the DUP leadership and membership that further transfers of powers to local political institutions are needed?

After the analysis of how the DUP moved from opposition to power-sharing in the first two chapters, the third chapter explores the base of unionism's seemingly hegemonic force. This section provides the first detailed data-base of the demography of the DUP membership. Chapter 6 gives a detailed analysis of the religious base of the party, so this chapter concentrates upon other aspects, such as the party's age profile; its social class base; the large graduate-level influx of joiners since the Good Friday Agreement; the geographical concentrations of members—and what those members do for the party, in terms of leafleting, canvassing, and attending meetings. This chapter provides a comprehensive analysis of the strengths (and weaknesses) of the DUP's activist base. Beyond the demography, the chapter assesses the concerns of members. The DUP is required to act as a responsible party of government, not protest. This section thus explores the priorities of party members for post-conflict Northern Ireland. To what extent do they prioritize education and health issues, for example, over older constitutional questions? Do those members now see the defence of cultural (Protestant) Britishness, illustrated by, for example, disputes over Orange Order parades, as being of lesser importance than so-called 'bread and butter' issues, such as employment prospects, university tuition fees, or pensions? Chapter 4 analyses how the DUP has portrayed itself as the safer custodian of unionist interests than its rival, the UUP, before and after the Belfast and St Andrews deals. The DUP's presentation of the Belfast Agreement was primarily through a discourse of concessions to republicanism and losses to unionism. This was accompanied by the claim that the UUP had betrayed unionists under the original terms of the power-sharing deal. The DUP insists that it was responsible for a new deal that forced the Irish republican movement to accept the institutions of partition, to abandon violence, and support the state's police force. In understanding the political position of the DUP, it is important to conceptualize the development and utilization of the notion of 'negotiation through strength' within the party. The DUP was amenable to change, but on its terms. This section examines how such a position was articulated to party members before assessing how change was sold internally and exploring how far the DUP's own membership base has been stretched. The internal discourse offered was that the DUP had successfully identified and removed the major threats to 'Ulster', via the ending of the Provisional IRA's armed campaign and the willingness of Sinn Féin (following the St Andrews Agreement) to support the Police Service of Northern Ireland. This notwithstanding, leading a robust, avowedly hardline party membership towards power-sharing with republicans cannot have been an 'easy sell'. Indeed, the party leadership acknowledges in interviews that the DUP leadership underprepared its support base for the dramatic change which ensued. Moreover, the membership survey data confirms that the DUP base continues to perceive the Union as under challenge, from mainstream republican politics and through dissident republican violence. The latter is classified as a 'major threat' by a majority of DUP members and 'securing the Union' remains the number one priority for most DUP members—not 'bread and butter' issues.

The fifth chapter analyses the identity of party members. Devolution offers greater scope for the restatement of regional Ulster Loyalism, which the DUP often appeared to represent. However, this chapter argues that the party may have moved closer to offering a formation of Britishness more closely aligned to that found elsewhere in the UK than had previously been the case. This proposition was tested via a battery of survey and interview questions to party members. They overwhelmingly preferred a British to Northern Irish or Ulster identification, but their Britishness remains more Protestant and socially conservative than that found elsewhere in the UK. This chapter assesses the rival pulls of national Britishness versus regional Northern Irishness at both leadership and grassroots levels of the party. The chapter also highlights the exclusiveness of identity, in terms of the outright rejection by DUP members of any sense of Irishness.

Historically, the DUP was strongly associated with the Free Presbyterian Church, given the position of Ian Paisley as leader of both, although how strong the connection was in terms of policy influence had long been disputed. Chapter 6 assesses how the DUP remains a highly religious party, using data to show the extent of Protestant denominational identification and observance. Free Presbyterians are the largest single denominational category of member, but their rate of entrance to the DUP is in marked decline. The chapter then discusses the religiously conservative attitudes of members, the data showing very strong opposition to homosexuality and abortion. The survey data show that most party members believe that 'Faith and Church' *should* play a substantial role in the party. These members are hostile to 'mixed' (Protestant to Catholic) marriages and most believe that there is a significant level of prejudice against Protestants in Northern Ireland.

Despite its appeal to Catholic unionists to support the party, the DUP leadership continues to offer 'unionism as politicised Protestantism'. Yet some of the party's members are fearful that the post-Paisley era of the DUP may lead to further dilution of the Protestant principles which infused the party. This chapter assesses the extent to which the DUP is moving towards becoming a 'normal' secular party, no longer necessarily conditioned by a religious outlook. Do party members endorse or resist a diminution of religious influences with the party? Does this herald a switch of the DUP from an ethno-religious to an ethno-national organization, one whose support for the Union is now grounded in the contractual and pragmatic assertion of unionist Britishness, rather than a particular religious variant? The chapter demonstrates that most members still demand a religiously oriented party, but highlights significant differences between its highly religious wing and somewhat more liberal post-Belfast Agreement joiners.

The electoral rise of the DUP was far from inevitable. Indeed, the Belfast Agreement was constructed upon the expectation that the UUP would be the dominant unionist force. Chapter 7 thus explores how the DUP saw off the UUP to assume supremacy within unionist politics. The chapter's data show that one-quarter of DUP members used to belong to the UUP. The DUP has picked off the talent from its rival and outwitted the UUP with impressive internal discipline. The chapter analyses the data to examine the views of members on whether electoral alliances or full distancing from the UUP are seen as the most appropriate way forward. The data reveal the (lack of) willingness of DUP members to offer lower preference votes to other parties.

This chapter also considers also how the DUP has had to see off a challenge from harder-line unionists arguing that the DUP's compromises have betrayed unionists. Not everyone was impressed by the sharing of power with republicans, including a significant number of members who considered defection. Opposition has largely coalesced around Traditional Unionist Voice (TUV), under the leadership of former DUP MEP Jim Allister (one of the many interviewees for this book), who has been highly critical of the DUP's willingness to administer 'joint rule', with 'unrepentant terrorists in key posts'. The distance in understanding between the TUV (largely standing on a pre-devolution DUP ticket) and members of the DUP needs to be assessed if we are to understand possible future directions of unionist politics.

Chapter 8 looks at the problem of the under-representation of women in the DUP. The number of women in political life in Northern Ireland has increased in the past decade. Women form 19 per cent of MLAs in the Northern Ireland Assembly and 24 per cent of local councillors are female. However, in relation to other devolved institutions, where female representation is 43 and 37 per cent in the Welsh Assembly and Scottish Parliament respectively, progress has been more limited in Northern Ireland. The cleavages of nationality and religion tend to eclipse a cross-cutting gender cleavage in Northern Ireland. As a result, politics has centred on communal loyalties, providing little space for alternative agendas. The gender deficit is particularly stark within unionism, where women remain seriously under-represented at an elected level. Whilst being described as the 'backbone of the party' and actively participating at the membership level, very few women in the DUP enter the sphere of formal politics. This chapter accounts for the reasons behind this gender deficit in relation to the DUP and examines the role and opinion of women at various levels of the party. Evidence is drawn from quantitative survey data, focus group material, and interviews with DUP representatives and the party leadership to explore the supply and demand of female candidates, the opportunities for female participation, and the selection process within the party. Women have always been active within the DUP, but standing for election has been rarer. The chapter discusses the barriers to female participation and reflects upon the DUP's response to the gender deficit across the elected levels of the party.

The Conclusion assesses future directions for the DUP, as the party continues to replace its old Free Presbyterian trappings with broader appeal. Will the DUP continue to expand beyond its current position as effectively a 'catch-all' party within a particular ethnic bloc, even beginning to attract electoral support from beyond the Protestant community? What roles will the party play in removing the sectarianism which has bedevilled Northern Ireland amid the near-subsiding of the old violent constitutional conflict? And finally, what the will the DUP's membership look like in a generation's time? Will it much more broadly reflect the wider Protestant (or even wider?) population in Northern Ireland? Can it maintain the cohesion and unity which characterized the party of opposition for so long, before it acquired the burdens of government?

Notes

1. S. Bruce (1986) *God Save Ulster! The Religion and Politics of Paisleyism*, Oxford: Oxford University Press; (2009) *Paisley: Religion and Politics in Northern Ireland*, Oxford: Oxford University Press.
2. E. Moloney and A. Pollak (1986) *Paisley*, Dublin: Poolbeg; E. Moloney (2008) *Paisley: From Demagogue to Democrat*, Dublin: Poolbeg.
3. C. Smyth (1988) *Ian Paisley: Voice of Protestant Ulster*, Edinburgh: Scottish Academic Press; D. Cooke (1997) *Persecuting Zeal: A Portrait of Ian Paisley*, Dingle: Brandon.
4. B. Rowan (2005) *Paisley and the Provos*, Belfast: Brehon.
5. D. Gordon (2009) *The Fall of the House of Paisley*, Dublin: Gill & Macmillan.
6. G. Ganiel (2007) ' "Preaching to the Choir?" An Analysis of DUP Discourses about the Northern Ireland Peace Process', *Irish Political Studies*, 22/3, 303–20.
7. N. Southern (2005) 'Ian Paisley and Evangelical Democratic Unionists: An Analysis of the Role of Evangelical Protestantism within the Democratic Unionist Party', *Irish Political Studies*, 20/2, 127–45.
8. e.g. G. Walker (2004) *A History of the Ulster Unionist Party*, Manchester: Manchester University Press; A. Maillot (2004) *New Sinn Féin*, London; Routledge; I. McAllister (1977) *The Northern Ireland Social Democratic and Labour Party*, London: Macmillan.

1

'Never, Never, Never, Never': The DUP, 1971–2003

> Where do the terrorists operate from? From the Irish Republic! Where do the terrorists return to for sanctuary? To the Irish Republic! And yet Mrs. Thatcher tells us that the Republic must have some say in our Province. We say never, never, never, never!
>
> (Ian Paisley, 23 November 1985, following the signing of the Anglo-Irish Agreement)

The history of the Democratic Unionist Party (DUP) has been dominated by one major personality: the Reverend Dr Ian Paisley. One of the most extraordinary stories of the Northern Irish 'Troubles' is the journey made by Paisley, from a firebrand Protestant preacher who opposed every major political initiative to broker an agreement between unionists and nationalists (including sharing power with Catholics), to eventually becoming First Minister of Northern Ireland in a power-sharing executive, with a former Provisional IRA (PIRA) commander as the Deputy First Minister. This chapter charts that journey, outlining the oppositional nature of Paisleyism as a political and religious entity created to resist the supposed treachery of governments, ecumenists, and internal 'enemies of Ulster'.

The Origins of Paisleyism

Paisley's political career went hand in hand with his religious vocation. He formed the Free Presbyterian Church in 1951—itself part of a schism with another congregation that many have seen as a metaphor for Paisley's relationship with other unionists in Northern Ireland.[1] He first came to prominence with his opposition to the ecumenical movement. In 1966, for example, Paisley sent a telegram to the Queen over the proposal that a Catholic priest should speak at Westminster Abbey during a prayer week for Christian unity because: 'The visit constitutes a grave violation of the terms of your Coronation oath, is contrary to the [1689] Bill of Rights and...is an insult to the martyrs whom Rome burned. As Protestants we reaffirm that the Pope of Rome has no jurisdiction in this realm.'[2] For Paisley, Northern Ireland was the last bastion of evangelical Protestantism in Western Europe: 'we must not let drop the torch of Truth at this stage of the eternal conflict between Truth and Evil...We are a special people, not of ourselves, but of our Divine mission.'[3] Paisley warned against the 'diabolical principles of popery increasingly working to exterminate Protestantism and the truth for which Protestantism stands. We can but glance at the dark page of Rome's butcheries in Ulster', a reference to the slaughter of Irish Protestants in the 1641 and 1798 rebellions. In the 1960s, Paisley believed the papacy was exploiting the situation that had arisen in Northern Ireland 'because our leaders in church and in state today have either lost the great vision of our Protestant heritage or else are practising deliberate treachery to that which our fathers won for us at such a tremendous price'.[4]

From the beginning of his political career in the 1960s, Paisley was associated with opposition to the reformist tendencies of Captain Terence O'Neill, Prime Minister of Northern Ireland. From 1921 until 1972, when the UK Government suspended devolved government at Stormont and imposed direct rule from London, one party ruled Northern Ireland under its majoritarian system, the Ulster Unionist Party (UUP), with the Catholic Nationalist minority bereft of influence. O'Neill disturbed the unity of this unionist hegemony when he began to make overtures to the minority and across the border to the Irish Republic, which had seceded from the UK in 1922. So when, in 1965, O'Neill met with his counterpart from the Republic of Ireland, Taoiseach (prime minister) Seán Lemass, in an effort to improve North–South relations, Paisley accused O'Neill of 'treason': 'It was not even mere politics. It is a matter of our faith and our heritage...He is a bridge builder he tells us. A traitor and a bridge are very much alike for they both go over to the other side. It was the bloody hand of a traitor that he (O'Neill) held'[5]—referring to Lemass's role as a former member of the IRA which had fought a bloody guerrilla war against British rule from 1919 to 1921.

The fiftieth anniversary of the Easter Rising, in 1966, was a particular focus of tension between the two communities in Northern Ireland. Paisley attacked the celebration of 'a Papal plot to stab England in the back while she was at war with Germany', claiming 'It was an insult to the constitution that people should be allowed to flaunt the Irish Tricolour and celebrate what was a great act of treachery against the Crown on our own doorstep.'[6] Paisley's response to what he perceived as threats to 'traditional Unionism' was to begin what became a series of loose associations with quasi-paramilitary elements—although he had no proven involvement in the instigation of violence. The first such move was his own creation, the Ulster Protestant Volunteers (UPV) which, in 1966, were to be formed in every Northern Irish parliamentary constituency as a group of men 'who are prepared to stand together in this day of crisis and in this evil age'. The UPV would be 'constitutional, democratic and legal'. At the UPV's formation he observed: 'They say Thompson machine-guns will be handed out tonight. I don't see any machine-guns.'[7] A secret intelligence report, by the Inspector-General of the Royal Ulster Constabulary (RUC), in 1966, described the illegal Ulster Volunteer Force (UVF) as the 'militant wing' of the 'Paisleyite Movement',[8] something denied by Paisley. It is noteworthy that Gusty Spence, the leader of the UVF who was convicted for killing a young Catholic barman in 1966, later stated: 'I have no time for Paisley's type of religious fervour or his politics but he had no involvement in re-forming the UVF though he stirred up a lot of tension at that time for his own ends.'[9]

The relationship of Paisley to violence is clear. In 1973, for example, he argued it was 'wrong for Protestants to contemplate taking the law into their own hands and meting out justice to those whom they believe guilty of atrocities... "avenge not yourselves" is the unmistakable teaching of Scripture. Romans 12, verse 19, goes on to remind Christians that "Vengeance is mine; I will repay, saith the Lord"'.[10] This did not mean, of course, that Protestants could not defend themselves, their homes, and their families from attack. It did mean that the punishment of offenders must and should be left to those holding official authority to judge and punish. There were, however, circumstances in which the use of force was justifiable. Paisley offered the example of the 'wicked, immoral murderous brute of a father' cited by John Knox in the sixteenth century; subjects had the right to resist the tyrannical ruler as they would a frenzied father. Knox supported his claim by appeals to scripture.[11] Paisley's view was that the British Government could not impose a Roman Catholic regime on a Protestant majority or transfer Northern Ireland into a united Ireland.[12] This contractual relationship, which might be broken by the British Government failing to protect its citizens—Ulster Protestants—manifested itself in the constitutional threat to Northern Ireland's position within the UK and the lives of its citizens. Hence Paisley demanded that the IRA be 'exterminated from Ulster... [T]here are men willing to do the job of exterminating the IRA. Recruit them under the Crown and they will do it. If you refuse, we will have no other decision to make but to do it ourselves.' But Paisley also qualified this when, at the head of a 'Third Force' (the RUC and the British Army were the first and second forces), in the early 1980s, he declared: 'This force proposes to act entirely within the law and will in no way usurp either the work or the activities of the crown forces.'[13]

While Paisley has stated that he has never advocated violence, it was his electrifying rhetoric predicting the selling out of Protestant Ulster by rival unionist politicians and successive British Governments, combined with the theatrics, from the UPV in the 1960s to his inspection, in the 1980s, of hundreds of men waving firearm certificates on a hillside, that led critics to attack him as a demagogue. For others, Paisley was a prophet who fore-warned correctly that the dangers of O'Neill's 'appeasement'—and that of his successor Major James Chichester-Clark—would lead to a renewed IRA campaign to destroy Northern Ireland's position within the UK. The outbreak of the Troubles, with communal violence between Protestants and Catholics in 1968, leading to the intervention of British troops a year later to preserve order, presaged the formation of the Provisional IRA, which began its 'armed struggle', in 1970, to drive the British state out of Northern Ireland. Paisley saw the IRA campaign in religious as well as political terms, claiming: 'The Provisional IRA is in reality the armed wing of the Roman Catholic Church. Its real aim is to annihilate Protestantism.'[14]

This was the background to Paisley's political advance, although the UUP remained the dominant political force in unionism. After being elected to Stormont in 1970, he launched the DUP in 1971. Among those who joined the new party, in its early years, was Peter Robinson, a future party leader and First Minister. The factor that was Robinson's 'calling into politics' was the killing of his schoolfriend, Harry Beggs, by an IRA bomb: 'we had a lot in common. We enjoyed playing football and we enjoyed the lessons. We both left school at the same time. He went to work for the Northern Ireland Electricity Board as it was known then and I went into estate agency.'[15]

This catalyst came at a time when Robinson saw the UUP 'flounder-ing...uncertain and didn't have answers and was regarded as "softly, softly". I think that was the term being used in those days. They didn't seem to be prepared to take on what was a virtual insurrection.'[16] The DUP's demand for a tougher security line and stronger defence of the Union attracted Robinson. In contrast to UUP leaders, such as Chichester-Clark and his successor Brian Faulkner, Ian Paisley was someone 'who had a very clear view of the way forward', recalled Robinson, who was also attracted by new party's interest in 'social justice and...reputation for working for people on the ground and constituency work. That was something that had been absent from Unionist politics.'[17] Robinson claimed his predecessor as MP in East Belfast

used to get his chauffeur to drive his car to the end of the street, then the chauf-feur would knock on a few doors and ask if they would like to see their MP. That was during the election; that was canvassing in those days. All you had to do was wave the flag and people came out to vote. They did nothing by way of serving the electorate. We changed all of that building up a network of advice centres; other parties then had to follow.[18]

13

The Reverend William McCrea, who went on to become a DUP MP, remembers how he 'got into politics simply because I was brought up in [a] strict Presbyterian home outside Cookstown'. He was a Free Presbyterian minister who, because of his background as a civil servant in the Department of Health and Social Security, found people asking him to help them with such issues as housing or benefits: 'They'd say that there is nobody to help us', recalled McCrea, who 'started a little advice centre' in response, where people could come along and get help.[19] Following a reorganization of local government in 1973, he stood as a United Loyalist candidate for Magherafelt council and then joined the DUP, his first foray into electoral politics, although he had earlier worked for Paisley. For McCrea, 'Dr Paisley was enunciating things that I believe, strong Christian standards and also in the political scene, stand[ing] against the trend...of compromise and appeasement to Republicanism which seemed to be evident at that time and have continued to be evident down through the years.'[20] He 'genuinely felt that what Dr Paisley was saying both religiously and politically was something which I strongly believed in and I became a member of the party'.[21] McCrea argues that the UUP did not govern in the interests of either Protestants or Catholics:

> The myth that was spread around was the Roman Catholic community in Northern Ireland had been discriminated against by the Ulster Unionists. To be honest, the unionists were discriminated against by the Ulster Unionists. It wasn't Roman Catholic versus Protestant. It was the Ulster Unionists who looked after their own.[22]

The failure of the UUP to stem the growing tide of violence was also a factor in the politicization of Gregory Campbell, later MP for East Londonderry. He recalls:

> I suppose I had three choices. I was 15, 16 at the time of the Troubles...to join the Loyalist paramilitaries, because I could see mayhem, destruction and protests...that wasn't for me; I didn't want to go down that route. Once I was closing off the paramilitary violent route, or the response to violent route, however you would describe it, then there were two choices...the Young Unionists, the UUP's youth wing [or]...go off to some of these fringe groups that were cropping up in the late 60s early 70s.[23]

Campbell preferred to 'have some sort of influence' and so joined the Young Unionists, but soon realized 'there was a need for a DUP or something like it...I just didn't feel at home in the party of the middle to upper classes, the retired generals and big business people, large farm holdings. None of that fitted my social class.'[24] Moreover, whilst the UUP 'looked as though it was the proverbial rabbit in headlights—didn't respond, took everything in its stride and lazily', the DUP said: 'this is what is happening out there—we need to confront it, we need to oppose it'. Like McCrea, Campbell was a member of the Free Presbyterian Church, joining just before he became a party member.[25]

Son of a lorry driver and factory worker, David Simpson, elected MP for Upper Bann in 2005, joined the party partly because of Paisley's religious approach, but also because of social class issues, claiming the DUP

> represented my core values from moral values right up to working class values. I am very proud of the fact that I am working class...that class issue, that really bugged me and as a child I didn't understand it. I remember many years ago, whenever I was in school, I was invited into places, I wasn't good enough because I was from a working class background to play or engage with children from parties that were perceived as Ulster Unionist, middle class and it was just that stigma thing that really annoyed me.[26]

Growing up in the 1960s, Sammy Wilson, also later to become a senior party figure, thought that Ian Paisley was 'very charismatic and he resonated with a lot of the things that I would be brought up to believe anyway, being brought up in a traditional, evangelical Protestant, working class background'.[27] (Wilson is a Baptist, not a Free Presbyterian.) Wilson found embryonic Paisleyism appealing because there was a real fear that Northern Ireland was under threat again. 'There had been previous IRA campaigns. There was always this paranoia amongst unionists that attempts were always being made to shake us out of the Union.' The Northern Ireland Civil Rights campaign, dominated by Catholics, was

> seen as a kind of Trojan horse by which a lot of Republican personnel were involved at the higher echelons of it....a 'cover for a lot of civil disorder and eventually some terrorist activity against the police. It was all seen as part of the campaign [to destroy Northern Ireland] and of course coming from a Unionist background [I] would have been angry about that and...where you saw this as a threat...[I] wanted to react to it.[28]

Wilson recognized that Paisley shared a lot of the views that he had been brought up with through church affiliation and 'his message was much clearer. It was focused on certainties whereas some of the messages you were getting from Terence O'Neill and Brian Faulkner were much more waffley...when you are young certainties really capture your imagination much more as well.'[29] The UUP could never be a natural home:

> if you wanted to be anybody in it you had to be a businessman: there is no way at that stage I would have ever been regarded as the kind of person who would be seen and fingered for advancement, my background was not the right background. Whereas a new party is open to everybody.[30]

The DUP at that time were looking around for people to stand in elections who were active locally and who were deeply rooted in their own community;

Wilson, living in a working-class redevelopment area and being involved with about fourteen housing associations, fitted the bill. The DUP's association in its early days with being more on the left of socio-economic issues led to Wilson being called 'Red Sam' by his party colleagues, a label 'That still comes back to haunt me'.[31]

The DUP Says No

Paisley's DUP opposed virtually every major initiative championed by the British and Irish Governments to ameliorate the Northern Ireland crisis. In 1973, the two Governments brokered a deal with local parties in Northern Ireland broadly similar (notwithstanding significant differences) to the Belfast and St Andrews Agreements a quarter of a century later. The 1973 agreement established a power-sharing cabinet of unionists, led by Brian Faulkner (UUP), alongside the constitutional nationalists of the Social Democratic and Labour Party (SDLP), the most prominent figure in which was John Hume. It was the first time in Northern Ireland's history that Protestants and Catholics shared executive power at Stormont. At the following Sunningdale conference, in England, the two Governments, together with the UUP and the SDLP, agreed to the formation of a Council of Ireland that would be composed of ministers from Northern Ireland and the Irish Republic. Under its original formulation, the Council was to possess executive powers, fuelling unionist concerns that it, rather than the Irish Parliament and the newly established Northern Irish Assembly, would implement decisions on an all-Ireland basis. It was thus perceived by critics as an embryonic all-Ireland government. Reflecting on this period, William McCrea saw his opposition to power-sharing and Sunningdale as partly motivated by a distrust of British Government intentions:

> many of the politicians across the water, in Great Britain, would have happily...got rid of us. They had little loyalty to Northern Ireland, even though Northern Ireland was very loyal to Britain. Westminster was not very loyal to Northern Ireland. So there was a constant drip, drip, drip appeasement to Republicans (the IRA) and Nationalists which I was personally against.[32]

The power-sharing agreement and Sunningdale was brought down by the Ulster Workers' Council strike in 1974, during which those unionists opposed to the settlement, including the DUP, worked alongside loyalist paramilitaries to paralyse Northern Ireland and force the British Government to back down. In the aftermath of the UWC Strike, the British Government threw the Northern Irish problem back to the Province's politicians and established a Constitutional Convention to establish a system of government. When Bill Craig's Vanguard Party (which included the young Queen's University law lecturer, later UUP leader, David Trimble) proposed a 'voluntary coalition', consisting of anti-Sunningdale unionists and the SDLP, for the period of the current 'emergency' in Northern Ireland, it was a resolution by Ian Paisley against 'Republicans taking part in any future cabinet in Northern Ireland' that rejected the scheme. Instead, anti-Sunningdale unionists, including the DUP, demanded a return to majority rule at Stormont and no North–South institutional connection with the Irish Republic.

The DUP remained true to this position. The party's 1982 manifesto for the short-lived Northern Ireland Assembly declared: 'There will be no power-sharing nor Irish Dimension if the Assembly is controlled by those resolved to oppose these twin evils.'[33] In the absence of a unionist willingness to share power with nationalists and, in the wake of the electoral advance of the PIRA's political wing, Sinn Féin, in 1985 the British and Irish Governments signed the Anglo-Irish Agreement (AIA). This established an Inter-Governmental Conference (IGC) which, for the first time, gave the Irish Government a direct input into the internal affairs of Northern Ireland. Unlike the 1973 dispensation, the AIA did not require unionist participation. It was an agreement between two sovereign governments.

The problem for unionism now was how to get rid of the AIA. The strategy of the UUP, led by James Molyneaux, and the DUP, was to engage with the British Government. By the 1990s, this led to the inter-party 'Brooke-Mayhew' talks (named after the respective Secretary of States for Northern Ireland who chaired them) with the SDLP and the two Governments, and divided into three strands: Strand One referred to the governance of Northern Ireland; Strand Two to North–South relations between Northern Ireland and the Irish Republic; and Strand Three on East–West relations between the United Kingdom and the Republic of Ireland. In these talks Paisley rejected a return to the 1973 model: the ill-fated 'Power Sharing As-Of-Right Executive' or an institutionalized Council of Ireland.[34] Instead, there might be a system of committees to run the various Northern Ireland Departments, but no overall cabinet. As there would be no executive there could be no executive power-sharing. There might also be an External Affairs Committee, which would be a non-departmental committee drawn from any assembly, to monitor and consider affairs external to Northern Ireland and make appropriate representations when necessary.[35]

The talks broke up without agreement in 1992. The following year, the British Government agreed with the Irish Government a Joint Declaration that acknowledged a settlement might take the form of a united Ireland, but also stated it was for the people of Ireland, 'by agreement between the two parts respectively'—Northern Ireland and the Republic of Ireland—to 'exercise the right of self-determination in the basis of consent, freely and concurrently given, North and South, to bring about a united Ireland, if that is their wish'.

17

This meant Northern Ireland deciding its own constitutional future, regardless of what the Republic did: concurrent referenda, North and South, on any settlement, still permitted Northern Ireland to self-determine its constitutional future and consent, or not consent, to a change in its status, regardless of how the Republic of Ireland voted. The Declaration was thus designed to square the circle of offering nationalists all-Ireland self-determination while at the same time preserving the unionist concept of self-determination for Northern Ireland.[36]

While the UUP gave the Declaration a measured response, Ian Paisley warned of treachery and a Protestant backlash. According to Paisley, the Declaration signed by Major and Taoiseach Albert Reynolds—the 'Dublin liar'—was 'a tripartite agreement between Reynolds, the IRA and you [Major]. You have sold Ulster to buy off the fiendish republican scum', also claiming that the IRA had got 50 per cent of what it wanted, and that 'when we have the process under this document, they (will) get the other fifty per cent'.[37] Unionists of all persuasions were united in their opposition to the next Anglo-Irish proposal—the 'Framework Document' for a North–South body, composed of Ministers from the Irish Parliament, Dail Eireann, and a future Northern Ireland Assembly. The body

> would discharge the functions agreed for it in relation to consultation, harmonisation and executive action.[38] Thus, the envisaged North–South body was a return to model of the Sunningdale Council of Ireland, reviving fears of an embryonic all-Ireland government.

Following the IRA ceasefire, its political wing, Sinn Féin, was represented by Gerry Adams and Martin McGuinness at multi-party talks in 1997. Just before the republicans were admitted, Paisley and the leader of the UUP, David Trimble, drew up principles that would guide them in the talks. The two leaders identified two issues that they said were fundamental. One was the principle of consent, the right of the people of Northern Ireland alone to determine their own future. The second was decommissioning, Trimble and Paisley agreeing that the handing over of illegal terrorist weaponry must be resolved to their satisfaction before there could be substantive political negotiations.

Following, as Paisley saw it, the IRA's inclusion in the talks, the DUP, in accordance with its mandate, left the process. Trimble's UUP remained, to the chagrin of Paisley, whose view was that the entire process was fundamentally flawed. The chairmanship of the talks was determined before the process commenced. Far from the participants having a 'blank sheet of paper', the agenda was 'designed to produce the Framework Document outcome'. Participants had little function in the process other than to agree to an already produced deal between the two Governments in anticipation that the IRA would accept it. According to Paisley, the process was to appease terrorism.[39]

A criticism levelled at the DUP is that, had it remained in the talks, it might have prevented the resultant Belfast Agreement emerging in its final form, by preventing Trimble from signing up to its terms. Some party interviewees concurred, but only a minority. A more typical view is that offered by the Reverend McCrea, that the UUP 'were pushing us aside' because they were the biggest unionist party; the DUP 'couldn't prevent' the sort of deal which emerged because the British Government, whilst having 'no intention of pulling the plug on Northern Ireland', was 'completely sold on it [the deal]; they were the masters at divide and conquer for years. They have done this for a very long time...no-one could stop it being signed.'[40] Even those who believed the DUP could have stayed are not particularly regretful. Lord Morrow opines:

> In hindsight now, we probably should have stayed in, but that is hind-sight...I don't think I could have ever lived with myself if I ever played a part in the destruction of the RUC and the release of the prisoners...those were two big ones that were very difficult to swallow...I take any comfort my hands are not tainted with that. Could we have changed that if we had been in there? I don't know. I honestly don't know.[41]

The Belfast Agreement: The Battle for Unionism

The Belfast or Good Friday Agreement is the defining document in modern Irish history, on a par with the Government of Ireland Act, which partitioned Ireland in 1920, and the Anglo-Irish Treaty, under which twenty-six counties of Ireland seceded from the UK to form the Irish Free State. It also laid the basis for the DUP's transition from a party of protest to a party of government. Paisley's opposition to the Agreement, in contrast to Trimble's support, was the central factor in this process. It set the scene for a battle for the heart of unionism.

Strand One of the Belfast Agreement established a Northern Ireland Assembly at the core of which there was to be a power-sharing executive. The executive and assembly were to be governed by 'sufficient consensus' or a double veto. Decisions would require substantial support from unionist and nationalist representatives. Although there was a First Minister (unionist) and a Deputy First Minister (nationalist), they were co-equal and neither was subordinate to the other.[42] Trimble's justification for agreeing to this system was that he had secured some degree of unionist control over their destiny and that that any safeguards would be equally applicable to defend unionist interests.[43]

Paisley, on the other hand, objected to the mechanisms agreed in Strand One on the grounds that these were 'undemocratic' and gave nationalist parties an absolute veto on any key decisions. The assembly's existence depended on the maintenance of an all-Ireland North–South Ministerial Council (NSMC) set up under Strand Two. Without the all-Ireland body, the Northern Ireland Assembly had no role. The new assembly would not operate on the democratic basis of Westminster, or even Northern Ireland's local councils, where a simple majority vote was sufficient. In this assembly, 'key' decisions were to be taken on a cross-community basis. Paisley and the DUP protested at how the First Minister and Deputy First Minister were to be elected jointly, with the former having no role independent of his deputy. The DUP also objected that the assembly would not be in the control of the party with the majority of votes, but would be in the control of the nationalist community. Paisley complained that 'David Trimble has agreed to an Assembly that will permit nothing to pass into legislation without the approval of Gerry Adams!' and insisted that the UUP leader's 'false allegation' of a 'Unionist veto' was 'therefore the height of hypocrisy'.[44]

In Strand Two of the Agreement, the North–South Ministerial Council agreed to cooperation on matters of mutual interest within the competence of administrations, North and South. The assembly agreed to six areas of North–South cooperation, so that nationalists were reassured that the Council would have areas to discuss. All decisions would be by consensus.[45] As far as Trimble was concerned, he had secured a consultative body that was the antithesis of the proposed Framework Document, which had executive powers. He argued that the 1998 all-Ireland body, unlike the 1973 proposed Council of Ireland, had 'no supra-national characteristics'.[46] For Trimble, it was essential that it should clearly draw its authority from the Northern Ireland Assembly and Dáil Éireann and be accountable to these democratic institutions. So for Trimble, the NSMC was not a supra-national body and, as any Northern Ireland delegation to it had to be balanced between unionists and nationalists, this gave the former an assurance that nothing would happen in the NSMC without their consent.

Trimble's sanguine take was dismissed by Paisley, who claimed that an all-Ireland Ministerial Council with executive powers had been created. It was to be set up by Westminster and Dublin, so it was a free-standing body independent of the Northern Ireland Assembly. The assembly would cease to exist if the all-Ireland body ceased to function. The purpose of this all-Ireland body was threefold, namely, to develop: (*a*) consultation, (*b*) cooperation, and (*c*) action on an all-Ireland basis, via agreement on the adoption of common policies. As it had the ability to take decisions, it was, therefore, a body with executive powers, according to the DUP critique. There was to be a series of all-Ireland bodies set up subservient to the all-Ireland Ministerial Council to implement decisions taken by the Council. Membership of the Council was organized so that there would always be a permanent unionist minority. Decisions could be taken in the Council without reference back to the Northern Ireland Assembly. The only time that the assembly would be required to give approval to any decision of the Council would be in the unlikely event of a minister going beyond his departmental responsibility. If he stayed within it, there was no approval of the assembly needed.[47]

Strand Three saw a British-Irish Council (BIC) established. It was to be made up of all devolved administrations within the United Kingdom, Crown dependencies within the British Isles, and the sovereign governments in London and Dublin.[48] A British-Irish Intergovernmental Conference (BIIC) 'replaced' the Anglo-Irish Intergovernmental Conference set up by the AIA. British and Irish ministers and officials would be unable to discuss matters devolved to the assembly, while Northern Irish ministers would be allowed to attend Conference meetings as observers.[49] The BIC 'balanced' the NSMC, in Trimble's estimation, and reflected his view that the relevant context was the British Isles as a whole. It could develop the same type of implementation body already being created within the North/South context. Trimble thought it significant that, for the first time since 1921, the Republic of Ireland had come into an institutional relationship with the British Isles.[50] Paisley focused on the second institution created in Strand Three—the BIIC. This body took over the role of the Anglo-Irish Conference 'set up under the Diktat of 1985' and as such, Paisley argued it was 'wrong to claim that the Anglo-Irish Agreement has gone. It is simply being renamed and recreated.'[51] The only difference was that (as provided for in the AIA) those areas that were now devolved to a new assembly would no longer come under the jurisdiction of the BIIC. Paisley dismissed the BIC as nothing more than a revamped Anglo-Irish Council, claiming that 'what was previously overwhelmingly rejected by Unionists in 1985 is now falsely portrayed and rejoiced in as a Unionist victory'.[52] The BIC was at best, for unionism, a 'luncheon club, but at worst it is a council where the two Governments will continue to interfere in the affairs of Northern Ireland over the heads of the people of the Province'.[53]

In terms of 'Constitutional Issues', the Agreement had the principle of Northern consent at its heart: all parties agreed that there would not be a united Ireland without the consent of a majority of the people in Northern Ireland. Articles 2 and 3 of the 1937 Irish Constitution did not recognize Northern Ireland as part of the United Kingdom. Rather, its six counties formed part of Eire (the official title of the Irish state), as the whole island constituted the 'national territory'. This territorial claim was a long-standing source of resentment among unionists. British constitutional law, on the other hand, stated that Northern Ireland was, and had been, part of the United Kingdom since the Acts of Union in 1800. Now, in the Agreement, the Irish state recognized that Northern Ireland was not part of the Republic of Ireland, but was part of the United Kingdom. A new Article 2 recognized the right of persons on the island of Ireland to be part of the Irish nation if they so wished. A new Article 3 set out the aspiration of a united Ireland. It recognized, however, that this could be 'brought about only by peaceful means with the consent of a majority of the people, democratically expressed, in both jurisdictions'. The Government of Ireland Act 1920[54] was repealed, but a new Northern Ireland Act reasserted the sovereignty of Westminster.[55] As far as Trimble was concerned, he had secured the constitutional position of Northern Ireland within the UK. The first paragraph of the Agreement, argued Trimble, clearly recognized that it was for the people of Northern Ireland alone, without any outside interference, to determine the destiny of Northern Ireland.[56]

Paisley's assault on 'Constitutional Issues' was to focus on the abolition of the Government of Ireland Act 1920, which 'removed the title deeds of the United Kingdom's sovereignty over Northern Ireland', whilst the 'illegal' claims contained in the Irish Constitution would merely be amended. Furthermore, the changes in Articles 2 and 3 would take place only in exchange for all-island executive bodies. Paisley argued that it was 'clear that all the pieces of the jigsaw puzzle to remove Unionists from the Union have been identified and are now being put into place', whilst unionists were being asked to 'commit an act of collective communal suicide by voting themselves out of the Union'.[57] As far as the 'so-called principle of consent' was concerned, it was provided that it was 'for the people of the island of Ireland alone...to exercise their right of self-determination'; Paisley argued that the right to self-determination should be a matter for the people of Northern Ireland alone.[58]

Alongside the constitutional and governance aspects, the Agreement also established a Human Rights Commission to monitor and safeguard human rights in Northern Ireland. The European Convention on Human Rights was to be incorporated into Northern Irish law.[59] There was to be an end of emergency powers legislation, combined with a reform of policing and the criminal justice system, based upon the proposals of new commissions.[60] Two of the most controversial aspects of the Agreement—alongside the possibility of Sinn Féin serving in the executive—were those of decommissioning and prisoners. All paramilitary prisoners were to be released on licence within two years, provided their organization remained on ceasefire.[61] As for decommissioning, the Agreement stated merely that parties to the Agreement were to use their 'influence' with paramilitaries to achieve disarmament.[62] This was a particularly loose aspect of the Agreement, one which outraged the DUP. There was no guaranteed bar on Sinn Féin's taking places in the power-sharing executive, even if the IRA held on to all its weaponry. The Agreement maintained that those who held office should use only 'democratic non-violent means, and those who do not should be excluded or removed from office under these provisions'. However, because the support of the SDLP would be needed for unionists to remove Sinn Féin, Paisley argued this would not happen. In any case, Sinn Féin would argue, as they did in the talks, that they were committed to democratic, non-violent means, while the IRA were separate and carried out violent activity on their own behalf.[63] Paisley claimed that the Agreement 'actively *prevents* the decommissioning of terrorist weapons. In fact, there is not the remote possibility of the IRA's handing over its weapons.'[64]

The DUP was also concerned by what Sinn Féin called the 'demilitarization' agenda. Army surveillance installations were to be dismantled, military numbers reduced, and emergency powers removed. He also warned that policing changes would adversely affect recruitment, composition, training, and ethos, becoming a two-tier community service that incorporated ex-terrorists in the dispensing of justice within their communities.[65]

Finally, Paisley also attacked the 'equality agenda' in the Agreement as a euphemism for republican supremacy and reverse discrimination against Protestants. Unfair preference was to be given to the Irish language—a language 'of no merit', a 'weapon of cultural abuse', and one 'hijacked by the provisional IRA and spoken only by a minority of the minority community', whose deployment would 'lead to signs going up all around the country "Irish Language only-Protestants need not apply!"' [66]

Northern Ireland Says Yes, but the DUP Still Says No

The Belfast Agreement split the unionist community. In May 1998, 57 per cent of Protestants voted 'Yes' to the deal; Catholics voted overwhelmingly in support.[67] Protestant support for the Agreement then declined. The proportion saying that they would vote 'No', if asked again to vote on the Agreement, outstripped 'Yes' voters 38 per cent to 34 per cent by 2002.[68] Despite the initial setback of the referendum, the feeling in the DUP was that the Agreement would not be acceptable in the long term to unionists. Peter Robinson's initial reaction to its signing, as he recalls, was one of 'outrage. I knew instantly this wasn't something that was going to stand. It wasn't credible to get ongoing electoral support', given that the IRA would have had to 'bow down to him through the whole of the process for him to survive and that was never going to happen. At every level he got it wrong'.[69] Edwin Poots, later a Minister in the Northern Ireland Assembly, was 'devastated', but recalled:

I was quite shocked when I first read the Agreement and I was somewhat surprised at the overwhelming majority that it received. At the same time, there was 30 per cent [of voters] against it. That 30 per cent was almost entirely from the unionist community. There was a fair indication that almost half the unionist community wasn't going along with the Agreement, so I knew as a party we [the DUP] weren't finished, but I didn't like the fact it had such an overwhelming majority in the referendum that followed.[70]

Ian McCrea, the son of William McCrea and himself a Member of the Northern Ireland Legislative Assembly (MLA) established by the Agreement, was reassured by what he found when canvassing for a 'No' vote in the referendum, finding many people

absolutely incensed by it. So I knew there was a very large unionist community that would not, could not wear this...I knew that we could harness that, which we did...It was a shoddy and badly negotiated deal and there were absolutely crucial flaws in it. There was no link between decommissioning and the release of prisoners, which is an absolutely fundamental issue that wasn't addressed.[71]

One of the key criticisms offered by Peter Robinson towards Trimble is in respect of the terms of governance established in the new institutions:

He got it wrong in terms of setting up a system without any accountability. Each of the Ministers was completely responsible within their own department. That led to McGuinness's decision on education [abolishing selection]. It led to Bairbre de Brun's decision on health [the closure of a maternity unity], in spite of the Assembly voting that these things shouldn't happen, despite the committees voting against these things happening—no accountability whatsoever.[72]

Robinson also highlighted the failure to secure Sinn Féin's commitment to support the state's police force as a crucial flaw:

The killings still continued. The gangsterism still continued. There were still the attacks on the police, no support for the police, the rule of law, the courts. It was an untenable position to have people [Sinn Féin] in a government while they were still attacking and wouldn't give support to the police. It was a system that was never going to survive.[73]

Policing was indeed a key issue. The Independent Commission on Policing for Northern Ireland (1999), chaired by Chris Patten, made 175 recommendations, the most significant of which, in unionist terms, was symbolic: to rename the RUC to make it more acceptable to nationalists.[74] Under the provisions of the Police Northern Ireland Act 2000, the RUC was renamed the Police Service of Northern Ireland (PSNI). A Northern Ireland Policing Board (NIPB) was established in November 2001, its role being to secure the maintenance, efficiency, and effectiveness of the PSNI and hold the Chief Constable to account. Yet Sinn Féin refused to take up their seats on the NIPB and withheld support for the reconstituted force for several years. The Patten Report also recommended exceptional measures to address imbalances in the religious background of the membership of the police—50–50 Catholic–Non-Catholic recruitment for a temporary period.[75]

On several occasions, Trimble entered government with Sinn Féin in the hope of a reciprocal gesture of decommissioning by the IRA. Instead, the power-sharing executive had to be suspended four times, indefinitely on the final occasion, as republicans declined to destroy their full arsenal—although they made a 'gesture' of decommissioning in October 2001. A delegation from the DUP, led by Paisley, met with General John de Chasterlain, the Canadian chairman of the Independent International Commission on Decommissioning (IICD), which oversaw the 'event'. He was not permitted to reveal what or how much weaponry had been decommissioned or indeed where the event had taken place. Afterwards, the DUP declared that it was 'astounded' that David Trimble had recommended that his party re-enter the executive and that the Government were proceeding with the destruction of army installations and providing terrorists with an amnesty on the basis of 'an unspecified event, where an unspecified number of weapons, of an unspecified type, were put beyond use in an unspecified way, at an unspecified location'.[76]

Each time the executive was suspended, the credibility of Trimble and the UUP was undermined further. While this bolstered the DUP's position relative to the Ulster Unionists, a fundamental problem remained for the smaller pro-union party. This was the fact that the core institutions, established by the Belfast Agreement, were impossible to remove, given the support they enjoyed from not only Trimble, but all shades of Northern nationalism and the two sovereign governments. This was recognized by key personnel within the DUP. There was, as one adviser put it:

> some evidence of reflection...you might regard it as clarification of the Party's policy...By 2001 there was a clear view from ourselves that whilst the present arrangement was very unpopular, devolution wasn't unpopular and we didn't want to be seen to be running a policy which said we want to bring devolution down and replace it with nothing else—that wasn't going to do the job.[77]

Therefore, during the course of the election, the DUP developed the 'Seven Principles' which were:

> devised to look relatively positive and not to tie our hands in terms of a later agreement that could be reached. The Seven Principles were fairly broadly drawn. I think our view was there is no point in us putting out a document which said 'this is our alternative', but which would have been immediately rubbished by the other parties. Instead, we just put out principles against which any proposal could be judged—whether it was our proposal or somebody else's proposal, it gave us more room for manoeuvre and it showed us as being more constructive and positive. That played out quite well at the time.[78]

The DUP's 'Seven Principles' were:

1. The DUP is a devolutionist party. We believe in democratic, fair, and accountable government.
2. No negotiating with the representatives of terrorism, but we will talk to other democratic parties.
3. Those who are not committed to exclusively peaceful and democratic means should not be able to exercise unaccountable executive power.
4. Terrorist structures and weaponry must be removed before the bar to the Stormont Executive can be opened.
5. Any relationship with the Republic of Ireland should be fully accountable to the Assembly.
6. The DUP will work to restore the morale and effectiveness of the police force.
7. We will strive to ensure genuine equality for all, including equality in funding.[79]

In summer 2002, there was internal DUP discussion around what new arrangements might look like and 'subtly...we talked about renegotiation of the Agreement, as opposed to its complete removal...probably the view that some in the party would have had in 1998 about what a new agreement might look like was somewhat unrealistic'.[80]

Therefore, the DUP had to find a form of language which

> gave us a mandate for changes and spelt out what the changes needed to be, but were not so unrealistic that they could never be achieved and obviously that was a gradual job of bringing people along...to get us into a position that would be credible with the general public. If we were going out and saying we are going to deliver a voluntary coalition tomorrow, people aren't stupid, people know that given the way the mathematics of the Assembly were and the SDLP's continued unwillingness to move away from Sinn Féin, it was highly unlikely it was going to come about.[81]

In the run-up to the Assembly election of 2003, a Joint Declaration issued by the Governments stressed the necessity in this context of 'acts of completion' in the full implementation of the Belfast Agreement. This led to the establishment, by London and Dublin, of an Independent Monitoring Commission (IMC) to monitor the activities of paramilitaries.[82] The Assembly election itself was a watershed, as the DUP overtook the UUP for the first time in terms of seats. The party manifesto argued that 'It's time for a fair deal.' The UUP, it was claimed, 'had tried, failed, and lied'. The message to voters was that if David Trimble controlled over 50 per cent of the unionist seats in the Assembly, the Belfast Agreement would continue. If Ian Paisley controlled over 50 per cent of the unionist seats in the Assembly, there would be negotiations for a new agreement.[83] The message did not entirely convince, given that the UUP retained its vote-share lead over the DUP, but the higher number of Assembly seats won by the DUP (thirty, to the UUP's twenty-seven), accompanied by Sinn Féin's triumph in the nationalist bloc, ensured that the old UUP–SDLP pivotal axis for the Belfast Agreement was finished.[84] Paisley entered that election insistent that his party would never sit in government with Sinn Féin, but having overhauled the UUP in the Assembly, he was never again so adamant on the issue.

This seismic shift in unionist party preferences had been occurring for some time, given the fissures within the UUP over the Belfast Agreement. The DUP drew much talent across from its rival. The loss of popular and talented personnel, such as Jonathan Bell, Jeffrey Donaldson, Arlene Foster, Simon Hamilton, and Peter Weir, hugely damaged the UUP. Originally, Weir had been suspicious of the 'angry unionism' of the DUP, but eventually was happy to join.

> Within the Ulster Unionist Party there was a sort of fractioning post Belfast Agreement...that created a level of division, effectively it created two parties within the Ulster Unionist Party. I was eventually, sort of towards the end of 2001, kicked out of the Ulster Unionist Party. I felt, having worked and seen the DUP up close in the assembly, that the sort of views they were articulating were like my views and it would be a comfortable home for me.[85]

Regarding the Belfast Agreement, Weir's concerns reflected those he encountered more widely within the UUP:

> There were a lot of things that people weren't happy with. I suppose the initial focus [was] on the prisoners, a medium focus on the police, but the issue that continued to be greater was the entering of Sinn Féin into government and what conditions they would take to get in that. There was a concern that they would have their cake and eat it—get in, not decommission, and still have that threat of violence behind that. Those were the main concerns.[86]

A key moment in the intra-unionist rivalry was the defection of the leader of the UUP's dissidents, Jeffrey Donaldson, MP for Lagan Valley, to the DUP in January 2004. Donaldson had been a Trimble ally and part of his talks team in 1998. Interested in politics from an early age, his cousin Samuel Donaldson having been the first RUC officer to be killed by the IRA during the Troubles, Donaldson had been active in UUP politics since his late teens, as, variously, election agent for Enoch Powell, his local UUP MP, in South Down, chairman of the Ulster Young Unionist Council, elected member of the 1982–6 Northern Ireland Assembly, and, from 1997, a popular UUP MP. Donaldson's original party choice came because, despite being 'impressed by the charisma' of Paisley, the UUP leader, James Molyneaux, had a 'humble yet very strategic long-term approach to politics'.[87] Powell and Molyneaux had considerable influence over Donaldson in terms of scepticism over the possible ultimate direction of British policy and the risks of full devolution. Powell had 'very strong theories' concerning the Foreign Office and the Americans conspiring to bring about the circumstances whereby there would be a gradual transfer of power from Britain to Belfast, through devolution, and then to Dublin.[88] Donaldson tended towards this approach but subsequently came to the conclusion that it was possible to have high-level devolution without endangering the Union.

Donaldson's transfer to the DUP was

> all about the peace process and the UUP's handling of it. To be honest, I came to the realization that the UUP was not capable of delivering the necessary changes in order for unionists to buy into the whole Agreement. There were some key issues within the Belfast Agreement with which I had great difficulty. Not the constitutional arrangements...Without in any way beating my own drum, all of the flaws I saw and predicted came to pass...There was no chance that the Sinn Féin leadership was going to use their best endeavours to bring about IRA decommissioning within two years...Because of the decision to rush through the Agreement, it took us nine years to fix it.[89]

Donaldson was not alone in his hostility to a flawed deal and the approach of the UUP leadership. For Arlene Foster, another UUP 'dissident' close to Donaldson, political expediency had replaced principle, arguing: 'the deal did not offer justice...there is no justice in letting criminals and gangsters out of prison. They were trading justice for a political agreement.'[90]

Donaldson concluded that the UUP, under Trimble's leadership, were not capable of delivering the necessary changes to secure the peace process. That was partly because Trimble was 'not a good negotiator, he's an academic— and that's not a slight on academics. But I would not hire an academic lawyer to act as a negotiator.'[91] The UUP leader did not have 'the eye and the ear for the people. When people have concerns, what you don't do is isolate them. You try to address the concerns.'[92] As late as the November 2003 Assembly election, Donaldson had not decided to join the DUP. He sat in the House of Commons as an independent for a short period, but 'one man was the catalyst' for him joining the DUP 'and that man was Peter Robinson', the next DUP leader, who held several meetings with Donaldson.[93] In those discussions, Donaldson 'made clear that I hadn't fought as long and hard as I had to address the flaws of the peace process only to find myself outside the tent. I needed to know that the DUP were going to be fully engaged in attempting to fix the peace process.'[94] Donaldon's joining the DUP was conditional on an assurance from Paisley and Robinson that they were going to become fully committed to negotiating the outstanding unionist concerns with the peace process—and moving Sinn Féin on policing and justice.

Donaldson had become close friends with Robinson and the DUP's Nigel Dodds and was aware that the DUP was interested in renegotiating, rather than entirely abandoning, the 1998 deal.

I certainly knew there were people in the DUP at a very senior level who were pragmatic enough to understand that it wasn't possible to discard everything and go back to the drawing board... So I knew from those friendships and contacts that there was a pragmatism within the DUP; that if given the opportunity to sit at the table, they could deliver the kind of changes that were necessary. Unlike Trimble, they weren't likely to buckle under pressure. They were capable of sitting at the table and staring the other person out. Also, they weren't impressed with Bill Clinton or Tony Blair sitting opposite them. I also knew—and this was very important for me—that there was no one better at strategy than Peter Robinson. Intellectually, Trimble represented the best of Unionism. But Peter Robinson was a shrewd strategist, and that was what we needed at that stage. You will note that I haven't mentioned Ian Paisley very much in my responses. In Parliament, I was more likely to be in the company of Peter Robinson or Nigel Dodds. I knew Ian Paisley as the leader and as a very strong leader at that. But I didn't know him very well personally. It was people like Peter and Nigel that I related to. That personal connectivity is very important when making such a big decision. But I have never once regretted the decision to join the DUP. They have delivered all that I hoped for.[95]

Arlene Foster's defection was also highly significant, given that she came from Fermanagh, a county institutionally Ulster Unionist, where the DUP 'didn't really have a presence... if you talked about Unionism in Fermanagh, that was the Ulster Unionist Party'. After the 2003 Assembly elections, she found the attitude in some quarters of the UUP towards her and Donaldson 'very aggressive... I always remember [senior party figures] Michael McGimpsey and [Lord] Ken Maginnis being very aggressive... Maginnis sent an email... and... said "Time to say goodbye Jeffrey"'. After Foster left the UUP, in December 2003, the chairman of the local DUP Association in Fermanagh approached her with a view to joining the party (although she had also had separate conversations with Peter Robinson). This was a difficult decision for Foster, as the UUP was her 'political nursery':

That is where I had started, that is where basically I matured. I became a party officer when I was only 25, so I had been probably one of the youngest party officers ever and it was very difficult, and living where I lived in Fermanagh as well made it very difficult. If I had lived somewhere that was more DUP it probably would have been easier.[96]

Foster found that her experiences in the DUP were in sharp contrast to those in the UUP. She was particularly struck by the personality and personal kindness of Ian Paisley. Her defection to the DUP was the spark for others in the Fermanagh UUP Association to follow; as Andrew Walker, a former Ulster Unionist member who joined the DUP, put it: 'Where Arlene goes, I follow...there were three of us [that joined the DUP] that were very, very close to Arlene. I mean close, was at every meeting, down her house, up at our house, very close...her policies were the policies to follow.'[97] In Lagan Valley, over half of Donaldson's constituency association followed him over to the DUP. When Donaldson fought the DUP at the UK general election in 2001, he got 26,000 votes for the UUP and Edwin Poots got 6,000 votes for the DUP. But after joining the DUP, in the 2005 general election, Donaldson got the same percentage share of the vote in Lagan Valley as he had for the UUP. Donaldson insists he

> did not know which way those votes would go...I knew that many of my constituents voted for the Agreement but were cheesed off with the way things had gone since then. They were fed up with the drip, drip, drip concessions. It had worn thin with them. But it was still a big risk. I had no idea how those people would respond to my leaving the UUP to join the DUP...I managed to persuade them that my decision was not based on some sort of personal fallout between myself and David Trimble, but on the changes that the DUP was capable of bringing about. I brought a lot of people with me who had been loyal UUP members and supporters, some of them in their sixties and seventies. One lady in her eighties wrote to me to explain that she had voted for the UUP in every single election since she was first able to vote. But she told me that she would be voting for me in 2005 rather than the UUP candidate.[98]

While the new DUP intake were confident that a comprehensive deal could be negotiated in Downing Street, the mood there was gloomy, with Jonathan Powell, Tony Blair's Chief of Staff, recording how the Prime Minister was sceptical that Ian Paisley would ever do a deal. Blair's initial idea was that the Government's strategy should be to allow the DUP scope to reach an agreement, but also the space for their political ruin by obstructing one. Powell indicated to Adams and McGuinness that, since the election, the price of a deal had risen: if Sinn Féin wanted the British to carry out their commitments to them this had to be reciprocated.[99] When confronted with evidence of ongoing IRA activity, from criminality to intelligence gathering, Adams and McGuinness did not deny its existence, but focused on the lack of fighting capability within the IRA after years of ceasefire and the time required to wind the organization down.[100] As one DUP adviser recalled, while some saw the 2003 result as a setback, Peter Robinson made the point that it

> was actually a blessing in disguise. Blair...had commented, adapting the old Churchill line, 'Well if it was a blessing in disguise it was very well disguised', but my feeling at the time was, it was only when we were inside the process in a

meaningful way that we had a realistic chance of getting [issues] resolved...The last thing we wanted to do was to appear like a party that nobody could do business with. So quite a bit of our efforts in 2004 were in persuading the government that actually we were genuinely serious about doing a deal, if it was on the right terms.[101]

Conclusion

The DUP, from its inception in 1971 until 2003, when it became the dominant unionist party in Northern Ireland, was a party of protest. The career of its leader, Ian Paisley, was built on opposition to successive leaders of the UUP, from Terence O'Neill, in the 1960s; James Chichester-Clark and Brian Faulkner, in the 1970s; to David Trimble, in 1990s. Paisley's religious beliefs were a key factor in influencing his politics and evangelicalism formed a major component of the early DUP. What 'Paisleyism' represented, in political terms, was the preservation of traditional, robust, constitutional unionism, infused with a religious element in terms of the defence of the Protestant people. In essence, this meant that majority rule by the Protestant community was the optimum political solution, necessary as the best method of preserving Protestantism within Northern Ireland. Greater cooperation with the bordering Irish Republic, dominated by a Catholic-Gaelic culture, and which claimed Northern Ireland as part of its national territory, was rejected by Paisley. He regarded such moves by other unionists as the first stage in selling out Northern Ireland's constitutional position within the UK. The DUP was consistent in rejecting executive power-sharing within Northern Ireland, with nationalists, and any institutional link with the Republic of Ireland. The DUP also interpreted successive attempts at cooperation between British and Irish Governments, such as the AIA, as a slippery road to a united Ireland.

The DUP saw the Belfast Agreement as flawed in both constitutional provision and moral terms. The DUP argued that the Agreement had dismantled Northern Ireland's position within the United Kingdom; laid the foundations for the creation of an embryonic all-Ireland government; permitted the continuation of Dublin's interference in Northern Ireland's internal affairs; established undemocratic and unaccountable institutions across all three Strands; allowed terrorist representatives into government without decommissioning; laid the foundations for the destruction of the RUC; and initiated an 'equality agenda' process which aimed at discriminating against Protestants and unionist interests. Unionist discontent with the operation of the Agreement laid the foundations for the DUP to supplant the UUP in 2003; but this involved an acceptance that, in order to 'renegotiate' the Agreement, some of the shibboleths that defined the DUP since its foundation had to be compromised. In that sense, the battle for the form of 'traditional Unionism' that the DUP had long championed—such as a return to majority rule and no institutional link with the Irish Republic—had been lost.

Notes

1. S. Bruce (1986) *God Save Ulster! The Religion and Politics of Paisleyism*, Oxford: Oxford University Press, 24.
2. *Belfast Telegraph*, 13 Jan. 1966.
3. M. MacIver. (1987) 'Ian Paisley and the Reformed Tradition', *Political Studies*, 35/3, 368–9.
4. MacIver, 'Ian Paisley and the Reformed Tradition', 366.
5. *Belfast Telegraph*, 26 Jan. 1965.
6. *Belfast Telegraph*, 7 Feb. 1966.
7. *Belfast Telegraph*, 11 May 1966.
8. M. O'Callaghan and C. O'Donnell (2006) 'The Northern Ireland Government, the Paisleyite Movement and Ulster Unionism in 1966', *Irish Political Studies*, 21/2, 212.
9. S. Bruce (2001) 'Fundamentalism and Political Violence: The Case of Paisley and Ulster Evangelicals', *Religion*, 31/4, 392.
10. Bruce, 'Fundamentalism and Political Violence', 390.
11. MacIver, 'Ian Paisley and the Reformed Tradition', 375.
12. MacIver, 'Ian Paisley and the Reformed Tradition', 378.
13. Bruce, 'Fundamentalism and Political Violence', 396.
14. Bruce, 'Fundamentalism and Political Violence', 399.
15. Interview with Peter Robinson MLA, DUP party leader, Stormont, 25 June 2013.
16. Interview with Peter Robinson, 25 June 2013.
17. Interview with Peter Robinson, 25 June 2013.
18. Interview with Peter Robinson, 25 June 2013.
19. Interview with Revd William McCrea MLA, Ballyclare, 24 Jan. 2013.
20. Interview with Revd William McCrea, 24 Jan. 2013.
21. Interview with Revd William McCrea, 24 Jan. 2013.
22. Interview with Revd William McCrea, 24 Jan. 2013.
23. Interview with Gregory Campbell MP, MLA, Stormont, 18 Oct. 2012.
24. Interview with Gregory Campbell, 18 Oct. 2012.
25. Interview with Gregory Campbell, 18 Oct. 2012.
26. Interview with Gregory Campbell, 18 Oct. 2012.
27. Interview with Sammy Wilson MP, MLA, Carrickfergus, 25 Jan. 2013.
28. Interview with Sammy Wilson, 25 Jan. 2013.
29. Interview with Sammy Wilson, 25 Jan. 2013
30. Interview with Sammy Wilson, 25 Jan. 2013.
31. Interview with Sammy Wilson, 25 Jan. 2013.

32. Interview with Revd William McCrea, 24 Jan. 2013.
33. Democratic Unionist Party (1982) *Assembly Election Manifesto*, Belfast: DUP.
34. Brooke-Mayhew Talks Papers: Annex B Speech by Dr Paisley MP, MEP at Plenary Session of Strand 1 Talks, June 1991.
35. Democratic Unionist Party (1992) *A Sure Advance*, Belfast: DUP.
36. HM Government and Government of the Irish Republic (1993) *Joint Declaration for Peace*, 15 Dec., London: HM Government; available at <http://cain.ulst.ac.uk/events/peace/docs/dsd151293.htm>, accessed Jan. 2014.
37. Cited in the *Irish Times*, 16 Dec. 1993.
38. HM Government (1995) *Frameworks for the Future*, Cmnd. 2964, London: HMSO.
39. I. Paisley (1998) 'Peace Agreement: Or Last Piece in a Sellout Agreement?' *Fordham International Law Journal*, 22/4, 1281–2.
40. Interview with Revd William McCrea, 24 Jan. 2013.
41. Interview with Lord Morrow, DUP Chair, Stormont, 10 Jan. 2013.
42. Belfast Agreement: Strand 1, Paragraphs 1–33.
43. D. Trimble (1998) 'The Belfast Agreement', *Fordham International Law Journal*, 22/4, 1158–9.
44. Paisley, 'Peace Agreement', 1302–3.
45. Belfast Agreement: Strand 2, Paragraphs 1–19 and Annex.
46. Trimble, 'The Belfast Agreement', 1155–6.
47. Paisley, 'Peace Agreement', 1291–2.
48. Belfast Agreement: Strand 3, British-Irish Council, Paragraphs 1–12.
49. Belfast Agreement: Strand 3, British-Irish Intergovernmental Conference, Paragraphs 1–10.
50. Trimble, 'The Belfast Agreement', 1576–7.
51. Paisley, 'Peace Agreement', 1292–3.
52. Paisley, 'Peace Agreement', 1307.
53. Paisley, 'Peace Agreement', 1307–8.
54. Belfast Agreement: Constitutional Issues, Paragraph 1; Annex A; Schedule 1; and Annex B.
55. Northern Ireland Constitution Act 1998, clause 43.
56. Trimble, 'The Belfast Agreement', 1152–3.
57. Paisley, 'Peace Agreement', 1284.
58. Paisley, 'Peace Agreement', 1287–8.
59. Belfast Agreement: Rights, Safeguards and Equality of Opportunity, Paragraphs 1–10.
60. Belfast Agreement: Security, Paragraphs 1–5; Policing and Justice, Paragraphs 1–5.
61. Belfast Agreement: Prisoners, Paragraphs 1–2.
62. Belfast Agreement: Decommissioning, Paragraphs 1–6.
63. Paisley, 'Peace Agreement', 1289–90.
64. Paisley, 'Peace Agreement', 1311.
65. Paisley, 'Peace Agreement', 1312–13.
66. Paisley, 'Peace Agreement', 1317.
67. J. Tonge and J. Evans (2002) 'Party Members and the Good Friday Agreement in Northern Ireland', *Irish Political Studies*, 17/2, 61.

68. R. MacGinty (2002) 'Unionist Political Attitudes After the Belfast Agreement', *Irish Political Studies*, 19/1, 90.
69. Interview with Peter Robinson MLA, DUP party leader, Stormont, 25 June 2013.
70. Interview with Edwin Poots MLA, Lisburn, 10 Jan. 2013.
71. Interview with Ian McCrea MLA, Stormont, 9 Jan. 2013.
72. Interview with Peter Robinson, 25 June 2013.
73. Interview with Peter Robinson, 25 June 2013.
74. Independent Commission on Policing (1999) *A New Beginning: Policing in Northern Ireland* (The Patten Report), Belfast: HMSO.
75. House of Commons (2006) Research Paper 06/56, *The Northern Ireland (St Andrews Agreement) Bill 2006–7*, 17 Nov. 2006, 42–3.
76. Note of the meeting between the Democratic Unionist Party (DUP) and the Independent International Commission on Decommissioning (IICD), 25 Oct. 2001.
77. Interview with confidential source.
78. Interview with confidential source.
79. Democratic Unionist Party (2001) *Leadership to Put Things Right: General Election Manifesto*, Belfast: DUP.
80. Interview with confidential source.
81. Interview with confidential source.
82. House of Commons Research Paper 06/56, 7.
83. Democratic Unionist Party (2003) *Fair Deal Manifesto*, Assembly Election Manifesto, Belfast: DUP.
84. House of Commons Research Paper 06/56, 8.
85. Interview with Peter Weir MLA, Stormont, 9 Nov. 2012.
86. Interview with Peter Weir, 9 Nov. 2012.
87. Interview with Jeffrey Donaldson MP, MLA, Lagan Valley, 8 Mar. 2013.
88. Interview with Jeffrey Donaldson, 8 Mar. 2013.
89. Interview with Jeffrey Donaldson, 8 Mar. 2013.
90. Interview with Arlene Foster MLA, Belfast, 24 Jan. 2013.
91. Interview with Jeffrey Donaldson, 8 Mar. 2013.
92. Interview with Jeffrey Donaldson, 8 Mar. 2013.
93. Interview with Jeffrey Donaldson, 8 Mar. 2013.
94. Interview with Jeffrey Donaldson, 8 Mar. 2013.
95. Interview with Jeffrey Donaldson, 8 Mar. 2013.
96. Interview with Arlene Foster, 24 Jan. 2013.
97. DUP Fermanagh Focus Group, 26 Apr. 2013.
98. Interview with Jeffrey Donaldson, 8 Mar. 2013.
99. J. Powell (2008) *Great Hatred, Little Room: Making Peace in Northern Ireland*, London: Bodley Head, 137–8.
100. Powell, *Great Hatred, Little Room*.
101. Interview with confidential source.

2

The DUP Says Yes

The road to the DUP entering a power-sharing government with Sinn Féin in 2004 was a long one, but the essentials of an agreement were in place as early as 2004. It was the precise terms of agreement that were difficult. The first stage was to convince the British Government that the DUP was serious about negotiating a deal. This became the 'Blair Necessities' formula. In early 2004, a DUP delegation met with the Prime Minister. Assisted by Clive McFarland, of the DUP's policy unit, Peter Robinson ran a powerpoint presentation, with one person connected to the negotiations recalling:

> I think Blair was relatively impressed... 'Blair Necessities' was Peter [Robinson]'s idea; the idea that we would throw back at the Government everything it had said about what Sinn Féin had to do and say that was our policy, which made our policy not dissimilar to their policy, the difference being we would hold them to their policy, whereas they would more than happily avoid facing up and confronting their policy. That's where 'Blair Necessities' came in.[1]

This meant confronting the Prime Minister with his own words on the requirements for Sinn Féin's admission into an executive. It included reminding Blair of his statement in 1998 that: 'I pledge to the people of Northern Ireland: Those who use or threaten violence [will be] excluded from the Government of Northern Ireland.' It also required holding the Prime Minister to his rather more detailed statement of May 2003: 'We need to see an immediate, full, and permanent cessation of all paramilitary activity, including military attacks, training, targeting, intelligence gathering, acquisition or development of arms or weapons, other preparations for terrorist campaigns, punishment beatings, and attacks and involvement in riots.' Thus, the DUP wanted a new agreement that was stable, accountable, effective, and efficient. There were, in addition to the Seven Principles, to be Seven Tests imposed by the DUP:

1. Any Agreement must command the support of both Nationalists and Unionists.

2. Any Assembly must be democratic, fair, and accountable. Any executive power must be fully accountable to the Assembly.

3. Only those committed to exclusively peaceful and democratic means should exercise any Cabinet-style Ministerial responsibility.

4. Within any new Agreement any relationship with the Republic of Ireland must be fully accountable to the Assembly.

5. A new settlement must be able to deliver equality of opportunity to unionists as well as nationalists.

6. Agreed arrangements must be capable of delivering an efficient and effective administration.

7. The outcome must provide a settlement within the UK, not a process to a united Ireland. It must provide stable government for the people of Northern Ireland and not be susceptible to recurring suspension.

In the 'Blair Necessities' the DUP took on the Sinn Féin accusation that it would not share power with Catholics; that they did not want to have a 'Fenian' (Catholic) about the place, as Sinn Féin's Martin McGuinness alleged. For the DUP, it was about not wanting a 'terrorist' about the place. The DUP rejected the pattern followed by the UUP, in which they entered government with Sinn Féin in parallel with an

> IRA decommissioning stunt—the extent of which is known to no one other than the IRA and the Decommissioning Body [and would] not take the IRA on its word nor accept an incremental process...no instalment will satisfy...Completion is what we require and no move to include Sinn Féin in an Executive or granting them executive power will precede the full delivery of the Blair Necessities.[2]

At a follow-up meeting, on 3 March, between Blair's Chief of Staff, Jonathan Powell, Jonathan Phillips, the Northern Ireland Office's political director, Peter Robinson, and Nigel Dodds, Robinson detailed the DUP strategy. The DUP would go into government with Sinn Féin once the Independent Monitoring Commission (IMC) on paramilitary activity had confirmed, over six months, that paramilitarism and criminality by the IRA had ceased, decommissioning was complete, and republicans accepted DUP changes to Strands One and Two of the Belfast Agreement. They also wanted the Government to open channels to Sinn Féin. The following month, April, Adams and McGuinness revealed to the British that the IRA were prepared to reach a deal, including acceptance of the changes the DUP wanted to the Belfast Agreement, if they were convinced the unionists would not erect new hurdles afterwards. They acknowledged that support for policing needed to be part of the deal, so as to end punishment beatings by the IRA. This, however, would require the DUP agreeing to a date for the devolution of control of policing to Stormont from Westminster. McGuinness had concluded that Paisley wanted to be First Minister before he retired.[3]

In articulating its proposed reforms of the Belfast Agreement, the DUP declared: 'One of the most fundamental flaws in the Belfast Agreement is that it permits the representatives of terrorism to sit in government and has no adequate or effective means of excluding them.'[4] Another fundamental flaw with the Belfast Agreement was that decisions were made by those who were not accountable to the Assembly. Following the signing of the Agreement, it was 'promised that Ministerial and Executive action would be subject to the scrutiny of the Assembly and Assembly members would be empowered to hold Ministers fully accountable for executive decisions'.[5] Any legislative proposal could be defeated on the floor of the Assembly and thereby not come into law, but the Northern Ireland Act 1998 devolved power to individual ministers rather than the Assembly. The DUP warned:

> Following an Assembly election, under the Belfast Agreement, it would be possible for Sinn Féin/IRA Ministers to opt for other departments. Republicans could be placed in control of allocation of housing, strategic development, or economic regeneration. Indeed, a Sinn Féin/IRA Minister could opt to change the language on road signs, creating bi-lingual Irish and English signs. It is also perfectly possible that powers over policing and criminal justice could be devolved. If this were the case, a Sinn Féin/IRA Minister could have partial or total control over both of these areas. [Sinn Féin's] Gerry Kelly, the man who bombed the Old Bailey, could be Policing & Justice Minister.[6]

The DUP also complained that, at the time of the Belfast Agreement, the UUP promised that the all-Ireland implementation bodies would be accountable to the Assembly, yet, in 2001, a DUP attempt to reallocate funding from these bodies had been deemed to be outside the scope of the Assembly: The DUP thus claimed:

> People in Northern Ireland are therefore paying taxes and rates without any ability to control how they are being spent. No taxation without representation has been a fundamental democratic principle for centuries, but is flouted today in Northern Ireland...They are politically motivated bodies, negotiated and designed to appease the republican aspiration of an all-Ireland Government...Once set up, these all-Ireland implementation bodies take on a life of their own. They are controlled not by the Assembly, but by the North/South Ministerial Council.[7]

The DUP insisted that any relationship with the Republic of Ireland should be fully accountable to elected representatives in the Assembly. It was 'clear from the provisions which established the NSMC and in practice, that the Assembly's role in controlling the NSMC is virtually non-existent'. The only check placed on any activity was that it needed to be agreed by the ministers present. The Assembly was reduced to a forum where questions could be asked but no effective action could be taken. The DUP still complained that virtually every decision taken by the Assembly was capable of being vetoed by nationalists. The party argued that the 'simple democratic majority in Northern Ireland counts for nothing but is reduced to equal status with the minority' and unable even 'to pass a motion banning hare coursing', yet the 'one issue for which there was no requirement for a cross-community consensus was the single most important matter for Northern Ireland—its constitutional status'.[8] If nationalists ever became the majority, a vote of 50 per cent plus one could lead Northern Ireland into a united Ireland.

On the wider constitutional issues, the DUP indicated that Articles 2 and 3 were still unacceptable. The change from the Republic claiming the territory of Northern Ireland had been transformed to now claiming the people who lived there: 'the claim is now more offensive than it had been. Unionists have achieved a meaningless change to the Irish Constitution in return for the setting up of a shadow all-Ireland Government.'[9] The DUP insisted that the Irish Constitution should not claim the people of Northern Ireland any more than it should have claimed its territory and needed to more clearly respect the constitutional position of Northern Ireland. The DUP proposed the formation of a successor to the British-Irish Council, encompassing the totality of relations within the British Isles. The 'failing' of the BIIC was its isolated function involving the British and Irish Governments outside the umbrella of the totality of the relationships, which led to a lack of transparency, accountability, and had 'at times created suspicion'.[10]

The Human Rights Commission established by the Agreement was seen by the unionist community as a pro-nationalist or, at best, a pro-Agreement institution which had an agenda alien to the ordinary unionist. There was not a single recognizable person from an anti-Agreement background on the Commission, despite anti-Agreement unionists representing over 50 per cent of the unionist community. The Equality Commission, established by the Agreement, appeared to have become fixated on the removal of Union Flags from local government facilities, which had fed into the negative image it had in the unionist community. The Northern Ireland Victims Commission, another outgrowth of the Agreement, had not delivered: 'victims have been marginalised and former prisoners elevated'.[11] Alongside this was the fudging of decommissioning and the scaling down of security: 'There can be no doubt that the Belfast Agreement destroyed the force which stood against terrorism for 30 years whilst it elevated terrorists into government and released them from prison. It appears that it is only a matter of time before Sinn Féin/IRA come on to the Police Board and seek to control the police they once tried to slaughter.'[12]

Elements of Agreement

The first formal meeting of all the relevant parties to a potential successor deal was at a gathering in Lancaster House, London, in June 2004. Little emerged from these exploratory meetings apart from a private meeting, asked for by Paisley, with Blair and Taoiseach Bertie Ahern, where the DUP leader gave an assurance that, if republicans did indeed give up paramilitarism, 'everything would be possible'. He would then be prepared to 'go into government with them'.[13] It was at this time that Gerry Adams, in a private meeting with Blair, sketched out his idea for unilaterally standing down the IRA. A further meeting with Blair saw Adams and McGuinness reveal that the IRA would not agree to cease all paramilitary activity or decommission under the conditions set by the Independent International Commission on Disarmament (IICD). In September, Adams and McGuinness informed the Prime Minister that the IRA had finally agreed to put their arms beyond use—decommission—but they had to be convinced that the DUP were serious about entering government with Sinn Féin.

This was the preamble to a summit at Leeds Castle, in Kent, also in September, where the DUP delegation—Paisley, Robinson, and Dodds, plus an adviser—met with Blair and Ahern. During these meetings, the Taoiseach would say little, a reticence interpreted by the DUP team as a deliberate policy not to antagonize. Paisley's initial enthusiasm, in a private meeting with Blair, raised hopes among the Governments that a deal was close. As one participant recalls, from that first meeting at Leeds Castle, 'the Prime Minister would have been convinced that Dr Paisley would have wanted to do a deal if the terms were right'.

The DUP 'raised the stakes' on decommissioning by asking for a Protestant clergyman to observe the decommissioning event alongside General de Chastelain, the chairman of the IICD, with the unrestricted right to take photographs. When this was reported to Gerry Adams, he described the idea of third-party observers as a step too far. What the DUP were also seeking was accountability in Northern Irish and cross-border governance alongside 'mutually assured obstruction', whereby both unionists and nationalists could block something they did not like in the executive. The talks broke up, amid recriminations between the DUP and Sinn Féin, without agreement. In Powell's view, agreement was lost 'largely on technical points'. By this he meant the Irish, in particular their Foreign Minister, Brian Cowen, was 'unyielding' on the DUP's proposed changes to Strands One and Two: the Irish and the SDLP were convinced Paisley and his party were seeking a return to majority rule. By the time the Irish had begun to modify their position, the impetus had gone out of the talks.[14]

For some in the DUP, it was a relief that there was no agreement. One adviser's 'clear memory from Leeds Castle was that looking back, we were not being told directly or terribly honestly what the position of Sinn Féin or the IRA was on decommissioning'.[15] The Prime Minister continued to indicate that things were possible on decommissioning and on institutional structures when it would subsequently appear that there was never any prospect of what was being talked about being possible, and the DUP team suspected he was doing the same to Sinn Féin in reverse. Blair concluded that what the DUP were specifically asking for in the institutions was specifically what Sinn Féin were not prepared to concede. Leeds Castle thus ended in failure. A senior DUP member of the negotiating teams acknowledged that 'a lot of our people left Leeds Castle more than happy that things hadn't worked out', whereas the Governments

> probably saw from Dr Paisley's demeanour in the first meeting that Doc was in the mood to do a deal, but I think the fundamental difficulty was that the Governments were not well enough prepared in terms of what was needed to be changed in terms of institutional arrangements: I think they sort of assumed if they could get devolution all these other so-called 'minor' things will go away. Though as one member of the delegation pointed out, we would not be prepared to sign up in 2004 for arrangements we rejected in 1998.[16]

The sense that the British were unprepared is borne out by Powell's account, which records Blair accusing him of not being prepared enough for the discussion.[17]

At the end of the talks, Gerry Adams accused the DUP of not engaging or negotiating and remaining 'unwilling to accept equality' with Sinn Féin.[18] Despite republican frustrations, the DUP were not prepared to move first. This is what appealed to new DUP members, such as Jeffrey Donaldson, who claimed of senior DUP figures such as Robinson and Dodds that they had 'something that I did not see in David Trimble', adding:

> Sinn Féin weren't as clever as they were made out to be. There was a capacity for walking straight into the traps that Sinn Féin had laid for us. They do it so cleverly...Constructive ambiguity was as much as they had to do and the two Governments would build this up as significant movement when, in reality, Republicans didn't really have to do much beyond ceasefires. People like Peter Robinson and Nigel Dodds...realized that it wasn't enough to bang the drum and be the loudest voice in unionism. You had to be tough in cutting a deal, but nevertheless you had to cut it...That was a steely determination and a strategic approach to politics. Sinn Féin would have had to get up very early to get one over them. They brought the two Governments to realize that they were going to have to do business with the DUP, that David Trimble was a busted flush. Once Tony Blair saw that, Sinn Féin came to realize that they were going to have to start

delivering. That's exactly what they did in terms of decommissioning and policing and justice.[19]

Arlene Foster was also impressed by her experience at Leeds Castle, claiming:

When I was in the Ulster Unionist Party, I remember talks like Weston Park, and every time there was a round of negotiations…we always came out, Unionism always came out worse off. There was always something that had to be given to try and achieve decommissioning, or to try and achieve movement in relation to policing…It [Leeds Castle] was the first time we couldn't agree—so we are not agreeing, just for the sake of the optics. We are just going to leave and say we couldn't reach an agreement because that was much better than giving way and ceding something. So to me, it showed the strength of the DUP.[20]

Following Leeds Castle, the British and Irish Governments put pressure on Sinn Féin to clarify a proposed IRA statement that would deal clearly with decommissioning and the ending of all paramilitary activity. The 'obfuscatory' language used by the IRA in its statements and refusal to accept the clarifications put forward by the Governments could no longer continue. Adams informed the British that the IRA had now agreed to two independent observers for decommissioning, but not to photographs. He also wanted the British to prepare a 'Plan B', giving the Irish Government a greater say in the affairs of Northern Ireland. McGuinness laid great stress on a 'backchannel' between Sinn Féin and the DUP. He claimed the backchannel passed on some potential IRA language for its proposed statement and the DUP had responded that it was 'in the ballpark'.[21] The communications involved several very senior DUP figures, but also a small number of mid-ranking, ostensibly very hardline MLAs. One person close to the DUP leadership describes what has been reported as the 'backchannel' in the following terms:

I think there was always an understanding that people would talk to Sinn Féin and people would talk to us, and in those circumstances, there would have been an understanding of where Sinn Féin were at generally…to describe it as a back channel would be to overstate its importance. It certainly was not the way that the real business was being done.[22]

Following an invitation from Ian Paisley, Powell began shuttle diplomacy between Adams and McGuinness, mainly via Hillsborough, and with the DUP, using Jeffrey Donaldson's constituency offices in Lisburn. Sinn Féin handed over an IRA draft of a proposed statement to Powell to give to the DUP.[23] As one of the DUP team explains, the sight which then greeted Powell in Lisburn was

almost certainly not the way that the government would have done negotiations in the past. There must have been at least twenty people in Jeffrey Donaldson's office. It was totally unsuitable to any form of serious negotiation but it had the

41

advantage of making sure that as many people as possible were directly involved. I suspect Jonathan Powell had never experienced anything like it, with one person after another on our side taking the opportunity to ask questions and probe details.[24]

The DUP made amendments to the IRA draft, which were then taken by Powell to Adams and McGuinness, who accepted some of these while agreeing to take other suggestions back to the IRA.[25] The DUP gathering eventually broke up in the early evening, with Powell and Phillips returning the next morning for a smaller, more private meeting, where it was agreed that a solution was not on the cards and the two sides should reconvene in London with smaller numbers of people. Despite the large body of people at Lisburn, there was no leak from the DUP that they had been shown an IRA statement.[26] Powell persuaded the DUP to destroy the versions they had seen.[27]

Proximity talks in London followed, with the DUP in the Cabinet Office and Sinn Féin in 10 Downing Street. There was a door connecting the Cabinet Office and No. 10, and Powell and Phillips shuttled between the groups. It was a 'much more constructive day's work, or day and a half's work than the encounter in Lisburn', although the DUP MPs 'would disappear off every hour or so to vote in the House of Commons on some relatively obscure and unimportant vote to make a point about where their relative priorities lay in all of this'.[28] At these talks, Gerry Adams drafted a statement of Sinn Féin's position, which, although 'probably 80 per cent there' in terms of the DUP's demands,

> clearly was not written with the idea of reconciliation in mind and that sent our people over the edge, and I think Dr Paisley spent about 20 minutes lecturing Jonathan Powell on what a dreadful letter this had been and he wanted something drafted up in response...I think Powell concluded at the end of all of this that he regretted ever reading out what was in the document.[29]

Robinson and Dodds were the key players at this point because of their parliamentary duties in London, and considerable progress was made on the institutional changes that the DUP wanted. There was a long sequence of meetings, often away from the glare of publicity. Nigel Dodds recalled:

> Blair and Powell basically ran the show. What you would get was Powell would ring up and say 'can you come round? Use the Cabinet Office entrance, come round the back. Let's have twenty minutes, half an hour'. It would be two or three bullet points and he would say 'what do you think? what do you think? Let's touch base over the weekend.' That sort of thing...I think the thing about Blair that struck me was that he wasn't in the slightest bit interested in any kind of detail. He was always kind of [focused on the] 'great vision'. I remember when we were talking to him about things that Sinn Féin and the IRA were doing that

was causing difficulties and...he was, 'oh, I know and well, let's put that to one side for the time being'. He would never want to return to it.[30]

Dodds believed that the reason it took from 2003 to 2007 for the DUP to enter government with Sinn Féin was

> because we weren't prepared to take his [Blair's] word for stuff...one of the constant themes was, these people [Sinn Féin] are working in good faith, they don't believe that you are working in good faith, they don't really believe that you want to get in to government. We used to say to them [the Government] that policing, commitment to the rule of law, all of that is absolutely vital...Blair [was] standing up in the House of Commons telling me it was a pipe dream to think there could be any alternative to the conditions of the Belfast Agreement and we were absolutely adamant in the issues of policing. Ian Paisley...made it a very personal thing that this had to be delivered. I remember Blair telling me on numerous occasions that this was not going to be do-able.[31]

Dodds was nonetheless keen to continue robust dialogue and negotiation and to show that, given movement, the seemingly endless talks would not be wasted:

> I think the period that we spent with Powell and Blair...demonstrated that we were absolutely serious about entering government if we achieved what we wanted to achieve. I'm not sure they were convinced of that at the start at all. I think we convinced them of that, I think the Shinners [Sinn Féin] became convinced that: (a) we would remain the biggest party; (b) that we were serious; and (c) for them, they had nowhere else to go. The Shinners, for them to turn round and not follow through, meant that the whole project of McGuinness and Adams was a failure, so where did that leave them? They had committed everything to this sort of internal Northern Ireland strand, this North/South stuff which they made a lot of, which is of course now not a big issue, and the East/West stuff. They had committed an awful lot. They couldn't go anywhere else.[32]

Jeffrey Donaldson also believed that Sinn Féin was boxed in:

> Don't underestimate the amount of political capital that they [Sinn Féin] had invested in the peace process. They needed the peace process to work. If it didn't work, then the Adams and McGuinness leadership would have had to admit defeat to the hardmen. That was a very powerful influence at a leadership level. It's important to understand what your opposition needs. They wanted devolution, they wanted back in, they needed to be able to show that politics could work, and they needed to be in government. But we weren't going to give them that until they decommissioned and delivered on policing and justice, in principle at least.[33]

Symbolism remained important in the negotiations. In September, Paisley travelled to Dublin to meet with Ahern; Trimble noted, wryly, that when his predecessor, Jim Molyneaux, took another historic trip to the Irish capital, in 1992, to meet with Irish premier Albert Reynolds, he was 'denounced as a Judas by a Christian pastor. How Jim must have smiled to himself when he saw that same Christian pastor in Government Buildings in Dublin, taking tea and sandwiches with a Fianna Fáil Taoiseach.'[34] It was not all tea and sandwiches. After a brief spat, when Paisley told the Taoiseach to stop lecturing unionists about admitting 'Sinn Féin/IRA into the government of Northern Ireland at a time when his own party refuses to countenance Sinn Féin in power in the Republic',[35] the DUP leader turned his fire to republicans. Noting that Gerry Adams claimed the DUP wanted to humiliate the IRA over decommissioning, Paisley commented: 'There's nothing wrong with that. I think it's a very noble thing. The IRA needs to be humiliated. And they need to wear their sackcloth and ashes, not in a backroom, but openly. And we have no apology to make for the stand we are taking.'[36] Paisley highlighted the 'heartache the IRA has brought to countless homes across this province. The pride of republicans cannot be allowed to prevent progress and it is clear to me that Sinn Féin/IRA are scared of democracy because their republican ideology will be seen to be bankrupt stock.'[37] The prospect of a deal collapsed in the aftermath of Paisley's 'sackcloth' speech and his demand for photographs of the decommissioning event. The IRA condemned the latter as seeking an 'act of humiliation'.[38]

The two Governments had been confident they were really close to a deal, but a journalist was telling the DUP, about forty-eight hours out from the publication of the Comprehensive Agreement, that 'Sinn Féin aren't going to sign up for this; the process for now is over', which, to the DUP, 'came as a little bit of a surprise because we thought good progress has been made'.[39] Retrospectively, it was thought Sinn Féin had concluded the deal on the table was

> going to require too much for them at the time. And my sense is that they then used Dr Paisley's speech as an excuse for saying 'this is all too difficult, we will set it down now and come back to it again'. Clearly, the speech didn't help republicans manage their own people, but I think it was used as justification for them not proceeding.[40]

Having said this, the view of this participant was that, ultimately, it was good thing for the DUP that agreement was swerved:

> There was no doubt in my mind; looking back, it would have been a major mistake from our perspective to have done a deal in 2004 and sought to sell it then, as opposed to three years later...I think people were barely ready in 2006, 2007, never mind 2004. Obviously, what then followed, with the Northern Bank and the McCartney murder, robbed Sinn Féin of whatever credibility they might have

been building up. Certainly, I think we were not a million miles away from getting a deal in 2004, but fundamentally, it was too big an ask for Sinn Féin at the time.[41]

Prospects for a quick deal also faded following the robbery at the Northern Bank, in Belfast, on 20 December 2004, where £26m was stolen. The IMC report of 10 February 2005 concluded that the IRA had been responsible. The PSNI Chief Constable also indicated that, in his professional opinion, responsibility for that robbery should be attributed to the Provisional IRA.[42] This led to Bertie Ahern demanding 'commitments—both in word and deed— that the full spectrum of IRA paramilitary activities and capability has been brought to a definitive closure'.[43] The Governments were alarmed by bellicose IRA statements, in February, hinting republicans might return to violence. Intelligence indicated unusual levels of IRA activity. Adams, on the other hand, was informing the Irish that the IRA would not return to war because their community would not allow them.[44]

In fact, Sinn Féin found itself under more pressure following the murder, in a Belfast bar, of Robert McCartney in January 2005. A number of IRA volunteers had been involved in the killing. The campaign for justice by McCartney's family drew widespread support, even from President Bush in the White House. The Belfast murder was a blow to Sinn Féin because the McCartney sisters then became very powerful in terms of selling their message in the United States. Sinn Féin had gone from having been very close to a deal in 2004 to being in a position where they were

> beyond the pale for all mainstream politics and the only way they could get out of that hole was to do something much more dramatic than either of the two of them were prepared to do. This time they would have to do it without anything being reciprocated but the hope that, in time, people would come on board.[45]

Republicans were faced with implementing the logical outcome of the peace process. In April, Adams declared that the IRA was being used as the excuse not to engage properly in the process of building peace with justice in Ireland. In the past, he had defended the right of the IRA to engage in armed struggle: 'I did so because there was no alternative for those who would not bend the knee, or turn a blind eye to oppression, or for those who wanted a national republic. Now there is an alternative.'[46] Adams was laying the ground for the announcement, on 28 July, by the IRA leadership, that it was formally ordering an end to its armed campaign. All IRA units were ordered to dump arms, with all its volunteers instructed to assist the development of purely political and democratic programmes through exclusively peaceful means. The leadership also authorized a representative to engage with the IICD 'to complete the process to verifiably put its arms beyond use in a way which will further enhance public confidence, and to conclude this as quickly as possible'. As part of this process, it invited two independent witnesses, from Protestant and Catholic churches, to testify to this.[47]

Paisley's response to the IRA statement was to note that there had been similar republican announcements that were greeted with descriptions of 'historic', 'ground-breaking', and 'seismic', only to be followed by the IRA reverting to type. The DUP would judge the IRA's *bona fides* over the next months and years based on its behaviour and activity. He also noted that the IRA had failed to explicitly declare an 'end to their multimillion pound criminal activity and have failed to provide the level of transparency that would be necessary to truly build confidence that the guns had gone in their entirety'.[48] The British Government, meanwhile, reciprocated the end of the IRA campaign with its 'normalization programme' of reducing troop numbers and the removal of security fortifications, particularly in republican areas. Paisley described this as another 'surrender to the IRA' and more evidence of bad faith on the part of the Government.[49]

A further dramatic announcement came from the IRA, on 26 September, confirming that the 'process of putting our arms verifiably beyond use has been completed'.[50] Paisley's response to this was to attack the duplicity and dishonesty of the two Governments and the IRA, claiming that to call the IRA action transparent 'would be the falsehood of the century...We do not know how many guns, ammunition, and explosives were decommissioned, nor do we know how the decommissioning was carried out.'[51] The IICD, he complained, could only say that the proof that all the guns and material were decommissioned was an assurance given to them by the IRA. Not one iota of evidence was given to verify that assurance. The IICD message was to trust the IRA, as the IRA had indicated all weapons had been decommissioned. Paisley accused the Prime Minister of breaking his assurance that decommissioning must be transparent and verifiable and must satisfy everyone: there were no photographs, no detailed inventory, and no detail of the destruction of these arms. A meeting with the IICD chairman failed to reassure the DUP leader.[52]

As a senior DUP figure explained with regard to decommissioning:

Obviously, there was unhappiness that it was being done in a way which lacked visibility, other than the fact you had [the Reverend] Harold Good and [Father] Alec Reid attending. Our view was once it's done and it hasn't been filmed and pictured you can't do it again, but what it would require would be a longer testing period for people to be satisfied that the weapons genuinely...were off the stage.[53]

Reid and Good met with the DUP to answer questions 'or not answer questions' about what had gone on. One of the problems was that, as part of the secrecy surrounding the process, they were not in a position to divulge a lot of information. Good was 'very good at sticking to the script' and 'really saying very little other than he was satisfied', but Reid, whom DUP members preferred to try and talk to separately to gain information, was

> much more expansive...much more talkative and much more prepared to say things to convince us about what had happened; on a number of occasions during the meeting, when the priest wanted to tell us stuff, Harold Good would put his hand on...Reid's arm more or less to stop his saying too much more.[54]

Despite the conclusion of the Provisional IRA's campaign and the decommissioning of its weaponry, the DUP continued to refuse to share power with Sinn Féin. By January 2006, Powell recorded that 'Adams was getting desperate' and warned Blair that the current Sinn Féin leadership would be 'finished' by the summer if the executive had not been set up by then.[55] However, an IMC report, in February 2006, concluded that, while there were a number of definite signs of the IRA moving in the direction indicated in the 28 July statement, there were 'other signs which we would describe as neutral and some which are more disturbing. For example, some members continue to be engaged in significant crime and occasional unauthorised assaults.'[56] Although these assaults were not, in the IMC's view, sanctioned by the leadership, and might be directly against its wishes, the contrary appeared to be the case with some other criminal activities, such as the exploitation of financial assets the IRA had previously acquired or the illegal gathering of intelligence. Despite the IMC assessment, the view grew in Downing Street that something was needed to shock the DUP into moving towards entering power with Sinn Féin. Jonathan Powell began working on a 'Plan B' for greater British–Irish policy cooperation over Northern Ireland.[57] On 6 April, a Joint Statement was issued by the Prime Minister and the Taoiseach, with five main proposals:

- Recall of the Assembly to initiate the 6 week period within which a First Minister and Deputy First Minister should be elected
- Intensive party talks to ensure an Executive
- Second Assembly session from 1 September to 24 November, should no agreement be reached in June
- Cancellation of Assembly member salaries and allowances on 24 November, should no agreement be reached
- If no agreement, then the British and Irish Governments would develop partnership arrangements to develop the structure and functions of the Belfast Agreement[58]

As was seen in the Comprehensive Agreement, the essentials of a new agreement were already in place, but the sequencing of events was now the problem. The DUP refused to follow Trimble's example and make the first move of entering government with republicans. Sinn Féin's position was that they

could sign up to supporting the PSNI, by calling an Ard Fheis (party conference) to ratify this decision, but only *after* the DUP had entered the executive with them. The DUP's position was that Sinn Féin had to hold their Ard
Fheis *before* new Assembly elections and *before* they entered an executive with
republicans.

Into Government: The St Andrews Agreement and its Aftermath

In October, the Governments and parties gathered at St Andrews, in Scotland,
to find a solution. A possible resolution was suggested by Michael McDowell,
Bertie Ahern's coalition partner and Irish Minister for Justice: nominate the
First and Deputy First Ministers for 24 November; follow this by Sinn Féin's
endorsement of the police; and then hold new elections to the Assembly.[59]

Early indications that a deal could be done soon disappeared and late on
the penultimate evening, the government claimed to be preparing for collapse. Amid fears the talks would collapse, Peter Hain, the Secretary of State,
came to the DUP and warned:

> the Prime Ministers were going to wrap the whole thing up in the morning and
> say it couldn't be done; we would have to go to Plan B...we would reconvene at
> half eight in the morning. Peter [Robinson] said [to Hain] if we are just going to
> wrap it up in the morning, we will take a lie-in, we will see you near lunchtime. [60]

Hain's intervention was regarded as a

> fairly vulgar attempt to try and threaten...It didn't have a lot of credibility.
> I remember getting up on the final morning and at that point we went back up
> to see the Prime Minister in his room and by this stage, things had moved back
> in the right direction...it was almost as if the previous night hadn't happen with
> all the negativity.[61]

Nigel Dodds dismissed Hain's threat: 'No, I don't buy it, I didn't buy it at the
time...the idea that the British Government was going to throw everything
up in the air and wipe out the last 15–20 years of policy at the moment when
they had Sinn Féin and almost the DUP [agreeing], it was ludicrous in my
view.'[62] Robinson, however, whilst not believing Hain's specific threat that
evening, had concluded that, in terms of the broader long-term threat from
Westminster policy, the Secretary of State 'certainly wasn't bluffing...If we
hadn't reached an agreement we would have ended up with a much greener
[pro-nationalist] form of direct rule', adding that whilst he

> wasn't going to swallow everything that I heard from the British Government,
> we have sufficient friends inside to know what was being planned. There would

have been much closer cooperation between London and Dublin...That was the alternative. It wasn't a case of having majority rule with bells and whistles that some people longed for. The choices were either you are putting your hand on the steering wheel with the ability to put your foot on the brake or else you...sit in the margins and watch them taking you without having any control. Those are the choices that we had.[63]

Robinson's desire was 'always to get the deal done, and the right deal done, put slightly off course with the over-enthusiasm at the first session, but right at the end: we got a package put together that was broadly positive'.[64] Despite suggestions, from Jonathan Powell, that Dodds was more sceptical of signing up to a deal, this participant recalls that 'the view with Dr Paisley, Peter, and Nigel [was] that the thing looked relatively positive'.[65]

Dodds insists he was content with arrangements: 'What made us do the deal was [that] we had achieved to a large extent what we had set out to. There comes a point in politics when you finally get most of what you are asking for on all the big issues. There comes a point where it is right to say yes as opposed to saying no.'

It was crucial, of course, for Sinn Féin to sign up to the sequencing now accepted by the DUP. Officially, the DUP and Sinn Féin did not meet face to face until months later and dialogue 'didn't happen at St Andrews', according to Dodds.[66] That is true in respect of head-to-head formal talks, although an account published elsewhere has offered a slightly different perspective.[67]

The St Andrews Agreement was published by the Governments on 13 October. As it was an agreement between the two Governments and not the political parties attending the gathering, the DUP did not formally endorse it, but the party was happy enough. The largest party in the largest Assembly designation would nominate the First Minister. Whilst Sinn Féin could catch the DUP, this was unlikely and in any case, the slight risk helped the DUP, who could mobilize votes to stop Sinn Féin achieving this. A revised Strand One made ministers more accountable, mainly via Section 28A of the Northern Ireland Act, to the executive and the Assembly by creating a legally binding Ministerial Code, at the heart of which was collective responsibility in the executive. The First and Deputy First Minister (FM/DFM) could determine that an issue should be dealt with by the executive as a whole, rather than by an individual minister (Section 20(4) of the Northern Ireland Act permitted the First Minister significant autonomy in this respect). The executive was also to seek consensus on all decisions; however, where this was not possible and a vote was taken, three ministers could ask for the vote to be taken on a cross-community basis and if thirty MLAs were unhappy with a ministerial decision of public importance, they could refer it back to the executive for review. In Strands Two and Three, the Ministerial Code required that draft decision papers be circulated to all executive members in advance of a scheduled NSMC or BIC meeting. Any member of the executive would have the right to seek an executive discussion on such a paper. Crucially there was also to be a new Ministerial Pledge of Office referring to support for the 'rule of law' including policing and the courts. Policing and justice were to be devolved at a point unspecified. The immediate timetable was that the Assembly would meet on 24 November to nominate the FM/DFM, followed by executive nominations and the devolution of power in March. It was left to the parties to decide whether an election or referendum was preferred to provide legitimacy.[68] The DUP and Sinn Féin were (unsurprisingly) happier to consolidate their own respective bloc dominance and Assembly representation via elections in March, whilst it was deemed that the deal would not require ratification by a referendum in the Irish Republic, as it held no significant variations from the constitutional aspects agreed in 1998.

For the DUP, proof of Sinn Féin's support for the PSNI would be provided by the insertion of relevant words in the Pledge of Office that ministers in the executive would have to take. At first, McGuinness informed the British that he would refuse to take the new Pledge of Office, as proposed by the DUP, because it referred to the police. Eventually, it was Sinn Féin that conceded the essentials of the language demanded by the DUP in the Pledge of Office, which stated that a Minister was committed 'to uphold the rule of law based as it is on the fundamental principles of fairness, impartiality, and democratic accountability, including support for policing and the courts'. There was another near collapse of the process when Paisley reneged on using a sentence he had promised the Prime Minister he would employ, on 24 November, when the shadow Assembly met and the FM/DFM were nominated. Paisley had promised Blair he would he would declare that if the St Andrews Agreement was adhered to and implemented by all the parties, then he would take the office of First Minister, reassuring Sinn Féin things were going ahead. Following a difficult party meeting, Paisley decided not to use the words he had agreed upon with the Prime Minister. Instead, the Speaker of the Assembly read out a statement, drafted for her by the NIO, saying that Paisley had indicated his intention to be First Minister—which he clearly had not. Disaster was averted by the botched attempt of a convicted loyalist killer, Michael Stone, to break into Stormont and kill Adams and McGuinness. Peter Hain described the interruption as 'divine intervention'.[69] Hain managed to get Paisley to clarify his position by issuing a press statement containing the crucial sentence in it and told the DUP leader how the Prime Minister felt personally let down by his failure to deploy the sentence as promised.[70]

The problem had arisen because some in the DUP still baulked at going into power with Sinn Féin. Dodds agrees that the party was not fully prepared: 'In the case of the famous moment when the camera pans back and there is Ian Paisley and Gerry Adams sitting at the apex of this table—that took a lot of people by surprise, to put it lightly.'[71] One MLA, Sydney Anderson, articulated the feelings of many. Although in favour of St Andrews, he admitted:

It was a culture shock...It wasn't that we didn't trust the party leadership, but things were moving a wee bit too quick. There needed to be more discussion. It might have come slightly early for us, but Dr Paisley said here is the list and then when you meet these we will go to government...We weren't kept fully abreast. There was a difficulty at that time. The party leadership stepped forward and simply expected the Assembly Group to simply follow—like it or lump it. The strong leadership of Peter Robinson and Dr Paisley brought the party forward. Those who felt aggrieved or concerned needed that extra time.[72]

Another MLA, Gordon Dunne, made a similar point, arguing that it was 'Dr Paisley's leadership...I don't think many other people could have done it' that swung things in favour, as far as he was concerned.[73] A North Down MLA 'didn't take any pleasure in sharing power with Sinn Féin' and felt it was a 'very difficult decision' which was 'on my conscience', but 'confidence in Peter Robinson' helped him accept the Agreement.[74] Senior party figure Edwin Poots accepts there 'probably could have been a bit more effort' to soften the landing for DUP members, but also states that 'there were probably senior members of the party who didn't read the change in Sinn Féin's position...had we spent a lot of time preparing the party, that would have weakened our negotiating hand at St Andrews, so that would have been a problem as well.'[75]

Even after Sinn Féin's Ard Chomhairle (party executive) and Ard Fheis ratified support for policing, the DUP refused to meet the March deadline to enter government, wanting more time. The solution was a face-to-face meeting—the first official one—with Sinn Féin. It would be up to the DUP to convince the republicans that they were serious about entering government with them—and that May, rather than March, should be the date for going into the executive. The lure, for Adams and McGuinness, of this formal contact with the DUP was decisive in overcoming their objections to a further delay. In reality, the DUP now had to decide whether or not to bite the bullet and enter the executive—or risk the British pulling the plug on the Assembly and moving to 'Plan B'. This led to a series of meetings. DUP officers met on the Thursday night of a frenetic week. There was then a meeting with the Prime Minister in London on the Friday, in which it was provisionally decided to enter government with Sinn Féin. The party executive agreed to this and the date of entry—8 May—on Saturday morning, a move followed by the historic meeting with Sinn Féin a day later. The decision to enter government with Sinn Féin was too much for some party members. Jim Allister MEP left the DUP to form his own party, Traditional Unionist Voice (TUV).

Claim and counter-claim are made over whether certain prominent DUP members were completely opposed to sharing power with Sinn Féin or merely wanted a longer decontamination period for republicans to demonstrate their commitment to exclusively peaceful and democratic means. In terms of a deal to share power with Sinn Féin, Allister insists his rejection was based upon 'principle' rather than, as suggested by DUP sources, timescale. 'I didn't want it at all. I didn't think that Sinn Féin had demonstrated themselves as fit for government. I didn't think there had been testing or anything else of that...all of a sudden it was now or never.'[76] Allister remembers 'very distinctly' being invited, with his wife, to a garden party at Buckingham Palace; also attending were Nigel Dodds, Willie McCrea, and their wives: 'Afterwards we went off for a bite to eat. Obviously, things were coming to a head, but Mr Dodds and Mr McCrea were as resolute as I was, or at least I thought they were, that we weren't going to bend or budge on this issue.' There then followed a party officers meeting the following week, when the proposition was put to call the DUP executive together, at the weekend, to agree to enter government. 'To my amazement', stated Allister, 'I was the only person voting against it. So what happened between the Tuesday night [when Dodds and McCrea were seemingly against entering government with republicans] and the Thursday night I have never discovered, but something happened.'[77]

For his part, Willie McCrea disputes the TUV leader's assertion that the latter was completely opposed to power-sharing with Sinn Féin.

> You see, I don't believe that was what Jim Allister's policy was. Jim Allister stated at a meeting that I was at that he would be willing to go in to power [with Sinn Féin], that the DUP should go in to power-sharing if they [republicans] were willing to recognize the police, were willing to not only recognize the police, but support the police, and that they were to give their weapons up. If I thought that by beating my chest I could somehow benefit the condition for the Ulster people and the unionist population, then I would have taken a similar view, but I did not believe that he [Allister] had actually anything to offer in that stance. I wish I could see another way.[78]

As far as Allister was concerned, it was 'quite clear Robinson was quite mercilessly using Paisley as the front man to get the deal, to sell the deal, because he knew he could never sell it. Once he had sold it, he [Paisley] got elbowed out of the way.' Paisley could sell St Andrews 'on the credit that he had with the unionist community; that was his essential role. Ian Paisley was...never was a detail man. He was well beyond that by then.'[79] The 'prime movers', claimed Allister, were the DUP leader's son, Ian Paisley Junior, 'who was bursting for office' and Robinson. Even though 'neither men like each other, they both had that mutual interest'. Allister found Dodds 'the biggest disappointment...I think Dodds bottled it in the end. The DUP would not be in government today if Nigel Dodds had stood his ground. I am totally convinced of that. He had the standing and the capacity to block it, but in the end, he bottled it for whatever reason.'[80] When asked why other seemingly hardline DUP MLAs, such as Jim Wells and Ian McCrea, did not resist the deal, Allister dismissed them in a blunt manner:

> Ah, the intellectuals now...The DUP is their passport, it is their meal ticket...All you have to do is turn up at an election and say, you might have your problems with us, but it is us or Martin McGuinness. Vote for us to keep Sinn Féin out. That is the meal ticket for Ian McCrea and other worthies like him. Let's be brutally frank. Where would Ian McCrea, or several others you could name, find an employer who would pay them £48,000 a year?[81]

In his defence, Ian McCrea states 'it was a difficult day' when the decision was taken to enter government, but 'everything we demanded was achieved, we got and that's the reality of it...there was nobody jumping up and down, but I think that again it goes back to the alternatives...we set up government with Sinn Féin or faced joint British-Irish rule'.[82] The DUP had campaigned for years against no Dublin interference in Northern Ireland's affairs and therefore if it could control what happened in Stormont, then that benefited unionism. Jim Wells was one of the few MLAs who voted against going into the power-sharing executive with Sinn Féin. Had Wells and other MLAs left the DUP at that stage, the party would have been in serious trouble. Wells was 'not against St Andrews', as it offered local control over crucial 'moral' issues such as abortion, but felt

> there were still issues outstanding that needed to be dealt with. I did not like the timing. I did not feel like we had consulted our grass roots sufficiently. I was extremely uneasy with it. I then agonised about what I was going to do. Should I go or should I stay in the Party? Some went, some stayed. My view is I felt it was a democratic decision and I would stay in...I was a waverer at the time; I am still not the most enthusiastic. I detest having to share government with those that I know have killed my kith and kin, but I also know that the alternatives are much worse and I have to just bite my lip and get on with it. This is not a choice between a good option and a bad option. It is the choice between a bad option and a worse option...There are men down the corridor here that have committed the most atrocious deeds. But an agreement was made in St Andrews which at least means we can control what they do and they are in here rather than out on the streets murdering people.[83]

On 8 May 2007, Ian Paisley became First Minister; Martin McGuinness Deputy First Minister. In his speech following his pledge of office, Paisley declared the Union 'is today stronger than ever'.[84] A demonstration of the DUP's ability to block unwanted measures was evident in October, when Edwin Poots, as Minister for Culture, Arts, and Leisure, announced that the proposed Irish Language Act, promised as part of the negotiations leading to the St Andrews Agreement, would not go ahead.[85]

Paisley did not remain as First Minister for long. On 4 March 2008, he announced that he would stand down as Northern Ireland's First Minister and leader of the DUP. Peter Robinson succeeded him in both roles. At the time, Paisley denied that he had been forced from the headship of the party he had founded and dominated. Given that dominance, there was no formal mechanism for his removal. Whilst it may be exciting to assume a deep inner conspiracy, the duller reality is that there was no elaborate coup. There was a reluctance to deal the fatal blow to a leader still admired (and feared) at the time—and a lack of knowledge of how it might be struck in any case. Nonetheless, there was impatience amongst some senior party figures for Paisley to step down, a growing feeling, increasingly articulated by unattributable sources, that change was needed for the party to adjust properly to its new role and flourish in government.[86]

Although Paisley Senior's political antennae remained intact, his bombast, contrarian utterances, rhetorical flourishes, and lack of attention to detail (the lattermost had certainly been on display at St Andrews) were more suited to an opposition role than that of First Minister and the (often dull) routines of governance. Yet Paisley was long accustomed to being leader, rather than team-playing, or not playing at all, and adjustment to a non-dominant position was difficult. The partial catalyst for his departure, which was not enforced, but gently encouraged as inevitable and appropriate, was an internal survey of MLAs, undertaken by Paisley's special adviser at Paisley's behest, which revealed some criticisms of his style and role. More than five years later, Paisley claimed that the survey was used by the most senior party figures to recommend that he departed.[87] Paisley's ire at the modest criticism contributing to his exit was exacerbated by a feeling that his son had been unfairly treated by party colleagues, leading to his resignation as a junior minister in 2008. Paisley's criticism was extended to Robinson's loss of the DUP's East Belfast seat in 2010 and to the personal difficulties which embraced his successor, the insistence that 'his [Robinson's] ways are not my ways',[88] marking a final parting of the ways between party founder and successor. Paisley had already severed relations with a party that was clearly moving on, declining to attend party conferences, even prior to voicing criticisms of his 'ousting' and of the current leadership.

The early years of the Robinson era saw a long struggle with Sinn Féin over the devolution of policing and justice powers. Following the intervention of Prime Minister Gordon Brown and Taoiseach Brian Cowen, the Hillsborough Castle Agreement, devolving these powers, was concluded on 4 February 2010. David Ford, leader of the cross-community Alliance Party, became the Justice Minister.

Reflecting on the whole process leading to, and beyond, entering government with Sinn Féin, Robinson acknowledges that the 'party wasn't travelling at the same pace…if there had been a clearer view beforehand of what we were prepared to settle for, then you could have prepared people a lot more readily'.[89] He learnt from this when dealing with the devolution of policing and justice:

> We sat down to negotiate. We started talking about the issue, publicly indicating what we would and what we wouldn't accept in this area…Jim Allister was 'scaremongering' with literature claiming Gerry Kelly was 'going to be the policing and justice minister, Martin McGuinness was going to be appointing judges', and policing and justice was going to be brought under the auspices of the NSMC. In spite of all of that, we prepared people for what we were prepared to do. We stated very clearly what we were not going to accept and when we did the deal there…was never any difficulty because there was an election immediately after it and it was never raised once on the doorstep. Now that is how you prepare your support base for something that you know is going to happen, provided that it happens on the basis that you want it to.[90]

Are the Members Happy with the Political Institutions?

Following the restoration of devolved government, the DUP feels itself to be in control of Northern Ireland's destiny. The unease amongst senior party members over doing and selling the deal has largely dissipated. Is this sanguine feeling replicated amongst the party membership as a whole? Almost two-thirds concur with the proposition that 'political deadlock has finally been broken in Northern Ireland' and there is overwhelming support among DUP members for the devolved executive. As Figure 2.1 shows, more than four-fifths back the administration.

Yet joined-up government has been difficult. First Minister Peter Robinson would prefer a 'system where people can voluntarily work together because they have common policies and a common outlook', finding power-sharing with republicans a 'woefully slow and difficult' system to operate:

> Insert the word 'Northern Ireland' into a document and there are people down the bottom end of the corridor who are crying their eyes out, even though they are in a Northern Ireland Executive as part of the Northern Ireland Assembly. If we have difficulty at that level then you can imagine that every day is a negotiating day.[91]

Robinson complains about the inability of republican ministers to make a quick policy decision. He describes Sinn Féin as

> not a normal political party. If I was dealing with any other political party…I would sit across the table and would say here is the issue, let's resolve it, and we would sit there and try and work it out. They [Sinn Féin] will never take a decision with you in the room. It always has to be taken out. It goes into this labyrinth

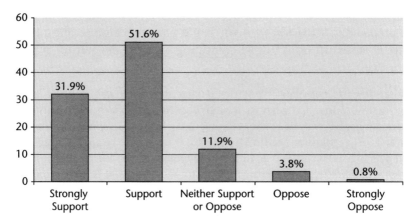

Figure 2.1 DUP members' views of the Northern Ireland Executive

of an organization. Whether it goes to Connolly House [Sinn Féin's Belfast Headquarters], whether it goes to the Dáil, or whether it goes to their Assembly group, or where in the circle of advisers decisions are made, nobody is quite clear. You will never get a decision for a very long period of time...because of the process that Sinn Féin has in government.[92]

Despite the First Minister's opposition to mandatory power-sharing, more than half of party members surveyed take the view that the First and Deputy First Ministers should be provided by the DUP and Sinn Féin, as shown in Figure 2.2. Moreover, as Figure 2.3 indicates, a majority (albeit a similarly non-overwhelming one) also believe that unionist and nationalist parties are cooperating well in the Northern Ireland Assembly.

In terms of enforced cooperation, what is surprising is that, within a party historically opposed to power-sharing, 61 per cent of members agree that ministries should be shared between unionist and nationalist parties. Indeed, slightly more than half (52 per cent) accept that legislation should require the consent of a majority of unionist and nationalist Assembly members. The DUP no longer supports majority rule. Given that 60 per cent of members agree it is necessary for political stability that the DUP and Sinn Féin provide the First and Deputy First Ministers, it would appear that voluntary coalition is not supported either. More than three-fifths of the membership feel nationalists are now more content that Northern Ireland should remain in the UK. Not only has Northern Ireland been transformed since the Belfast Agreement, so has the DUP.

Some old views die hard. Unsurprisingly, given the DUP's historic opposition to North–South institutions, hostility to the cross-border element of the Belfast Agreement remains. Over half of the membership does not support them, although a quarter of respondents did offer some degree of support (Figure 2.4).

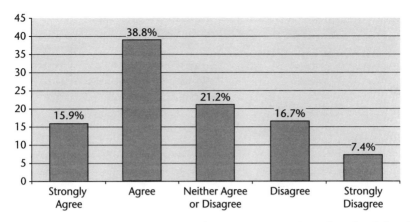

Figure 2.2 DUP members' views on whether it is necessary for political stability that the DUP and Sinn Féin provide the First and Deputy First Ministers

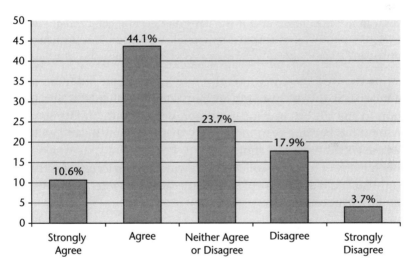

Figure 2.3 DUP members' views on whether unionist and nationalist parties are cooperating well in the Assembly

According to the DUP leadership, the all-island dimension of the political arrangements has been rendered harmless. Peter Robinson even views North–South cooperation in terms of getting 'things done the way it was in Craig's time', referring to Northern Ireland's first Prime Minister (1921–40) and claiming:

> We have muted the development of the North–South institutions...you can go along to North South meetings now, if you can stay awake during the course of them, and you would see that they are basically discussions, reporting sessions,

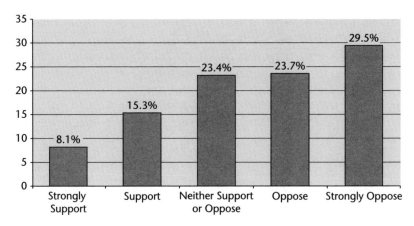

Figure 2.4 DUP members' views on North-South/All-Ireland Bodies

there is no executive action...if I want something done, I will lift up the phone and speak to the minister or if it is a particular departmental thing, I will get our [Northern Irish] minister who is responsible to speak to their [Irish Republic] counterpart.[93]

Following the DUP's re-entry into government on improved terms after the St Andrews deal, the membership are very confident that Northern Ireland's position in the UK has become even more secure, with almost 80 per cent believing it has become even more likely that Northern Ireland will remain part of the UK, as Figure 2.5 shows.

As with many of his party colleagues, Edwin Poots no longer sees the Union under threat and is dismissive of Sinn Féin's call for a border poll, insisting the constitutional question

is settled now and I am happy to leave it settled. [A border poll] is pointless and will only open requests for coming in on a semi regular basis from here on in. So, you can call Sinn Féin's bluff and...call a border poll and they go away, but they will go away and come back and say it is OK, we will get one in ten years' time again and maybe get two or three better per cent at that point: 'we are going the right direction' and so forth.[94]

Conclusion

When the DUP became the largest unionist party in Northern Ireland, it entered a negotiating process. Once it entered that process, the realpolitik of what was achievable and what was unachievable became apparent. Negotiation involves compromise. What defined the parameters of what could be negotiated was the Belfast Agreement. In 1998, the DUP regarded

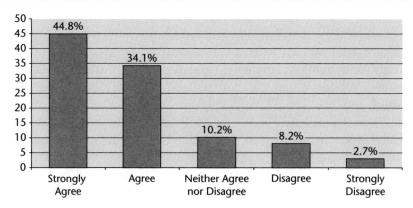

Figure 2.5 DUP members' views on whether it has become more likely since 2007 that Northern Ireland will stay part of the UK

that Agreement as unacceptable in its entirety. By 2007, when the DUP entered into power with Sinn Féin, the fundamentals of that Agreement remained in place. There also seems to have been an unspoken acceptance by elements of the DUP that parts of the Belfast Agreement which were anathema in 1998 have proven to be less toxic in practice. For example, on constitutional issues, the DUP took the position that Northern Ireland's place in the UK had been diluted—but Northern Ireland clearly remains a part of the United Kingdom because of the Act of Union and not in spite of the repeal of the constitutionally irrelevant Government of Ireland Act. The DUP's position, in 1998, was that the changes made to Articles 2 and 3 were cosmetic rather than actual. The party argued that the offending provisions may have ended the Republic's claim to Northern Ireland's territory, but the Irish Constitution now claimed its people instead as part of the Irish nation. Yet in 2013, Ian Paisley acknowledged that the

> removal of the articles in the Irish Constitution laying claim to Northern Ireland as that jurisdiction's territory, was, we should never forget, hard won...It was a substantial act of goodwill by the people of Southern Ireland to vote to have the claim removed from their constitution in order to facilitate neighbourly relations. It played no small part in disarming the political justification of the Irish Republican Army's reign of terror.[95]

Similarly, the NSMC remains in the form it was in 1998—a consultative body with no executive powers that lead to a united Ireland. The NSMC never was— and could not have become—an embryonic all-Ireland government, such as the Council of Ireland or the Frameworks North–South body might have. The smaller North–South bodies have proved to be mirror images of the Foyle Fisheries Commission—a subsidiary North–South body with executive power set up by the Unionist Government in 1956—and no one ever suggested that Lord Brookebourgh, then Prime Minister of Northern Ireland, would agree to anything that would have led to a united Ireland. Perhaps most significantly, the British-Irish Intergovernmental Conference (BIIC), which replaced the Anglo-Irish Intergovernmental Conference of the Anglo-Irish Agreement, and which the DUP claimed was merely an old wine in a new bottle, remains intact. The original IGC was the manifestation of the outrage concerning the Irish Government's right to be consulted, by London, over the internal affairs of Northern Ireland and the focus of Ian Paisley's famous 'Never, never, never, never' speech. The BIIC's significance was diminished by the Belfast Agreement in that the new institutions allowed for direct North–South cooperation and transparency, but it remains, as does the actual or potential Irish governmental consultation with the British Government in non-devolved matters. It is debatable whether, had the DUP stayed in the original talks process, in 1997–8, they would have prevented Trimble from signing up to the Belfast Agreement in its original form or whether it would have strengthened unionism's bargaining position. Another cogent historical argument concerns whether, had unionism in general, and the DUP in particular, been more flexible in the past, initiatives such as the AIA might never have been implemented. In a revealing comment, in 2012, Peter Robinson admitted how: 'In Northern Ireland, unionists were slow to accept or appreciate that after the fall of the majority rule parliament at Stormont in 1972, some form of power-sharing was inevitable', although he added that, 'when they did, constitutional nationalists set the bar too high to achieve it'.[96]

None of this, however, should diminish the achievements of the DUP in the period after 2003. The legislation in the Northern Ireland Act 1998, giving effect to the workings of the Belfast Agreement, neutered the executive and the Assembly in terms of the democratic accountability of ministers and North–South/East–West bodies to the devolved institution. The DUP's reforms increased accountability, both collective and institutional, to the executive and Assembly respectively. A more significant achievement was the DUP's role in forcing Sinn Féin and the Provisional IRA to accept the logic of the peace process: that violence and the modalities to execute it were a thing of the past. The UUP could not do this. That party's leader, David Trimble, needed to make the institutions work, in order to demonstrate that the DUP was wrong in its criticisms of the Belfast Agreement. Yet Trimble's need to prove this, by entering government with Sinn Féin, meant less pressure on the IRA to decommission and formally end its armed struggle. At the same time, when the DUP supplanted the UUP, it benefited from the fact that unionists had entered into government with Sinn Féin without much reciprocation: thus, it was republicans, not unionists, who had not delivered on the Agreement. The DUP could afford to wait for Sinn Féin and this, in the end, illustrated how much Adams and McGuinness needed the process to work in order to survive. Sinn Féin's direction of travel would probably have been the same without the DUP, but the DUP emphasized there really was no alternative route.

Forcing Sinn Féin to support the Police Service of Northern Ireland, in the explicit and unambiguous manner it did, is probably the most impressive achievement of the DUP. The acceptability of the police in a society is a fundamental recognition of the legitimacy of that society and its institutions. For a quarter of a century, the IRA had been killing Northern Ireland's police officers as representatives of what republicans regarded as an illegitimate state. Now Martin McGuinness was condemning dissident republicans as 'traitors to Ireland' when members of the security forces were killed by these groups. The decision of the IRA to stand down and formally end its campaign was also something which might have occurred on Trimble's watch eventually, but republicans knew for sure there would be no power-sharing with the DUP whilst the Provisional IRA remained intact. With regard to decommissioning, however, the DUP achieved no more clarity on the logistics of what or how many weapons were 'put beyond use' than the UUP earlier, when the DUP directed withering criticism at Trimble. Nevertheless, these gains were achieved by the hardline position of the DUP that it would not enter government with Sinn Féin before republicans had demonstrated their commitment to exclusively democratic and peaceful means. The essentials of a deal between the DUP and Sinn Féin were, in fact, agreed quite early on in the process—certainly by late 2004. The dragging out of the process centred on how republicans demonstrated acts of completion in an unambiguous manner. In the end, the DUP played a critical part in guiding the peace process to its logical conclusion. Ultimately, it is hard to disagree with the views expressed by one perceptive commentator on Northern Irish affairs that, in constitutional terms at least, 'the St Andrews Agreement is just the Belfast Agreement in a kilt', notwithstanding other important aspects.[97]

Notes

1. Interview with senior DUP adviser, 8 Feb. 2013.
2. Democratic Unionist Party (2004) *Devolution Now: The DUP's Concept for Devolution*, Belfast: DUP.
3. J. Powell (2009) *Great Hatred, Little Room: Making Peace in Northern Ireland*, London: Vintage, 239–41.
4. Democratic Unionist Party (2003) *Towards a New Agreement: DUP Analysis Vindicated: A Critical Assessment of the Belfast Agreement Five Years On*, Belfast: DUP, 7.
5. DUP, *Towards a New Agreement*, 10.
6. DUP, *Towards a New Agreement*, 13.

7. DUP, *Towards a New Agreement*, 16–17.

8. DUP, *Towards a New Agreement*, 25.

9. DUP, *Towards a New Agreement*, 26.

10. Democratic Unionist Party (2004) *North South East West: Northern Ireland's Relationship with Other Regions of the British Isles*, Belfast: DUP.

11. DUP, *Towards a New Agreement*, 28–30.

12. DUP, *Towards a New Agreement*, 33.

13. Powell, *Great Hatred, Little Room*, 244–8.

14. Powell, *Great Hatred, Little Room*, 252–3.

15. Interview with senior DUP adviser, 8 Feb. 2013.

16. Interview with senior DUP adviser, 8 Feb. 2013.

17. Powell, *Great Hatred, Little Room*, 252.

18. Statement by Gerry Adams, President of Sinn Féin, Leeds Castle, 18 Sept. 2004.

19. Interview with Jeffrey Donaldson MP, MLA, Lagan Valley, 8 Mar. 2013.

20. Interview with Arlene Foster MLA, Belfast, 24 Jan. 2013.

21. Powell, *Great Hatred, Little Room*, 254.

22. Interview with confidential source.

23. Powell, *Great Hatred, Little Room*, 254.

24. Interview with confidential source.

25. Powell, *Great Hatred, Little Room*, 254.

26. Interview with senior DUP adviser, 8 Feb. 2013.

27. Powell, *Great Hatred, Little Room*, 254.

28. Interview with confidential source.

29. Interview with confidential source.

30. Interview with Nigel Dodds MP, Westminster, 3 July 2013.

31. Interview with Nigel Dodds, 3 July 2013.

32. Interview with Nigel Dodds, 3 July 2013.

33. Interview with Nigel Dodds, 3 July 2013.

34. Leader's Speech by David Trimble, Ulster Unionist Party Annual Conference, Newcastle, County Down, 13 Nov. 2004.

35. Statement by Ian Paisley, then leader of the Democratic Unionist Party (DUP), at Westminster, in reply to a speech by Bertie Ahern, Taoiseach (Irish Prime Minister), 9 Nov. 2004.

36. Speech by Ian Paisley, then DUP leader, at the North Antrim DUP Association Annual Dinner, 27 Nov. 2004.

37. Speech by Ian Paisley, 27 Nov. 2004.

38. Text of IRA Statement, 9 Dec. 2004, in response to 'Proposals by the British and Irish Governments for a Comprehensive Agreement' (8 Dec. 2004) <http://cain. ulst.ac.uk/othelem/chron.htm>, accessed Aug. 2013.

39. Interview with senior DUP adviser, 8 Feb. 2013.

40. Interview with confidential source.

41. Interview with confidential source.

42. Statement by Paul Murphy, then Secretary of State for Northern Ireland, on the Northern Bank robbery to the House of Commons, 11 Jan. 2005, <http://cain. ulst.ac.uk/othelem/chron.htm>, accessed Aug. 2013.

43. Statement by Bertie Ahern, then Taoiseach, regarding comments by Hugh Orde, then Chief Constable of the PSNI, on the Northern Bank robbery, 7 Jan. 2005, <http://cain.ulst.ac.uk/othelem/chron.htm>, accessed Aug. 2013.
44. Powell, *Great Hatred, Little Room*, 265.
45. Interview with DUP adviser, 8 Feb. 2013.
46. Statement by Gerry Adams, President of Sinn Féin, calling on the IRA to end the 'armed struggle', Belfast, 6 Apr. 2005, <http://cain.ulst.ac.uk/othelem/chron.htm>, accessed Aug. 2013.
47. Text of the IRA statement on the ending of the armed campaign, 28 July 2005, <http://cain.ulst.ac.uk/othelem/chron.htm>, accessed Aug. 2013.
48. Statement by Ian Paisley, then DUP leader, on the ending of the IRA armed campaign, 28 July 2005, <http://cain.ulst.ac.uk/othelem/chron.htm>, accessed Aug. 2013.
49. Statement by Ian Paisley, then DUP leader, on the British government's plans for security normalization in Northern Ireland, 1 Aug. 2005, <http://cain.ulst.ac.uk/othelem/chron.htm>, accessed Aug. 2013.
50. Text of IRA statement on putting arms beyond use, 26 Sept. 2005, <http://cain.ulst.ac.uk/othelem/chron.htm>, accessed Aug. 2013.
51. Statement by Ian Paisley, then DUP leader, on the decommissioning of weapons by the IRA, 26 Sept. 2005, <http://cain.ulst.ac.uk/othelem/chron.htm>, accessed Aug. 2013.
52. Statement by Ian Paisley, then DUP leader, on the decommissioning of weapons by the IRA, 26 Sept. 2005.
53. Interview with confidential source.
54. Interview with confidential source.
55. Powell, *Great Hatred, Little Room*, 274.
56. House of Commons Research Paper 06/56, 11.
57. Powell, *Great Hatred, Little Room*, 276.
58. House of Commons Research Paper 06/56, 13.
59. Powell, *Great Hatred, Little Room*, 285.
60. Powell, *Great Hatred, Little Room*, 285.
61. Interview with confidential source.
62. Interview with Nigel Dodds, 3 July 2013.
63. Interview with Peter Robinson MLA, DUP leader, Stormont, 25 June 2013.
64. Interview with confidential source.
65. Interview with confidential source.
66. Interview with Nigel Dodds, 3 July 2013.
67. E. Moloney (2008) *Paisley: From Demagogue to Democrat*, Dublin: Poolbeg, 456–7, states that 'two senior figures, both MPs, met Martin McGuiness'. Our understanding from a senior elected representative is that three people were involved on the DUP side and chatted informally with more than Martin McGuinness. However, it is important to stress that (*a*) this was an unofficial gathering, not formal dialogue and (*b*) it involved merely the DUP side indicating genuine interest in a deal, but only on the terms their party had already publicly demanded.
68. House of Commons Research Paper 06/56, 21–2.

69. P. Hain (2012) *Outside In,* London: Biteback, 348.
70. Powell, *Great Hatred, Little Room,* 294.
71. Interview with Nigel Dodds, 3 July 2013.
72. Interview with Sydney Anderson MLA, Craigavon, 5 Nov. 2012.
73. Interview with George Dunne MLA, Stormont, 4 Dec. 2012.
74. Interview with DUP MLA, Stormont, 4 Dec. 2012.
75. Interview with Edwin Poots MLA, Lisburn, 10 Jan. 2013.
76. Interview with Jim Allister MLA, Party Leader, TUV, North Antrim, 18 Apr. 2013.
77. Interview with Jim Allister, 18 Apr. 2013. See also Moloney, *Paisley.*
78. Interview with Revd William McCrea, 24 Jan. 2013.
79. Interview with Jim Allister, 18 Apr. 2013.
80. Interview with Jim Allister, 18 Apr. 2013.
81. Interview with Jim Allister, 18 Apr. 2013.
82. Interview with Ian McCrea MLA, Cookstown, 4 Dec. 2012.
83. Interview with Jim Wells MLA, Stormont, 9 Jan. 2013.
84. House of Commons Standard Note (2007) *Political Developments in Northern Ireland since March 2007,* SN/PC/04513, November, London: House of Commons, 3.
85. House of Commons Standard Note, SN/PC/04513, 10.
86. See D. Gordon (2009) *The Fall of the House of Paisley,* Dublin: Gill and Macmillan, especially pp. 190–6.
87. BBC Northern Ireland, *Paisley: Genesis to Revelation,* interview with Eamonn Mallie, 20 Jan. 2014.
88. BBC Northern Ireland, *Paisley: Genesis to Revelation.*
89. Interview with Peter Robinson, 25 June 2013.
90. Interview with Peter Robinson, 25 June 2013.
91. Interview with Peter Robinson, 25 June 2013.
92. Interview with Peter Robinson, 25 June 2013.
93. Interview with Peter Robinson, 25 June 2013.
94. Interview with Edwin Poots MLA, 10 Jan. 2013.
95. *Newsletter,* 25 Jan. 2013.
96. *Newsletter,* 28 Apr. 2012.
97. Alex Kane, 'DUP Gains Impossible without UUP', *Newsletter,* 24 Oct. 2011.

3

Who Are the Modern Members?

Having examined how the DUP moved from a party of protest to one of government, we now explore the demography and attitudes of those within its ranks. We offer a portrait of a party which, although still small in size, is vigorous in its levels of activism and enthusiasm. Addressing when and why people joined the DUP, this chapter also uncovers the social background, types of employment, and age profile of the members, whilst detailed consideration of religious and gender aspects of the DUP are dealt with in later chapters. This section dissects the modern membership base by providing an account of education background, age, the motivation for joining, social background, and socio-political attitudes. Beyond detailing who belongs to the DUP, this chapter also evaluates the primary policy concerns of those members, as the DUP consolidates its position as the dominant unionist arm of government. As the party's earlier incarnation as an organ of protest and dissent becomes an increasingly distant memory, what are the contemporary economic and social priorities of party members in a (very nearly) post-conflict Northern Ireland?

A Modest But Well-Formed Membership

The DUP is not a mass organization. Its size remains modest and the party is happy to attract registered followers, in addition to full members, in an attempt to boost numbers. The DUP's strength lies less in its size than in the quality of its membership, in terms of high levels of commitment and activism. Party membership has increased considerably since the Belfast Agreement, in an era where political parties are in decline more broadly. Only one per cent of the British electorate belong to political parties (a percentage still falling) and membership of Northern Ireland's political parties as a percentage of the electorate appears even lower.[1] In common with most other political parties, the bulk of the DUP's members are middle-aged, but, with an average age of

51, the party's base is youthful compared to the few other political parties surveyed in Northern Ireland and to the Conservative Party on the mainland.[2]
One-fifth of the party is aged below 35 and a further one-fifth is aged over 65.

The DUP's membership base is spread unevenly in gender and geography.
A majority (73 per cent) of members are male and there is a sizeable concentration of members located in the eastern counties of Antrim and Down, which
account for 29 per cent and 35 per cent of members respectively. Towards the
west of Northern Ireland, membership is significantly lower, with 11 per cent
of members hailing from Tyrone, a further 11 per cent from Londonderry,
8 per cent from Fermanagh, and 6 per cent from Armagh. As west of the
Bann has seen a significant reduction in the percentage of Protestants more
broadly, the DUP has struggled to build a sizeable membership base, even
though it has been helped by the wholesale defection of UUP branches in a
few localities. Even in the more fertile east of Northern Ireland, branch membership tends to be modest, one councillor in Antrim highlighting an increase
in membership in his sizeable town 'from three to fifteen' since the Belfast
Agreement as a major triumph.[3] Local aspects dominate methods of joining
the DUP, although this is changing with the growth of a central database and
centralized communication. Forty per cent of members joined via attendance
at a local meeting, with a further 6 per cent applying by post to a local branch.
Thirty-six per cent joined after being asked by a friend. Local canvassing also
assisted slightly, 3 per cent joining in response to this. Of the remainder, 8
per cent applied to join via postal application to party headquarters and 7 per
cent applied online. Localism also prevails in terms of funding: 84 per cent
pay subscriptions to their local branch, not party headquarters.

Little growth was experienced within the DUP, both in terms of electoral
success and membership, throughout much of the Troubles, amid stagnation
and frustration at unionism's political impotence and some suspicion of the
religious zealotry and oratory of the DUP leader. Many unionists stayed loyal
to the UUP and distrusted what they saw as a Free Presbyterian vehicle which
offered extreme, if constitutional, politics. New joiners were rare, although
original members remain an important dimension within the party, some 13
per cent having been there from the outset. There has been a huge upsurge in
recruitment of new members since the Belfast Agreement, with nearly 60 per
cent of party members having joined since 1998. Since that deal, there has
been a considerable graduate-level influx, almost 40 per cent of new recruits
having a degree or equivalent higher education qualification.

What the DUP lacks in quantity is seemingly compensated in terms of quality of membership. Seventy-five per cent of members describe themselves
as very or fairly active. In terms of their activities, leafleting and election
canvassing tend to be the most regular expression of this activism and a
slight majority claim to have attended the annual conference. More than

40 per cent of members claim to have been involved 'a great deal' in the traditional campaigning techniques of leaflet delivery and doorstep canvassing. Mobilization via social media appears considerably less advanced, a large majority of members never having used Twitter or Facebook.

The fracture between the UUP and the DUP had religious and socio-economic undercurrents. Alvin Jackson once argued that 'a gaudy Orange sash never fully conceals the stains of denominational conflict, or the patches of class division'.[4] Yet the class-based voting divisions within unionism have greatly diminished and DUP membership transcends financial and class strata. The economic background of the party members reveals an even spread across income bands, with median annual household income of approximately £35,000. Over half of the party are in full-time work, while a quarter are either in full-time study or retired. Of those who are in employment, two-thirds are employees, while the other one-third run their own businesses. Of those who are self-employed, most (two-thirds) run small businesses employing less than five people, focused overwhelmingly in the agricultural, legal, and retail industries. The economic breadth of the party reflects an all-encompassing social backdrop. Many elected representatives pride themselves on choosing the DUP because of its working-class ethos. In terms of class self-identification, 41 per cent of the party identify as working class, with 35 per cent viewing themselves as middle class. As might be expected, trade union membership, held by only 19 per cent of members, is positively correlated with working-class self-identification. The remainder claim not to think of themselves as belonging to a particular social class.

From UUP to DUP Membership

Extending their mandate and broadening their appeal across the unionist spectrum, the DUP supplanted the UUP amid the intra-unionist furore over the Belfast Agreement. The party limited defections to the Traditional Unionist Voice (TUV) after the risky St Andrews successor deal and have continued to fuse social conservatism with neo-liberalism. The Belfast Agreement was the catalyst for a mass influx of UUP members to the DUP. Twenty-four per cent of the party comprises former members of the UUP, with 62 per cent of ex-UUP members of the DUP joining their new party after the Belfast Agreement. During the period of mass defections from 1998 to 2006, almost 45 per cent of new entrants to the DUP were former UUP members. Although members who joined between 2008 and 2012 are somewhat less likely to be UUP switchers than those who joined between 1998 and 2007, the UUP has not entirely stopped the flow: 17 per cent of the most recent (i.e. post-2008) joiners are former UUP members. The DUP picked up very few members from the fringe, paramilitary-linked, loyalist parties of the Ulster Democratic Party and Progressive Unionist Party, amounting to 1.5 per cent of the party's total membership.

For those reluctant to opt out of political life after departing the UUP, the DUP became a natural home, as Belfast City Councillor Lee Reynolds remarked:

> When I was in the no camp after the Belfast Agreement, there was a sort of three-way division within unionism. There is the pushover unionism that will always say yes because they are afraid of what would happen if they would say no. Then there is Allister [the TUV leader], who says no to everything. There is a middle ground. This was a mistake Trimble made. He treated everyone who said 'no' that you were against making a deal. But, no, we weren't against making a deal, we just weren't happy with the one you are presenting us with. The DUP had evolved to be a practical unionist party.[5]

Assembly member William Humphrey, a former chair of the Young Unionists, found his way to the DUP from the UUP for similar reasons: 'I am not a rebel. The party became detached from the people. The party wasn't very relevant, even though it had the majority of the vote. I was reluctant to stay part of the party who had forced an issue that had divided the party.'[6]

Deep dissatisfaction with the Belfast Agreement triggered many to make the leap from the UUP to the DUP. The peace process is perceived as one of concessions to nationalists by many members, more than half (52 per cent) believing that nationalists benefited 'a lot more than unionists' (older members are significantly more likely to believe this), and a further 17 per cent arguing that nationalists benefited 'a little more'. The issue of prisoner releases was obviously emotive in a party in which a substantial proportion of DUP members (39 per cent) consider themselves victims of the Troubles. The Patten policing reform process established under the deal also triggered defections to the DUP from the UUP, even though the UUP were also critical of several aspects of the Patten changes. Very little support (only 6 per cent of members) could be found for the now-abandoned 50–50 Roman Catholic–Non-Roman Catholic percentage quota recruitment to the Police Service of Northern Ireland. Patten could claim vindication of changes though, in that 44 per cent of DUP members believe that most Roman Catholics now support the police, more than the 31 per cent dissenting. Thirty-six per cent believe that policing is benefiting from Sinn Féin's presence on policing boards, slightly outweighing the one-third of members dissenting from this view. Orange Order membership is a highly significant variable here, members of that organization much more likely to hold a jaundiced view of Sinn Féin's participation. Seventy-one per cent of DUP members do not believe that the PSNI is similar to the old Royal Ulster Constabulary, a belief which is clearly replicated amongst many nationalists, given the much wider support for the reformed force.

The contrasting experiences between the fracturing UUP, engulfed by chaos and internal dissent, and the burgeoning, tightly disciplined DUP meant that, for many former UUP members, it was a difficult decision emotionally to defect, but not a tough decision in political terms. Dissatisfaction with mainstream unionism allowed the DUP to position themselves as a protest party with the ability to offer a stronger line, which appealed to many, whereas, as one defector to the DUP put it: 'the UUP were prepared to give so much away; I think they could have done more. I felt the DUP was a more robust party.'[7] The UUP represented a political education for Arlene Foster, which honed her debating and negotiating skills, later deployed at a senior level within the DUP and the Northern Ireland Executive.[8] Her sentiment is echoed by a ministerial colleague, Simon Hamilton, who reflects upon his time within the UUP that 'a lot of the skills that I think I possess now I learned then, whenever I was agitating against David Trimble'.[9] The assimilation of the former UUP members has been largely unproblematic, but it has changed the nature of the party in terms of denomination and introduced a somewhat more liberal element. The influx has also markedly improved the DUP's professionalism and campaigning techniques. Patterson argued that the DUP's rhetoric, and critique countering aspects of the peace process that included decommissioning, prisoner release, and power-sharing, had the potential to alienate unionists, especially the apolitical 'Protestant in the garden centre' variety.[10] This was true amongst the broader apathetic electorate, but amongst the committed, the DUP's robust opposition to elements of the deal held great attraction and the DUP gathered hundreds of recruits, many of them UUP switchers.

Beyond the Belfast Agreement: Why Join the DUP?

Disaffection with the UUP's support for the Belfast Agreement was an important push factor for many current DUP members regarding their former party. What, though, of the DUP's pull? For many recruits, it is not the party's performance in government that motivates them to join, but rather the residual issues of the past, such as the constitutional question and opposing republicanism. The biggest single motivation for joining, offered by 36 per cent of members, is the DUP's defence of the Union, a much higher factor than each of the DUP's other policies. The consistent appeal to members on the basis of defending the Union prevails across the generations of DUP members and their year of joining is insignificant. This was the primary motivating factor before and after the Belfast Agreement. Historically, the DUP has been a strong advocate of devolution, offering strong region-alism within a UK framework bereft of concessions on governance to the Republic of Ireland. Unwilling to embrace direct rule from Westminster, the DUP dovetailed their Britishness and loyalism with a harking for devolved majoritarian rule, the latter only quietly dropped amid the dawning of the reality that devolved government meant power-sharing government. The influx of former UUP members has tempered the DUP's regionalism. Those joining the DUP from that party, with its more integrationist approach dur-ing the 1980s and 1990s, are significantly more likely to concede that the Westminster government should have a substantial say in the governance of Northern Ireland. Devolved government within the UK is the settled will of the vast bulk (84 per cent of the party), with the percentages favouring integration or an independent Northern Ireland in single figures.

One-sixth of the party's members joined because the DUP suited their Protestant values, the bulk of these members having signed up prior to the Belfast Agreement. It is not that Protestant values have been abandoned by post-1998 joiners, but they are less upfront about joining a party for overtly reli-gious reasons, or for the defence of a particular religious, rather than political, community. For one North Down councillor, the choice between the unionist parties was clear: 'In the 1980s you had the Ulster Unionists, who were kind of anything goes; the DUP were standing tall for the Protestant community'.[11] Historically, the DUP was embedded in a strong Protestant ethos, one also tied to the Free Presbyterian Church due to the cross-over of leadership under Paisley. From the outset, there was recognition by the party leadership that the promotion of Protestantism was a necessary, but insufficient, basis of appeal. The DUP was viewed at its inception as a 'coalition of the Protestant Unionist Party with a much more inchoate of disillusioned and radical members of the UUP'.[12] Against the backdrop of the main unionist party being unable to appeal to the urban loyalist communities with quite the same traction that Paisley harnessed, the DUP tugged at the power of the UUP, but with only modest effect. Seizing the opportunity afforded by a unionist party distinct from the UUP, some working-class unionists joined the religious evangelicals within the DUP. The DUP MP, David Simpson, articulated the reasons he chose the DUP over the UUP as a combination of religion and class sentiment:

> In those days, the Ulster Unionist Party would have been the largest party and therefore people would have been inclined to go to, at that time in Ulster history, the most successful party. I felt that the DUP represented my core values, from moral values right up to working class values...that was something that had been neglected for many, many years from the established perceived large parties.[13]

Eleven per cent of DUP members state their primary reason for joining as admiration for the party leader. This admiration as a factor is fairly equally distributed between joiners in the Paisley and Robinson leadership eras. For long-term members such as MLA Mervyn Storey, the influence of Dr Paisley on his political leanings was significant, 'I was brought up in that era that Ian Paisley was a dominant figure in politics... in a sense, I was immersed in that environment that Ian Paisley was the person my father respected as a political voice.'[14] A Strangford councillor claimed that 'the DUP is the party of the people. I was always inspired by Dr Paisley and by how hard he worked for the people'.[15] One MP insisted that 'the reason why I am in the DUP is Dr Paisley. Whenever I was a youngster, he would have been a hero of mine, I admired his courage: by his nature, by his actions, he created an interest in politics in me.'[16] Yet for many within the party who made the transition from the UUP, Paisley's appeal was not the factor causing them to break the ties that had bound them to the DUP's unionist rivals. For Jeffrey Donaldson, 'family ties and the local UUP influence had a greater bearing on my politics than any draw to a charismatic leader.'[17]

Paisley's leadership may have driven much of the recruitment for the pre-1998 member, but in more recent times, the strategic direction offered by the team of Robinson and Dodds offered a welcome alternative that also indicated, notwithstanding Dodds's Free Presbyterian membership, a weakening of the link between the Free Presbyterian Church and the political party. Robinson combined appeal to the party faithful with attention to negotiating detail. A woman MLA asserted: 'I thought, crikey, this is a man who can negotiate a peace with Sinn Féin... he had the vision to get us where we are today. I only joined the party because Peter Robinson was at the helm.' [18] A Belfast city councillor remarked:

> In terms of Peter Robinson, as a young person watching the news, I was just fed up with unionist representatives constantly being outsmarted and outfoxed by nationalists in debates and it seemed to me Peter Robinson was one person that nobody could outfox or outsmart. I thought that he was a very strong performer and was able to articulate our position very, very well.[19]

Indeed, Peter Robinson scores very highly within his party on the two measures tested, competence and trust. On a 0 (total incompetence) to 10 (total competence) scale, the DUP leader scored 9, nearly treble the score awarded by DUP members to the UUP leader, whose rating was on a par with that awarded to Martin McGuinness and below that given to the TUV leader, Jim Allister. On trust (0 equalled total distrust and 10 meant complete trust), Robinson was rated at 8.7. On the trust rating, the UUP leader at least managed a clear second to the DUP leader, but with only half of Robinson's score. Predictably, Sinn Féin's leadership duo of Adams and McGuinness received the lowest scores by some distance on the trust issue. Sinn Féin's leadership might be acknowledged, very grudgingly, as competent in office, but they are still not trusted by DUP members. Adams was rated at a mere 0.6 and McGuinness merited only a rating of 1 on the 0 to 10 scale.

Ten per cent of members express their reason for joining the DUP in terms of what it battles against, rather than what it offers directly, choosing 'to oppose republicanism' as their primary motivation. Given the context of the Troubles, this ostensibly negative mobilization may be rationalized. Such sentiment was articulated by a North Down councillor, in a typical offering: 'at that time [of joining the DUP], there was a terrorist campaign to undermine Northern Ireland's position in the UK. I was taking a robust stand against that campaign.'[20] Other negative primary cited motivations for joining the DUP were opposition to the Belfast Agreement (5 per cent) and 'disagreed with other Unionist parties' (9 per cent), with these two factors likely to be interlinked. Only 3 per cent of members were motivated to join the party because of 'social reasons', and the primacy of conflict-related, political, and constitutional motivating forces is evident.

Bigger and Better? From 'Family' Party of Opposition to Political Machine

The substantial growth of the DUP has created its own challenges, in retaining the warmth and unity of its 'family-feel', while broadening its support base to cope with the rigours of being the lead party in government, one whose success attracts members unfamiliar with the lean times and endurance experienced by older members. Whilst many members acknowledge that the party has changed as it has grown, most are sanguine over the 'arrivistes'. According to one Castlereagh councillor, in a typical view:

> The party is still, very much the same party. Some new fresh faces have come in and given their certain personalities, that has changed the party, but I think a lot of it goes down to the strategic mind of the leader and his view and foresight of where to take the party.[21]

For MLA Mervyn Storey, the burgeoning diversity is unproblematic:

> As far as the party is concerned, with all our diversity, it still has a family nature. It still has a sense of camaraderie that I don't think belonging to any other party gives you. You have a sense of history, you have a sense of association with people, and I can still look at people who are the in the party today and they were there throughout.[22]

According to another MLA, Jonathan Craig, the key to side-stepping the dangers of people joining the party for purely personal advancement is through the work ethic imbued in the principles of many in the party: 'Career politicians don't make very good politicians. If you haven't worked at grassroots politics then I would be of the strong opinion that you shouldn't be allowed to stand because it ends in disaster.'[23]

The growth of the party means greater choice in candidate selection and higher quality candidates, but the party also needs to maintain its internal discipline. This has not been a major problem, in that Paisley's force of character, Robinson's attention to detail, and their undisputed status as leaders largely inhibited solo runs or internal jostling for position in the past, but this might change. Party members appear desirous of continuing tight central control and mechanisms to ensure representatives remain 'on-message'. Eighty-three per cent agree that prospective candidates should receive formal training from the party and this aspiration to increase professionalism is matched by overwhelming support (86 per cent) for internal monitoring of the performance of elected representatives. Members are, however, evenly split on whether or not the DUP executive should approve lists of election candidates, a centralizing feature introduced by a change to the party rules by the DUP executive in the autumn of 2013.

This reflects ambivalence across the party on the merits of central selection, some preferring local autonomy and the right to determine, according to local circumstances, which election candidates to field—and how many. For one Antrim member, the process of central selection is harmful on two levels, financial and practical: 'I do not agree with the system that says we are sticking one in whether you like it or not. The association is out of money because of central selection.'[24]

The requirement for tough, often secretive, negotiations prior to the St Andrews deal and the need for difficult decision-making whilst in office have also tested the cosiness of the DUP, the luxuries of opposition unlikely to ever return. The necessary discretion involved in elite-level decision-making is juxtaposed with the need to involve the base in policy formulation and keep the members involved. Members seem very content on the broad thrust of policies, but organization and communication with members is rated below 7 on a ten-point scale, indicating perceptions that they can be improved. A Coleraine councillor asserted:

I know communication is difficult, but I think we could do more to communicate strategies and opinions rather than having a small hierarchy making all the decisions. Sometimes I get the feeling that a small nucleus at the top is making the key decisions. We have a good leadership, but I think you need to take on board the opinions of grassroots members, of councillors, MLAs, and MEPs. I think that could be improved upon, upwards and downwards. It's essential to the success of any party.[25]

In terms of how newer recruits feel, there is no significant difference between post-2007 joiners and the rest when it comes to opinions about organization and communication with members. Internal communication top–down and bottom–up remains problematic, despite recent initiatives such as the weekly email alert from the MPs and MLAs, or the regular Monday morning meetings between the MP and MLA teams. Barriers to communication remain. An Ards councillor declared: 'There will always be difficulty with communication and the ordinary members do feel detached. What has been attempted and works to an extent is an email from Stormont. The tensions of each tier of government have new dynamics.'[26] Whilst social media offers a potentially effective solution to overcoming the communication barrier, it has few takers. Forty-three per cent of members admit to rarely or never using the party website; 78 per cent rarely or never access the Twitter feed; and a majority fail to engage with the Facebook (68 per cent) or DUP blogs (73 per cent). Changes to party rules in 2013 sought to improve arrangements for communications across the party by placing specific responsibilities on certain post holders to call meetings.

In addition to communication issues, there have also been concerns over double-jobbing, as the dramatic rise of the DUP and the election of so many candidates to different institutions during the first decade of the twenty-first century created unforeseen problems, albeit ones that are hard for a party to address. It led to the holding of multiple posts by a number of elected representatives. In response, the party declared that anyone elected as a MP at the 2010 election would be obliged to quit the Assembly. Party members are hostile to double-jobbing, only 36 per cent believing that MLAs should also be allowed to be MPs. Members are almost evenly divided over whether Assembly members should also be permitted to be local councillors, 47 per cent in favour. Allegations of nepotism have also been evident. A 2013 *Irish News* report found that twenty-four of the thirty-six DUP MLAs employed family members, compared to four UUP representatives, three SDLP members, two from Alliance, and one each from Sinn Féin and the TUV.[27] Yet this does not appear to concern the majority of members, as 62 per cent believe that MLAs should be allowed to recruit family members. Whilst 69 per cent of members view MP's expenses as an important political issue and 75 per cent think likewise regarding MLAs, it has been the problem of double-jobbing, with senior representatives having to choose between influence at Westminster or at Stormont, that has been more difficult to resolve.

Political Attitudes

The DUP has managed to successfully recast itself to appeal to a broader swathe of unionism. Its profile and how it presents itself as a principled no-surrender party has been crucial in retaining most of its earlier members and securing new ones during a process of replacement of the UUP as the largest political party in Northern Ireland.[28] Robinson has moved the party from one rooted in fundamentalist Protestant rhetoric and standpoint towards one grounded in a more socio-economic narrative in defence of the Union. Under this casting, the Britishness of Northern Ireland is economically logical, an obvious political choice not reduced to religion. For Robinson, political stability will inevitably lead to greater investment, which, in turn, will further bolster the Union. As such, the old sabre-rattling rhetoric on behalf of the 'Protestant people' is no longer needed. What is required is quieter language concentrated upon the promotion of the message that Northern Ireland is very much open for business. As he put it: 'The legacy of violence and paramilitary activity has made the Province less attractive to potential investors than would otherwise have been the case . . . just try to visualise the surge that would attend political stability and a working assembly.'[29]

Members appear sanguine in terms of the broad thrusts of party policy. Asked to rate the DUP (on a scale of 0 to 10, where 10 is the maximum score) on social and welfare policies and the defence of Northern Ireland in the UK, members rank their party's defence of the Union at 9 and social and welfare policies at 8. Party leadership also scores very highly at 8.8. Members who joined the party earlier tend to give a higher rating on both questions, whereas newer members are somewhat less enthused. This is not to be confused with age. Older people tend to give a lower rating to party policy than their younger counterparts. Those DUP members identifying as right-wing are very strongly supportive of the party's approach.

In terms of the policy priorities of members, the political outstrips the socio-economic. Northern Ireland's place in the UK remains the number one priority, with 25 per cent of members viewing it as the single most important political issue. This constitutional question thus retains salience, despite the oft-repeated mantra that the issue is settled and despite members feeling very confident that Northern Ireland will stay part of the UK. Despite the regular utterance of another Northern Ireland cliché, that it is 'bread and butter' issues that matter most, none rank as highly as the constitutional issue. Eighteen per cent of members identified the economy as their priority issue, whilst other key policy areas include health (13 per cent), education and employment (each identified by 10 per cent), and crime (9 per cent).

Yet there is significant variation according to status here. Out of step with the membership in its entirety, councillors prioritized socio-economic issues more than the constitution. For many of these 175 councillors, a very sizeable chunk of the party's entire membership, there is an obligation to deal with local social and welfare issues affecting the unionist community of more immediate import than constitutional grandstanding. As one commented, in a very typical observation, 'working on the "bread and butter" issues is something that I hold very dear to my heart. It's about going out and helping people and getting things done. I have found that the DUP are a party that does really take grasp of the "bread and butter" issues.'[30] A North Belfast councillor, in another common observation, argued that the state of the economy had displaced the constitutional question in immediate salience, insisting that priority should be given to 'jobs and the economy because a lot of our young people now go overseas; Northern Ireland is losing a lot of good talent'.[31] The normalization of politics is taking root, according to the Speaker of the Assembly, William Hay, who claimed that 'politics is evolving in Northern Ireland. It is all about health now. It is all about education. It is all about the economy. It is all about job creation now. It is not so much now about the hard politics, it is not so much now about the constitutional issue.'[32] A Strangford councillor contended that 'when it comes to sustaining a region, you need employment and education and a learning process that correlates with its industry'.[33] This is echoed by an Antrim councillor, who argued that the socio-economic and political are indivisible, in terms of securing community provision:

> Priority should be given to employment, health, and education, which are all linked. We should be focusing on what we need to prosper and secure the health and well-being of the people we are in charge over. You can only govern by consent. Equality should be built into it, yes. Sinn Féin's equality is that Catholics should get their share, but there seems to be a lack of equality when Protestants aren't getting their share. We need to get real and look at what equality means, embrace the concept of equality in a genuine fashion.[34]

In the aftermath of Sinn Féin's challenges to academic selection, 60 per cent of the membership would like the DUP to be more vocal on education, the primary non-constitutional concern. The party remains largely supportive of academic testing, 81 per cent backing the idea, hence the desire that the leadership highlight the issue. Forty-two per cent of members believe that the DUP should be more vocal on policing and crime. On no other issue do more than one-third of members believe the party should be more vocal, the highest figure being the 31 per cent urging greater voice on welfare policy. There is very considerable unity of outlook on other issues beyond local control, such as opposition to the Euro, with less than 3 per cent of members in favour of its adoption.

Our Wee Country

The DUP's support for devolution within the United Kingdom is predicated upon the perception that Northern Ireland can govern itself, albeit with extensive funding provided by Westminster. This UK regionalism, fused with a robust defence of the Union, still struggles to accommodate Strand Two of the Belfast Agreement, the all-Ireland dimension, to which many members remain hostile, even though it seems anodyne. It is difficult to see Food Safety and Inland Waterways all-Ireland bodies as subverting the Union. For one Strangford councillor, in a not untypical broadside, North–South/All-Ireland institutions remain problematic:

> That was set up under the Belfast Agreement. I am opposed to it as a unionist. I believe that they shouldn't be there. We are part of the United Kingdom and that is where we hope to remain. I am not really opposed to the British-Irish Council because that also includes Wales and Scotland. I don't mind having a good working relationship with the Republic of Ireland, but I don't think that we should have the institutions there.[35]

A more pragmatic approach emerges when discussing the issue of North–South relations in relation to wider policy issues. In the context of the closure of Northern Ireland's children's heart surgery unit, support for the practical benefits of strong cross-border relations emerges. According to an Antrim elected representative:

> It's brilliant to have good manners, for want of a better word, with your neighbours. It's good to have cooperation. Take health issues, there is the classic example with the paediatric and cardiac issue [cross-border health cooperation] that was raised recently. It's common sense for the good of people's health. I have no issues with any type of cooperation. But it shouldn't be forced. It should be voluntary, based on goodwill and common sense, and for mutual benefit.[36]

Likewise, the way in which the DUP under Robinson's leadership engages with the Irish Republic offers economic advantages, but the voluntarism of the relationship is continually stressed:

> There are many areas where working together with the Irish Republic would be enormously to our mutual advantage and we should not allow politics to be an obstacle to such an advance. Equally, it would be a real threat to north–south relations if there were politically motivated attempts to enhance links where the merits of the individual proposals are lost in the politics of it all.[37]

This opinion echoes across the party in the context of a largely neutralized, non-dynamic North–South dimension formalized in Strand Two of the Belfast Agreement. The weakening of the North–South dimension, in terms of formal political and institutional cooperation, suits the DUP, as it was one of several unfavoured aspects of the Belfast Agreement. More North–South bodies can only be approved by the Northern Ireland Assembly, allowing a unionist veto over their growth. Despite North–South institutions being a neutered organ of the Belfast Agreement, antagonism prevails because for many 'they're only a waste of money'.[38] Although opposition to the North–South bodies is pervasive amongst the DUP membership, a member's year of joining is highly significant. Long-term DUP members are significantly more likely to oppose North-South/All-Ireland institutions than more recent joiners, who opposed the Belfast Agreement, but nonetheless recognize that the North–South bodies are not a major threat.

Conclusion

The DUP has a membership defined more by its quality, if judged on high levels of activism and a very significant proportion of elected representatives, than quantity. Given the relative youth of its members and their willingness to proselytize on behalf of their party, the DUP appears in good health. It is one of few political parties to be gaining members. The party has broadened its religious and social bases since 1998, helped by the influx of members from the UUP. That influx comprised many talented individuals who have further enhanced the DUP's position as a catch-all repository for unionist opinion, in the manner in which the UUP operated for several decades.

The sudden reversal in the DUP's stance on power-sharing with Sinn Féin, in institutions established by the Belfast Agreement, threatened to weaken the DUP's time-served core and, briefly, there was the prospect of widespread defections to the TUV, or members utilizing the exit option.[39] However, the leadership successfully rode out the storm and the party continues to grow, having kept most of its base. The continuing electoral strength of the DUP, the sizeable number of places held by the party in the executive, and the functioning Northern Ireland Assembly that emerged following the St Andrews Agreement all restored the faith of party members in the party's decision to enter into government with Sinn Féin. A majority within the DUP, albeit a far from overwhelming one, support power-sharing with Sinn Féin and accept that their republican rival must provide either the First or Deputy First Minister. There seems to be contentment, or at least acquiescence, over the sharing of executive positions between unionist and nationalist parties. Party policies are supported by the vast bulk of members and the leader is popular. Recent party conferences have been vibrant and positive.

There are, nonetheless, some difficulties for the DUP in respect of its membership. It remains small, and religiously and gender imbalanced (see Chapters 7 and 8 respectively), despite the process of broadening. The status of the DUP as the lead partner in the power-sharing government creates challenges. As its leader acknowledges:

> when the party is in government, its leaders are absorbed by the operation of government and don't have sufficient time to spend on party responsibilities. Which

means that communication, if not breaks down, slows down in terms of the regular meetings and so forth because everybody is too busy doing things. The party is reliant on its elected representatives, and we don't have the party grandees and the constituency structure that can operate, and the meetings go on without the elected representatives being there.[40]

The comparative diversity and talent of some of the new DUP recruits offers an opportunity for the party to appeal to a new generation of voters that are concerned with 'bread and butter issues', yet the resilience of the constitutional issues and debates over legacy issues threaten to undermine this opportunity. As the DUP has expanded and professionalized, it faces new challenges of further expanding its membership, a task set against an increasingly apathetic middle-class Protestant constituency and a seemingly disaffected section of the Protestant working class, concerned over flags and parades, which does not see conventional political party membership, as now represented by the DUP, as its route forward. The DUP's already busy membership will have to redouble its efforts to grow the party across the swathe of unionism, from catholic unionists to traditional loyalists.

Notes

1. F. McGuinness (2012) *'Membership of UK Political Parties'*, Westminster: House of Commons Library, available at <www.parliament.uk/briefing-papers/SN05125. pdf>, accessed Aug. 2013. Party membership surveys of the SDLP and Alliance Party respectively can be found in G. Murray and J. Tonge (2005) *Sinn Féin and the SDLP: From Alienation to Participation*, London: Hurst; and J. Evans and J. Tonge (2003) 'The Future of the Radical Centre After the Good Friday Agreement', *Political Studies*, 51/1, 26–50.
2. Evans and Tonge, 'Future of the Radical Centre'; Murray and Tonge, *Sinn Féin and the SDLP* ; J. Tonge and J. Evans (2001) 'Northern Ireland's Third Tradition(s): The Alliance Party Surveyed', *British Elections and Parties Review*, 11, 104–18; P. Whiteley, P. Seyd, and J. Richardson (1994) *True Blues: The Politics of Conservative Party Membership*, Oxford: Oxford University Press.
3. Interview with Antrim councillor, 3 Dec. 2012.
4. A. Jackson (1999) *Ireland, 1798–1998: Politics and War*, Oxford: Blackwell. See also E. Moxon-Browne (1983) *Nation, Class and Creed in Northern Ireland*, Aldershot: Gower.
5. Interview with Belfast City councillor, Stormont, 16 Oct. 2012.
6. Interview with William Humphrey MLA, Belfast, 9 Jan. 2013.
7. Interview with North Down councillor, Bangor, 25 Nov. 2012.
8. Interview with Arlene Foster MLA, Fermanagh, 24 Jan. 2013.
9. Interview with Simon Hamilton MLA, Strangford, 6 Nov. 2012.

10. Cited in A. Aughey (2006) 'The 1998 Agreement: Three Unionist Anxieties', in M. Cox, A. Guelke, and F. Stephen (eds), *A Farewell to Arms? Beyond the Good Friday Agreement*, Manchester: Manchester University Press, 89–108.

11. Interview with North Down councillor, Bangor, 12 Sept. 2012.

12. Smyth, C. (1986) 'The DUP as a Politico-Religious Organisation', *Irish Political Studies*, 1, 33–43.

13. Interview with David Simpson MP, Westminster, 3 July 2013.

14. Interview with Mervyn Storey MLA, Stormont, 8 Jan. 2013.

15. Interview with Strangford councillor, 11 Sept. 2012.

16. Interview with DUP MP, 3 Oct. 2012.

17. Interview with Jeffrey Donaldson MP, Lisburn, 8 Mar. 2013.

18. Interview with Lisburn MLA, 11 Jan. 2013.

19. Interview with Belfast City councillor, Belfast, 9 Oct. 2013.

20. Interview with North Down councillor, Bangor, 25 Nov. 2012.

21. Interview with Castlereagh councillor, Castlereagh, 27 Feb. 2013.

22. Interview with Mervyn Storey MLA, Stormont, 8 Jan. 2013.

23. Interview with Jonathan Craig MLA, Lisburn, 11 Jan. 2013.

24. Interview with DUP member, Antrim, 20 Nov. 2012.

25. Interview with Coleraine councillor, Coleraine, 5 Oct. 2012.

26. Interview with Ards Borough councillor, Newtownards, 16 Oct. 2012.

27. *Irish News*, 29 July 2013, 'More than Half the DUP MLAs are Employing their Relatives'.

28. G. Ganiel (2008) *Evangelicalism and Conflict in Northern Ireland*, Basingstoke: Palgrave Macmillan.

29. Peter Robinson (2006) Speech to KPMG's Management Conference, Europa Hotel, Belfast, 23 June, available at <http://cain.ulst.ac.uk/issues/politics/docs/dup/pr230606.htm>, accessed Aug. 2013.

30. Interview with Down councillor, Ballynahinch, 11 Sept. 2012.

31. Interview with Belfast City councillor, Belfast, 30 Nov. 2012.

32. Interview with Speaker William Hay, MLA, Stormont, 8 Jan. 2013.

33. Interview with Ards Borough councillor, Newtownards, 16 Oct. 2013.

34. Interview with Coleraine councillor, Coleraine, 5 Oct. 2012.

35. Interview with Down councillor, Ballynahinch, 11 Sept. 2012.

36. Interview with Pam Brown MLA, Stormont, 2 Oct. 2012.

37. Robinson, Speech to KPMG's Management Conference, 2006.

38. Interview with Coleraine councillor, Coleraine, 4 Oct. 2013.

39. Ganiel, *Evangelicalism and Conflict*, 34.

40. Interview with Peter Robinson MLA, DUP leader, Stormont, 25 June 2013.

4

Changing Discourses

> If the DUP had not been in existence, then Northern Ireland
> would not have been in existence. This Party and this Party alone,
> led the Ulster people to save the Union.
>
> (Ian Paisley, DUP party leader, Annual Conference 2001[1])

> At the heart of the St Andrews Agreement was the knowledge and
> strength that what was agreed allowed politics in Northern Ireland
> to move away from issues about the existence of the border.
>
> (Peter Robinson, DUP party leader, Annual Conference 2012[2])

It is sometimes easy to forget just how young the DUP is as a political party. In a little over four decades, the DUP underwent a remarkable political journey: from a vehicle established in the early 1970s to give expression to the 'politicized Protestantism' of Ian Paisley and the Free Presbyterian Church to a modern structured political organization; and from a conduit to channel the politics of self-positioned 'outsiders' to one at the heart of the government. Following eventual engagement in a political process that it once claimed was designed to ensure a political weakening of the Union, the party has moved from a position where its central claims included smashing the Irish republican project, to sharing power with Sinn Féin in the devolved administration of Northern Ireland. Indeed, at times, the DUP now espouses an identifiable seemingly post-ethno-nationalist discourse with its claim to be 'the Party for Northern Ireland'.[3]

Throughout these transitions, there has been both consistency and change in the dominant narratives and discourses emerging from the DUP leadership. Although it has taken various forms, one constant discourse has been the insistence that it was the party best representative of the 'true voice' of unionism, direct inheritors, as they see it, of the spirit of Edward Carson,[4] ensuring the continued constitutional position of Northern Ireland and the fulfilment of the democratic will of the 'Ulster people' (by which the DUP meant Protestant unionists in Northern Ireland). Further, throughout its existence, the DUP has presented itself as representing a politics based on moral values and as a political grouping capable of successfully identifying and opposing every major threat presented to the constitutional position, from both within and without, thus ensuring the continuing existence of Protestant British culture in Northern Ireland.

Political Discourse and the DUP

The construction of discourses that, on the one hand, bond the party and its members, guiding reactions to key events and issues while, on the other hand, projecting the public face of the party to harness and consolidate wider support, has been central to the political and social positioning of the DUP. Such discourses are complex and multi-layered, and the party's core messages and arguments have often involved a seemingly seamless interweaving of religious text, secular politics, moral stance, and political ideology.[5]

While at various historical points the emphasis has differed, these discourses are linked through a whole series of interrelated texts, both written and spoken, finding expression through public pronouncements and internal debates. They take shape through a variety of narratives and ideas produced formally and informally by the DUP leadership, its elected representatives, members, and supporters, and in exchanges with political opponents. It is through such discourses that DUP members give meaning to and organize their social lives, and structure forms of political action. Crucially, for the DUP, this includes the categorization of other social groupings, through the construction of wider social relationships and conceptual understandings that, in turn, steer reaction to political events and proceedings.

Within the DUP, discourses and narratives function to maintain and preserve ideological coherence, to frame political choices, and indicate what are and what are not seen as legitimate and desirable responses to particular circumstances. They also, in part, outline idealized futures and indicate the possibilities for change, or at least the likely boundaries within which change is deemed justifiable. Thus, DUP discourse is important in helping to frame the ways within which contemporary events are interpreted, in providing the justification for positions taken by the leadership on particular issues and in guiding members and activists in reactions to events.

In this way, discourse can act to both shape common-sense beliefs and to reinforce (or much less frequently transform) existing beliefs and understandings. Culture and consciousness are fashioned through discourse, and collective patterns of thought and narrative provide the prevailing conditions to structure social realities and perceptions. That is not to say that prevailing discourses provide intellectual enclosures from which there is no escape, or that dominant discourses cannot be challenged, but as we shall see with DUP members and activists, more often than not it is reference to established discourses that determines the ways in which people act.

Essentially, as Stuart Hall reminds us, discourses understood in this sense are 'ways of referring to or constructing knowledge about a particular topic of practice...which provide ways of talking about, forms of knowledge and conduct associated with a particular topic, social activity, or institutional site in society'.[6] Following on from this, Katy Hayward suggests that the two key dimensions within the political arena are: 'discourse as political action' and 'politics as discursive action'.[7] Viewing both in relation to the DUP, we adopt a wide-ranging view that links discourse with ideology, recognizing that, through the construction of knowledge in different ways, discourses can both enable and inhibit social and political change.[8] Within the DUP 'discourse is used to convince voters and to give legitimacy to actors'[9] and to actions.

DUP Political Discourses

Discourses are not important merely because of the narrative they convey, but also because they reveal much about the values, beliefs, and underlying strategies of those using them. In a newspaper article marking the twenty-fifth anniversary of the DUP's formation, Steve Bruce suggested that the party had directly reflected Ian Paisley's personal concept of politics and found its initial expression through a set of public discourses candidly reflecting the founder's worldview. This discourse emphasized the threat from popery without; the fear of treachery by liberal Protestant churches within; the evil to be found south of the border; the fear of betrayal by Westminster; and, the possibility of divine intervention to guide Ulster Protestants.[10]

While much of this is still recognizable amongst the views of DUP members today, not all of the components of this discourse have remained static in importance. The party's journey through oppositional politics, rise to power, change in leadership, and its role in the government of Northern Ireland have all led to subtle changes in discourse. To illustrate this, we concentrate on the major framing discourses, of faith and politics, resolute unionism, fear of betrayal, and eternal vigilance.

Faith and Politics

The extent to which religion, denomination, and politics are linked within the DUP will be dealt with in much more detail in Chapter 7. Here, however, we wish to highlight the role of evangelicalism, particularly as expressed by the Free Presbyterian Church, in constructing the original political discourse of the DUP. This was manifested within the policy and public messages emanating from the DUP, most obviously through Ian Paisley's expression of 'the Reformation tradition in both his theology and political beliefs'[11] and his targeting of the Roman Catholic Church as being at the core of the conflict. It has been suggested that Paisley's record of railing against change, real or perceived, across religion, politics, and society[12] allows him to be characterized as an 'ideal type' of Northern Irish evangelical.[13]

It was Paisley's interpretation of biblical writings and his representation of the social position of the Catholic Church[14] that largely gave form to both the Free Presbyterian brand of evangelicalism and to the DUP. As a consequence, many political issues surrounding Northern Ireland society were also characterized as both religious and moral. When Paisley came to prominence in the mid- to late 1960s, his presence represented an exploitation of a 'distinctly Ulster political tradition'[15] of public preaching that overtly mixed reference to scripture and politics.[16] Paisley made overt challenges to the unionist party surrounding its alleged willingness to compromise and expressed open hostility to the development of ecumenical tendencies within the Protestant churches in Ireland.

Paisleyism proved seductive to sections of Protestant society and found focus in opposition to Prime Minister Terence O'Neill's attempts to improve community relations. In conjunction with Paisley's highlighting of class differences within the unionist bloc,[17] by seeking to 'communicate and articulate the concerns of...ordinary grass roots unionists',[18] and providing 'a voice for the working class',[19] Paisleyite rhetoric achieved rising popularity amongst sections of the Protestant community, harnessed by a new grouping, Ulster Protestant Action (UPA). The momentum for the 'Paisleyite movement' was set in train by events that began in 1966,[20] following a series of demonstrations organized by Paisley and his supporters, who were protesting at the decision to allow celebrations marking the fiftieth anniversary of the Easter Rising. Political protests were accompanied by public rallies hostile to the ecumenical movement, which Paisley argued 'amounted to a Rome-led offensive on Protestantism'.[21]

After the emergence of the Civil Rights movement, which was dismissed as 'the latest IRA campaign to reunite Ireland',[22] the size and potency of populist political opposition coalescing around Paisley grew. Such protest 'grew more political in appearance' as the 'pulpit orator became the stump politician'.[23] 'Paisleyism' developed through the Ulster Constitution Defence Committee (UCDC) and eventually made possible the formation of the Protestant Unionist Party (PrUP), under which banner Paisley was first elected to both the Stormont and Westminster administrations in 1970.

As the Scarman Tribunal observed of Paisley, his 'spoken words were always powerful and must have frequently appeared to some as provocative: his newspaper was such that its style and substance were likely to rouse the enthusiasm of his supporters and the fury of his opponents'.[24] The PrUP was dissolved, to re-emerge as the DUP in 1971. As Clifford Smyth observes, the 'dual role of Paisley as pastor and politician was reflected in the type of person mobilised',[25] including those who became members, 'because they believed that supporting the DUP was "doing God's work"'.[26]

Many of the party's core activists were drawn from the Free Presbyterian Church and hence were well attuned to the interpretation of events that Paisley offered and understood politics being read directly 'from the pages of Scripture'.[27] As one current member put it, at its formation 'the Free Presbyterian Church...would all have been in the DUP',[28] while another recognized that 'in the early days it was very much a Paisleyite party[29] (see Chapter 7).

Evangelicalism and Politics

It was apparent that the overlap between Free Presbyterian Church and DUP was a direct one[30] and that the other, less religious, faction headed by the party's co-founder Desmond Boal was progressively more marginalized.[31] The role of evangelicalism in the construction of Ian Paisley's personal politics and the Paisleyite social movement is uncontested,[32] and there can be little doubt that Paisley's charismatic leadership and the form in which he expressed his politics drew many to the party in its early days.[33] Ed Moloney and Andy Pollak suggest that, at times of perceived crisis for unionism, 'thousands of fundamentalist Protestants turned to [Paisley] religiously as hundreds of thousands of less fundamentalist Protestants have done so politically'.[34]

What is important for the direction of later events is to assess the continuing centrality of evangelical views in structuring policy and discourse and the capability of that discourse to mobilize beyond Paisley's personal influence and the Free Presbyterian Church. This allows identification of the legacy of Paisleyism in contemporary DUP discourse and politics. It is necessary to assess how much influence the Free Presbyterian Church and Protestant faith, more broadly, continue to have upon party and policy discourses and in what ways this structures contemporary DUP politics. Two questions immediately arise: what is the relationship between the evangelical and the secular in determining party political positioning, and has this relationship changed as the party membership has expanded, the party 'modernized', and its leadership changed?

The effect of religion on the party can be seen in both narrow and broad terms. For some members and activists, this manifests in highly personalized ways. From interview material, it is apparent that those who hold strong evangelical beliefs often justify their political views within a distinct framework of religious precepts, and their political action within the DUP is usually legitimized through reference to biblical teachings, whereby members are seen to 'share the same aims and read the same scriptures'.[35] Take, for example, the views of these local councillors, one recently joined, the other of thirty years' membership:

> I think the Biblical principles are still there. It's what the party was founded on. The core principles are still there. I think they still hold in the main.[36]
>
> I am a born-again Christian. I believe that faith is where we must base our policies; basically, get back to decency and respect for one another. I personally, believe that we, by and large, stand by very straightforward biblical stands and biblical teaching. That may not come across all the time, but what I mean by that is we have to work with others that probably don't hold that view or that stance, part of the teaching of scriptures is to respect the views of others.[37]

Another long-standing member and MLA argued:

> I still think that the values that the Free Presbyterian Church brought to the DUP in those early days are still very prevalent and still very important to the party, those Christian values, and I think that it is vitally important that they remain as an integral part of what the DUP is about.[38]

Many interviewees recognized, however, that within this wider frame of Christian influence, which remained core to contemporary party values, the influence of the Free Presbyterian Church had weakened considerably, as the following observations highlight:

> The atmosphere has changed over the years within the DUP. Previously, people would have said 'It's the Free Presbyterians in Prayer'. It is much more open now, not necessarily a party that could or should be seen as exclusively Free Presbyterian....In times gone past, it was the Free P's political arm, but it is much broader now.[39]
>
> There are more secular people coming into the party. That is something we would need to deal with as a party. [But] they do sign up to the DUP's values and beliefs.[40]
>
> Today, it is not the DUP that I became involved with. I think the influence of the Free Presbyterian Church has diminished greatly, but I think the influence of faith is still strong within the DUP. I think it is pretty strong within politics in Northern Ireland in general.[41]

The changing base of DUP activists was recognized by one senior party member, Nelson McCausland, who described some of the differences from the early days of the party:

> In those days, [we] preserved Sunday because it is the Protestant thing to do, it wasn't so much, it is a good thing it has social benefits, whatever. Policies were quite often framed in those terms, people I knew around here who were in the

DUP in North Belfast were all very much into it. The Protestant aspect was still very strong.[42]

Asked if, in his view, that 'was something that stayed with the party, or if the situation had changed?', he responded:

We are in a different world today. We are in a much more secular world. We are in a world where we have to broaden the support for the Union, but it is important that we do not abandon core principles...how things are presented quite often is the key to it. You can put forward a message in a way that attracts and has a broader appeal than it might otherwise have. I think there is a need for that. We need to broaden the thing out. We are essentially in Northern Ireland, I think, a fairly socially conservative society. Therefore, certain things that might in the past have been pushed quite strongly within the party on the ground...the Evangelical Protestant position...held back a few people who never darkened the door of a church, they tend to be socially conservative and how you frame your message, present it, is the key to that. We would lose a lot of our core support if we abandoned those things.[43]

McCausland suggests that broad engagement with religion or Christian values plays a core role in framing understandings of politics and identity for many Protestants. Elsewhere, Claire Mitchell demonstrates how the active expression of faith remains central to the sense of politics and identity for many Protestants,[44] while Bell identifies how Protestantism can play a role in shaping identity and 'attitudes to Catholics, even for those Protestants who are not of theological conviction'.[45] While theological views may not transfer directly into politics, they do help structure retorts to political events and frame reactions to political change.[46] Mitchell further argues that politicized Protestantism represents a specific identity that seeks to place Protestantism at the core of senses of belonging, such as unionism and Britishness, through what Sean Farrell refers to as 'religious nationalism'.[47]

Although Christian values and teachings remain at the heart of the party for many, classic Paisleyite discourse interweaving religious and biblical reference with political analysis of contemporary events has largely disappeared from DUP public repertoire. It resurfaces in the public area only in moral debates surrounding issues such as abortion or gay marriage, as detailed in Chapter 7. One MLA gives an accurate overview of the contemporary party:

There are some people who have incredibly strong views and those are entirely based on their faith perspective on it. But there would be those who are less evangelical, maybe not even religious at all, who still take that view and agree. On...social [issues] there is little divergence of opinion within the party. Yet the party is not that homogenous Free Presbyterian bloc that people think that it is.

...I just think we are, as a society, for whatever reasons, largely religious. We are also incredibly conservative. That is reflected then in the membership. The party is reasonably united in this, and the fact that the party isn't united religiously, or denominationally, suggests that there is more to it than simply [that] we are an evangelical group of people.[48]

Conservatism and Protestantism now find expression in a more personalized form, rather than through a desire to impose all aspects upon others. Thus, according to one member:

I am conservative in how I live my own personal life, as opposed to how I feel about others living their lives. So I don't believe in imposing how I do things on others. It is up to people to decide how they live their lives. I suppose that is more reflective of how the DUP went about things in the early days, which was to impose their viewpoints on how other people actually...hoping to close play parks and things on a Sunday...that isn't an issue any more. It's up to people to make their own personal choices.[49]

The diminution of overt religiosity has not weakened affection towards Ian Paisley and the effect 'the Doc' had on the party, its politics, and on individual members. MLA Mervyn Storey gives some feel for this:

Ian Paisley had such an influence in those early days...my father became a member of the Free Presbyterian Church, but he was influenced by Ian Paisley and his politics first. As a result of that, he went to the Free Presbyterian Church...in the early days, there was more of that. It is not the case so much now because people from different religious denominations...join the party and they join the party not because of the Free Presbyterian Church, they join the party because of the DUP...Ian Paisley will go down in history for being the most unique individual that this nation has ever had and he follows in the succession of other great leaders for different reasons. I don't think there is any other individual who will ever be able to claim that they formed their own political party, they formed their own religious denomination, and both of them became a very big success[50].

The contemporary period has witnessed attempts to broaden the DUP's base by emphasizing its political robustness and social conservatism, rather than its evangelical religious credentials. This is reflected in a changing set of public discourses from the party, acknowledged by one elected representative who claimed to 'see a great change in the DUP...the DUP had a reputation of blood and thunder and very strong lines of where they would go, what they would do. It didn't really suit my make-up...the DUP is now a bigger party, and with [that] comes new ideas.'[51]

The new discourses of the DUP are not secular, but they represent a new, less evangelical form of Protestantism, still socially conservative, but more personalized and based more upon persuasion than coercion.

Resolute Unionism: Opposition to 'Treachery' and the 'Evil to Come'

For some unionists, defence of the Union and Protestantism were obviously linked, but even those who could see beyond the charismatic evangelical leadership of Paisley, who did not share his belief that he was anointed by the Lord,[52] or cared little for his reading of contemporary events from biblical texts, were often drawn to the strength of his political analysis, his warnings of the possibility of imminent British sell-out, and wariness of the enemy within, whether republican or liberal fellow unionist.

Hence, another core organizing discourse from the DUP surrounds the notion that they are the sturdiest custodians of the Union. This is most obviously found in oppositional discourses to Irish republicanism, but it is also manifest in relation to the stances taken by other factions of unionism (most notably the UUP) and through opposition to the governments of the Irish Republic and the UK, the Irish-American lobby, and the US government. Thus, a central discourse from the party has been that the DUP 'offers the surest guarantee' and the 'firmest stand against all attempts to force Ulster down the Dublin Road'.[53]

The electoral success and political importance of the DUP was built upon antagonism to the Belfast Agreement and the party's ability to harness subsequent discontent within the Protestant unionist community. The notion that Northern Ireland faced a constitutional crisis long formed a core DUP discourse central in mobilizing unionists to engage in oppositional politics.[54] Episodic attempts to find a settlement by the British and Irish Governments, supported by moderate factions from within unionism and nationalism, repeatedly incurred the wrath of the DUP, which vehemently contested new political initiatives.

Throughout the 1980s and 1990s, all attempts at legislative change, most notably that of the Anglo-Irish Agreement (signed in 1985), the 'Joint Declaration on Peace' (often known as the Downing Street Declaration, signed in 1993), the 'Framework Documents' (published in 1995), and the 'Belfast [Good Friday] Agreement' (signed in 1998), were met with hostility from the DUP and regarded as attempts to negotiate away the very future of Ulster. Take, for example, the views of this councillor on the Anglo-Irish Agreement:

> In 1985...every Unionist of every persuasion felt betrayed. We felt betrayed by...Thatcher. We were totally opposed to the Agreement, there was huge opposition to it. There were huge rallies at the city hall. There was a sense, in Unionism, that we were sold out by the British government and that created all sorts of problems...by democratic means you opposed the agreement...you had opposed the intervention of a foreign state.[55]

The emphasis on the dangers of treachery from without and betrayal from within marks key continuities in DUP discourse. This is highlighted in the following interview with a local councillor:

> I felt betrayed...since Margaret Thatcher at the Anglo-Irish Agreement, I had no real trust in the English because right throughout history, the government have had no real allegiance to Northern Ireland. At the end of the day, I'm only too pleased to see our own government in power.[56]

Part of the appeal of the DUP has always rested upon its particular 'apocalyptic view' of the future.[57] The discourses of fear were broad, covering the demise of Protestantism, the undermining of the constitutional position, and a hollowing out of British culture. Concerns over the constitutional position remain central to the views of the membership. Crucial to this perspective is the identification of imprudent and injudicious unionism—the enemy within. Every UUP leader has come under direct challenge from the DUP, portrayed as weak, lacking in political leadership, and incapable of presenting a political programme capable of defending the constitutional link. For the DUP, the UUP's support for the Belfast Agreement marked its ineffectiveness in countering plans designed 'to sacrifice Ulster's constitutional position on the altar of political expediency',[58] further illustrating that those 'who should be in the front line defending the union are in cahoots with the enemy'.[59] At the DUP's annual conference in November 1998, Ian Paisley unleashed a fearsome verbal assault upon the then UUP leader, David Trimble, pointing to what he called 'the worst and most loathsome person in society—the traitor—Judas, the Iscariot' and highlighting Trimble's decision to sign the Belfast Agreement as a direct betrayal of Protestant Ulster.[60]

The DUP's resistance, representing the Belfast Agreement as a pact designed to deceive unionism and betray the Union, became a central discourse. Ian Paisley declared: 'we are not going to allow the IRA/Sinn Féin to rule over us. We are not going to pull down our flag and join with the Trimbleite slaves in the tents of republicanism.'[61] For the DUP, the UUP had surrendered the principles they were supposed to uphold in an unholy partnership with the 'perfidious and discredited Government', and in so doing, failed to recognize that the 'so-called' peace process was little other than another republican tactic.[62] For the DUP, it was the strength of their resolute opposition that eventually led to a reworking of the terms of the Belfast Agreement at St Andrews.

The DUP's consistent highlighting of 'evil to come' and the 'approaching menace' was at the heart of its political discourses until the party entered government. The Belfast Agreement was described by a DUP MP, the Reverend William McCrea, as 'the mother out of whose womb the endless concessions to republicanism flowed'.[63] Ian Paisley insisted in 2001 that 'Ulster is to be made a prey to Republican domination' and in response, 'it is vital that a body blow is struck now against the conspiracy and treachery afoot',[64] and he declared that 'the IRA is the instrument of the entire Judas Iscariot strategy. Treachery is their order of the day.'[65]

For the DUP, the 1998 peace deal represented yet another betrayal of principles by the British Government, amid fears that a secret deal had been struck with Irish republicans in return for a guarantee that the IRA campaign would end (particularly in Britain). The DUP placed the blame upon Tony Blair's Labour administration, claiming it had 'misled the people of Northern Ireland' through 'deceit and incompetence',[66] and presented a view that unionists were dealing with a 'nest of traitors at Whitehall'.[67] Paisley argued that the Westminster government had 'psychologically abandoned' Northern Ireland[68] and was now 'in cahoots with Dublin, Washington, the Vatican, and the IRA'.[69] Together, they had conceded to the IRA/Sinn Féin strategy 'to extort bottomless concessions from the government',[70] and surrendered 'to the murdering thugs of Irish Republicanism'.[71]

Following the Belfast Agreement, many Protestants succumbed to DUP claims that the political and cultural rights of unionism were being undermined, that Protestants had not benefited equally in the post-Agreement period, and that the Union itself might be threatened. There were reminders from the DUP that many of its divinations regarding the political future of Northern Ireland could be seen as correct. Amid consistent warnings from the DUP that they could not trust the Westminster government, Stormont had been closed in the 1970s, the Anglo-Irish Agreement signed in the 1980s, and a much closer set of relationships with the Irish Government developed. Now the Belfast Agreement and associated side deals of the 1990s added a catalogue of non-constitutional concessions, including prisoner releases, policing changes, and parade restrictions.

The DUP also reminded the electorate that the 1994 ceasefire was a pretence and noted how the IRA had returned to 'war' in 1996–7. Hence, claims from the DUP that the peace process marked little more than a conditional surrender to the IRA and an attempt to introduce 'Irish unity by stealth'.[72] Many unionists considered that nationalists had benefited much more from an Agreement created from pan-nationalism,[73] a sentiment fostered by the DUP. A 2002 survey claimed that fewer than one in ten supported the Agreement in some loyalist areas.[74] Amid feelings of alienation, the critique offered by the DUP resonated with many unionists.[75] Following the Belfast Agreement, the task for the DUP was to undo the 'damage' and continue to put political pressure on the UK Government to change its position of 'appeasing' republicanism.

Sentinels Against Ulster's Enemies: The Security Discourse

Successful projection of the DUP as 'sentinels against Ulster's historic enemies', and as the only *true* guarantors of traditional unionist values, drew support to the party. The traditional security-oriented discourse of the DUP—one in which the Union is under perpetual threat and its enemies need to be tackled robustly—was married to moral outrage over the release of 'terrorist' prisoners and bitter opposition to the recasting of those who had attempted to deal with those terrorists: the police service.

As these members, who were post-1998 joiners, explain:

> I joined the DUP because I didn't agree with the Belfast Agreement. I felt North-South bodies could lead to a united Ireland. It gave a role to the Irish government. I didn't like what they did to the Royal Ulster Constabulary and it was an erosion of my culture.[76]
>
> With the Belfast Agreement, I didn't think people who were in jail for murder and who committed crimes should be released early on licence. The guy who shot my friends had already escaped dressed as a woman on Christmas morning. He went on the run and is still on the run. Even when we decided to go into government, I decided to speak with their families...I didn't want them to think I was doing some back door deal behind their backs.[77]

What emerged in the aftermath of the Belfast Agreement was a new police service, rebranded as the Police Service of Northern Ireland, which retained the title deeds of Royal Ulster Constabulary, but represented a departure. Only 10 per cent of members concur with the proposition that the 'Police Service of Northern Ireland is very similar to the old Royal Ulster Constabulary'. The changes to the name, size, and ethos of the police force, instigated following the 1999 Patten Report, all concerned DUP members.[78] As the Reverend McCrea articulated:

> The gallant and honoured RUC/RUCR were sacrificed on the altar of the Belfast Agreement and whilst false and empty promises were made that the RUC would not be done away with, the Unionist population knows the reality of the situation...Murderers and gangsters now lord over the long suffering law-abiding people of Ulster, law and order has broken down, and sadly, integrity and truth lie scattered in the dust.[79]

Throughout the implementation of Patten's recommendations, until the devolution of policing and justice responsibilities to the Northern Ireland Executive in 2010, local influence upon policing was slight. Although district policing partnerships established as part of the changes offered some input, strategic control by local parties was impossible.

In a typical criticism of the policing changes, an Antrim councillor remarked:

> Patten left the force weak and spineless and intelligent-less going forward. So they had to bring back some of their best guys to bolster the thing up again. It was the best police force in the world. People were asking RUC men to go over and tell them how they were so successful in tackling terrorists. People all over the world

were asking their advice and a lot of them are still finding employment in other countries because their skills are so precious.[80]

An Antrim MLA similarly claimed, 'We've lost a lot of really good experience and it's probably cost an awful lot of money.'[81] An Ards councillor insisted that the PSNI 'don't have sufficient manpower. There are issues arising around public order and general crime fighting and human trafficking that are under the radar.'[82]

Focusing on the reform of the RUC, another councillor personalized the experience as follows:

> 50/50 recruitment [following the Patten reforms] was something I had a big prob-lem with. I myself...applied to join the police. I got in. But because of 50/50, because I was a Protestant, I didn't get it. I'm not trying to blow my own trumpet, but there was a Catholic friend of mine who got into the police and wouldn't have made as good a policeman as me. I'm not trying to be egotistical. I just know. They're friends of mine and they would tell you they wouldn't have the aptitude. They got it because of who they were. That's discrimination, which is what we are trying to get away from, what the Good Friday Agreement was trying to stop. In terms of the RUC itself, my father-in-law was a sergeant in the police. For him, it was a bitter pill to swallow. It was an insult to some of his comrades. At the same time, I think there had to be a change in membership. You can't have an organisa-tion that is all...we had to encourage Roman Catholics to join the police. That's not an issue. Just the way they went about it, I think, wasn't the right way.[83]

A councillor expressed the following views, typical of many interviewees:

> The release of terrorists, some of whom had committed heinous crimes, murder and all that sort of thing, some of them that were sentenced to 25 years, were out in two years under the Belfast Agreement. I was unhappy about that part of it. I was certainly unhappy about the RUC, that it was going to be done away with. We were happy with the old RUC and we didn't want it taken away. So there were a number of things. Then there were the cross border bodies without any control over them. What we did at St Andrews was to make them answerable to the Assembly, which is not ideal by any means, but it does mean we have some control over them.[84]

Overall, the bulk of members do support the PSNI, notwithstanding its dif-ferences from the old RUC. Forty-four per cent declare that they 'strongly support' the service, with a further 34 per cent offering 'support', and only 7 per cent declared opposition to the reconstituted force. However, many changes have met with the wrath of DUP members. Sixty-one per cent believe the reform of policing has gone too far, whilst 34 per cent think that the changes have been 'about right' and only 5 per cent argue that they 'need to go further'. However, beneath this high overall hostility to change there are significant internal party differences according to age. Older members are

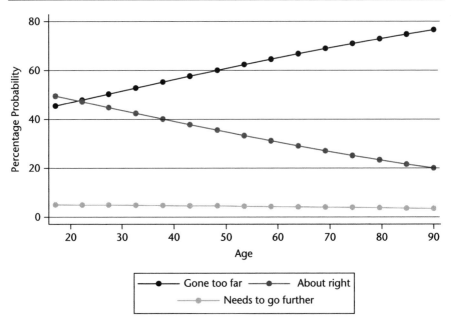

Figure 4.1 DUP members' views on policing reform, by age

much more likely to assert that policing reforms have been excessive. Very young members (aged 24 and under), in contrast, are almost equally divided between those thinking the reforms have been about right and those thinking they have gone too far. Figure 4.1 demonstrates the age effect.

A mere 6 per cent of DUP members view the 50–50 Roman Catholic and Non-Roman Catholic recruitment by the PSNI, utilized during the first decade of the new force's life, as a good initiative, with 81 per cent expressing opposition. A key feature of the Patten changes, the achievement of greater acceptability amongst nationalists via accountability mechanisms, meets with a mixed response. A majority of DUP members (61 per cent) do believe that 'most Roman Catholics now support the PSNI', so Patten might be seen as a success in that respect. Age is by far the most significant variable; the older the DUP member, the less likely they are to be convinced that Catholics are offering such backing. At Table 4.1 shows, Sinn Féin's presence on policing boards is seen as helpful by a sizeable proportion (36 per cent) of the DUP membership, but nearly as many do not think that policing is benefiting from this development.

Opposition to the reform of policing is particularly pronounced among Orange Order members within the DUP, who are significantly less likely (0.468**, p<0.05) to agree that policing in Northern Ireland is benefiting from Sinn Féin's participation on policing boards. Given that the Orange Order

Table 4.1 DUP members' views on whether 'Policing is benefiting from Sinn Féin's participation on policing boards'

	%
Strongly Agree	7.7
Agree	28.3
Neither Agree nor Disagree	30.5
Disagree	21.4
Strongly Disagree	12.1

had hundreds of members killed by the Provisional IRA during the conflict and that a sizeable number of these were serving police officers (particularly during the early years of the Troubles), particular Orange antipathy to discussing policing alongside the onetime supporters (or even perpetrators) of IRA violence might be expected. Sinn Féin's backing for the police force of a state it supposedly wishes to end was perhaps the most dramatic of all republican transformations, one awkward for that party, but perhaps even more so for those whom the Provisional IRA once targeted.

Yet the post-2006 discourse on security concerns is necessarily tempered amongst the DUP leadership by the need to trumpet the biggest change from the Belfast Agreement—the requirement that Sinn Féin's signed up to supporting policing. To claim this was not working would be to undermine the basis of the St Andrews deal. Thus, the loudest criticism comes from beyond the DUP, from a predictable but highly articulate source. The TUV's Jim Allister asserts:

On their own terms, I thought they [Sinn Féin] would sign up [to support for policing]. It is [on] their own terms. They do not support policing in the sense that if there was a crime committed before 1998, they do not support the investigation of it. They do not believe that murder by the IRA before 1998 was murder. If someone was butchered by them before 1998, they do not believe they should be brought to justice...So it is a very selective, expedient support of policing.[85]

Allister's claim may ring true, but Sinn Féin's stance on policing causes more intra-republican (mainstream versus dissident) antagonism than it creates angst within the DUP. The shift on policing appears to be a notable DUP success, even if it was an inevitable ultimate consequence of Sinn Féin entering a government of Northern Ireland.

The Discourse of Continuing Vigilance: Perceptions of the 'Dissident' Republican Threat

Traditional security-related angst amongst DUP members has been exacerbated by continuing violence. Whilst the First and Deputy First Minister have highlighted the progress made in Northern Ireland, the threat of the old IRA bogeyman still looms in the unionist psyche, reflected in the fears expressed by DUP members of dissident republican activity. The need for eternal vigilance remains important in the discourse offered by party stalwarts. Dissident republicans were responsible for the bulk of the 314 shooting and 274 bombings incidents between 2007 and 2012, during which time they also killed two British Army soldiers, two PSNI officers, and a prison officer.[86] The continuing security threat, officially classified as severe whilst the DUP and Sinn Féin embedded power-sharing, provided an unwelcome backdrop to the new political stability. Moreover, the perpetuation of violence, albeit mainly at a low level, did nothing to assuage the anger of DUP members over earlier policing changes.

The perception of a significant republican dissident threat—seemingly beyond the actual level posed in recent years—is evident in the membership survey results and came across in numerous interviews. More than half (54 per cent) of members do believe that 'there is a lasting peace in Northern Ireland', whilst 37 per cent disagree. Older members are significantly more sceptical, but perhaps, following the lead of their onetime leader Ian Paisley, who believes that peace has descended upon Northern Ireland via divine intervention, Free Presbyterian members are (slightly) significantly more likely to be positive.

Despite this apparent optimism, views are gloomier across the party regarding dissident republican activity. Sixty-one per cent of DUP members believe that dissidents pose a 'major threat', with a further 37 per cent regarding the threat as 'minor' and a mere 2 per cent being entirely dismissive of the dissidents. The dissident threat ranked fifth when members were asked to identify 'the single most important political issue for you', being cited by 10 per cent of members. This placed dissident violence below Northern Ireland's place in the UK, the economy, the NHS, and employment, but alongside education and above crime, the environment, and housing. The chief concerns regarding the dissidents are in respect of their persistence, intelligence gathering, the potential for growth in support, defections from the old Provisional IRA, and the fear of loyalist retaliation. In a small number of cases, personal threats from dissidents were reported. Older members of the DUP are significantly more likely to view the dissidents as a major threat. Social class does not have any statistical effect upon threat perception. Threat perception is highest in the more rural western counties of Fermanagh, Londonderry, and Tyrone, where almost two-thirds of DUP members see the problem as 'major' (here, none see the dissidents as 'no threat') and lowest in Antrim, where 55 per cent of members think likewise.

In his assessment of the dissident threat, the DUP leader noted that the dissidents are 'well infiltrated' and 'don't have the organizational capacity, numbers, equipment, and indeed strategic thinking to be anything close to what the Provos were doing'.[87] Given these pressures upon dissidents, a certain amount of frustration at their continuation was apparent amongst many interviewees, evidenced in the comment of one following the killing of the Prison Officer David Black in 2012: 'I just don't understand—they [the dissidents] seem to be heavily infiltrated, but they still seem to be able to carry out these atrocities.'[88] Another insisted he was 'not convinced the police are on top of it [the threat]...with the police force as it is, I worry about the capability and capacity'.[89] One of the party's MPs opined: 'Are they strong enough for a full blown campaign? No, but they don't need to [be].'[90]

Some DUP members fear that there has been significant paramilitary drift from the Provisionals. A Fermanagh councillor insisted: 'They seem to be getting better equipped. Some from the Provisional IRA that was have come into the dissidents now. They are getting their expertise somewhere and they seem to be improving their bomb making.'[91] A sizeable number of party members expressed scepticism over whether the Provisional IRA fully decommissioned their weapons, arguing some had 'leaked' to the dissidents. Most favoured a tough security response against dissident groups, Lord Morrow, in a typical comment, arguing that if 'they are not dealt with very firmly they will get bigger and bigger'.[92]

In terms of the threat of escalation via retaliation, a Carrickfergus councillor claimed in the aftermath of the killing of two British soldiers by republicans in 2009 that 'Northern Ireland doesn't know how close it got to retaliation', and that 'I don't think we could hold that line again in today's climate', continuing:

> one personal friend of mine who was a former member of the security forces received death threats in the last couple of weeks. He hasn't been involved in the security services now for twenty years, so the information is there. I don't think they are actively much of a threat here, but I do know if they targeted someone here, particularly within the loyalist community, there is a groundswell out there that the loyalists will retaliate.[93]

A number of DUP interviewees believed that the extent of sympathy for dissidents was being deliberately underplayed for political reasons. A Strabane councillor asserted: 'I think there are more dissident supporters than the government cares to admit. To me, they are a threat to Northern Ireland. I can see a young nationalist generation or a young republican generation coming up that are going to go the same way the Provisional IRA did. In years to come that agenda will come forth.'[94] The DUP's William Hay, the Assembly Speaker, commented: 'I do think the threat is growing, there is no doubt about that. It surprises me to see in court young men of 25–26 who weren't even around when the Troubles were in sight.'[95] Perhaps surprisingly, even the First Minister conceded that 'I don't think you wipe out these organisations as having no support. There is a level of support—not the kind of support that would let them enjoy getting in an elected representative, but there is enough there to cause a real problem.'[96] Urging people to remember that the Provisionals 'started out as dissidents as well', a Belfast councillor believed that local council election votes for the dissident group éirígí (10 per cent of first preferences in two seats) in the 2011 local council elections 'came out of nowhere...there is clearly an element of the republican community who feel Sinn Féin sold out on a political level. I don't think they are ever going to be at a Stormont level of representation, but you could see them snatching a few council seats from Sinn Féin here or there.'[97] There was some acknowledgement of the potential of street protests to destabilize. As one respondent put it, 'when you [have] actual violence, rioting on the streets, it gives them [dissidents] a reason to exist'.[98]

DUP members are divided over the extent to which ex-Provisionals, Sinn Féin, and so-called dissidents can be considered 'fellow travellers'. More astute DUP councillors acknowledged the antipathy between Sinn Féin and dissidents. A Belfast city councillor who has observed the hostility as dissidents have tried to disrupt policing board meetings commented: 'There is a real hatred between them and the Provos, Sinn Féin. Some people would say it is a show. In fairness, my experience of it is, it is not a show, the things they were shouting at each other.'[99] The denunciation of dissidents by Martin McGuinness, who stood alongside the Chief Constable of the PSNI and labelled the perpetrators of the Massereene attack as 'traitors to Ireland', was so strident that, according to Peter Robinson, McGuinness's 'own party didn't even know the language he was going to use. There were, let's say, conversations that we saw taking place after the event was over.'[100]

Even the ferocity of McGuinness's comments on dissidents has not assuaged some scepticism, one councillor arguing that 'there is an umbrella—"We are all republicans. You are there fighting that corner. We are fighting in the council. You are fighting in the Assembly"'.[101] The chutzpah of Sinn Féin in condemning what they for decades condoned was also remarked upon by some interviewees. North Antrim MLA Mervyn Storey noted how 'the murder of David Black was condemned by mainstream republicans, but they justify all the other members of the prison service that have been murdered during the Troubles because they saw them as legitimate targets'.[102] One councillor was sceptical of the lessons from history arguments, insisting that whatever Sinn Féin say 'is not going to make a difference, as they were at it themselves'.[103] Another argued:

Yes, dissident republicans need to be condemned for what they have done—it's wrong—but mainstream republicans who are now in government can't come out and say 'it's wrong, but it's only wrong because we have the best strategy'. The problem is, the only difference there is a difference in political analysis...If Sinn Féin try to justify the Provisional IRA's violence, then new republicans coming up who feel very ideological will say 'I want my bit of the action'. Sinn Féin has failed to fundamentally deliver on their political agenda and they know that having a stable government in Northern Ireland is not how you deliver a united Ireland. Northern Ireland is working. They have to try and justify where they came from, but again, it leaves it open to other republicans who have a different political perspective, that violence is justified.[104]

Whilst maintaining the discourse of vigilance, other DUP members are more sanguine over the dissident threat, pointing to its limited capacity, absence of leadership, lack of backing, and the need to keep the dangers in perspective. One councillor, 'back to checking my car again', declared: 'Terrorists will always pose a certain amount of threat—it is where you place that in your own mind.'[105] The perception that the political challenge posed by militant republicanism is irrelevant was summarized by one MLA: 'They [dissidents] are a very serious threat to life and limb, but they are not a threat to the process. Short of an unknown, I can conceive of nothing that would now threaten the institutions here.'[106] In similar terms, a Fermanagh councillor declared that she did 'not think they are a political threat' and that in terms of the 'military' threat, 'my confidence in the police dealing with that has really grown...I think increasingly we are getting on top of it'.[107] One MLA called for '24/7' monitoring to defeat 'a small number of psychopaths'.[108] The MP Gregory Campbell, whilst describing dissidents as a 'big threat', opined:

> I don't think, and this might be famous last words, that they are a realistic threat, in terms of a sustained campaign, like the Provisionals. I think they will continue to cause problems and setbacks...but I don't think they will be pressing the rewind button by a series of things they do to take us back fifteen years.[109]

Another senior figure, Arlene Foster, concurred, noting the exceptionalism, rather than regularity, of contemporary killings through personal anecdote:

> When Ronan Kerr [the PSNI officer killed by a booby-trap bomb in 2011] was murdered, George [her son] was in the car with me and he was 'But why would somebody do that? Why would somebody try and kill a policeman mummy?' It just brought back to me my own childhood. Policemen and the army were being shot every week and it just said to me that they had grown up in a completely different time, and I was very thankful for it.[110]

A lack of support for dissidents is also noted by many DUP members. Lisburn MLA Paul Givan observed: 'I don't sense them gaining any traction in the republican community to the extent Sinn Féin was able to get whenever the IRA was at its height...I don't anticipate them growing, certainly not politically anyway.'[111]

An Antrim councillor, again, whilst far from dismissive of the threat, commented:

> I can't help thinking of the two soldiers who were killed. The immediate effect was that the whole congregation came out of the chapel and stood in support. I think that's fantastic. No matter what they could do now, they'll never garner the support they had before. I still think they could cause massive damage and a massive loss of life. But people like the degree of normality they now have. I don't think anybody wants to go back to that.[112]

Others noted the failure of dissidents to mobilize many in the republican community, one MLA arguing of their campaign: 'I think the media tend to ignore it. The dissident dirty protests in the prisons—very few people would know it's on. It's not a trendy thing anymore, terrorism.'[113]

Overall, the perspective of the DUP membership is one based partly upon the old IRA bogeyman. This is not articulated much at the leadership level, where there is an obvious need to portray Northern Ireland as 'open for business' and making great progress since the St Andrews Agreement brought about by the DUP. Amongst ordinary members, however, some scepticism over whether violence has finally been ended is more clearly evident, although there is a recognition that there will be no return to the level of difficulty once endured.

Pragmatism, Change, and Altered Discourses

The DUP line on the 2006 St Andrews Agreement suggests that it was their constant opposition to the inferior 1998 deal that was solely responsible for a renegotiated accord that forced the Irish republican movement to fully accept the institutions of partition, the workings of the Northern Irish state, including support for the state's police force, and to abandon violence. The internal discourse offered suggests that in so doing, the DUP successfully identified and removed all the major remaining threats to 'Ulster', and therefore, that St Andrews could be marked as a clear 'victory'.

This interpretation of a renegotiated settlement securing Northern Ireland's place in the United Kingdom is now deeply engrained across the DUP membership and the perspective is clearly highlighted in the following statements drawn from across the DUP membership:

> I was a fire officer for 33 years. I lifted bodies off the streets and I don't want to go back to those days. The best option for this country at that time was that we go to devolved government. The mandatory coalition has its problems, but we are in a better place than 50 years ago. . . . What the DUP is doing now is the right thing. We are trying to move our country forward . . . There was great trust in the

leadership; they had thought it all out. Peter Robinson had thought it all out. He has a great vision and is very forward thinking. I was very happy to go that way.[114]

[St Andrews] was to move things forward and some hope for the future. If the Shinners and us didn't get together, there would be no progress. There would be no peace until then.[115]

Beyond the claims of 'St Andrews as victory', another discourse has emerged, suggesting more pragmatic reasons for a settlement, 'the only option, as the only other was joint authority'.[116] Indeed, Ian Paisley has subsequently argued that the DUP had no alternative other than to do a deal with Sinn Féin, otherwise 'it was going to be curtains' with 'the Union destroyed and the setting up of a joint government by the south of Ireland'.[117]

This new notion of a pragmatic approach to politics that emerged from the DUP after St Andrews was also recognized and found support across sections of the membership. As one councillor argued:

Peter [Robinson] is a pragmatist, like. You have to be pragmatic. The way it was before, when the things weren't in place for us to go forward...What's the best way to put it? There was always that intransigence, I suppose. The wheels weren't in motion. Whenever things did change, and there was decommissioning and that, I had to take a pragmatic view. If you don't, you're not going to get anywhere. You just can't be as blinkered. That has maybe been the shift. I wouldn't say any more liberal; definitely not any more liberal—just more pragmatic.[118]

Another explained this new political disposition as follows:

The younger generation are trying to make their way forward. There is an element from the older generation who idolized Doc, and when he moved into government, it was like the rug was pulled out from under them—they don't know where to go; they have nobody to follow. They are stuck with an image of what Paisley would think today, not making up their own minds. The world is changing, and it changed in 1998 and in 2007....People within the unionist community are trying to acclimatize to the new environment where we can't get everything we want anymore...Peter [Robinson]...is...running the country and the party has got bigger; therefore, there is more room for a wider variety of views.[119]

The discourse from the DUP leadership is grounded in pragmatism. As Peter Robinson explains:

Many people are still coming to terms with the new political dispensation. It is an outlook of many contradictions. There is no single perspective. Some have moved on more than others. Many unionists recognize the need to move this region forward with the widest possible consensus. Other unionists don't like to see Sinn Féin in government, but know they have to be there. They want their representatives to stand up for their own community, but they know that we have to work with everyone to get things done.[120]

While this pragmatic discourse has become the dominant one emanating from the DUP leadership, it has not been adopted uncritically by the membership. Peter Robinson has suggested that when the St Andrews deal was announced, the main reactions from within the unionist community could be characterized as 'surprise and even astonishment'.[121] From the interviews, it is clear that there were other widespread reactions from DUP members, including fear and even anger.

Admittedly, leading a party membership that for so long had been driven by discourses that placed it in the frontline of Protestant unionist resistance[122] and challenging power-sharing with republicans was always going to be difficult. This is especially true of that generation of DUP members who were convinced that only total victory over republicanism would mark a legitimate end to the conflict. Moreover, even before Ian Paisley stepped down as leader, the membership had to be convinced that its future lay in 'the end of old-style Paisleyism, with its policy of permanent opposition to unbelievers, liberals, and political compromisers',[123] and through a new approach, whereby the DUP must be 'prepared to work with everyone and for everyone'.[124]

For some, the eventual willingness to enter into a power-sharing government following St Andrews raised serious concerns over the party's new direction and questions regarding their continued membership. As one councillor explained:

At that time, there was probably uncertainty of the way to go, what do we do? There was a hard line and a soft line, and I said I hope they actually do go in because the institution has been established and if we don't go in and get the best agreement possible, we are going to come out with a lot worse. So from that time, probably the very hard line ones would have left and they would say they were going back to what the DUP had traditionally been. There were hard line ones that said, they would stick at it and see how it goes. There were people like me who said, get the best agreement you can get to safeguard the union as much as possible.[125]

Others in the period immediately after St Andrews experienced levels of unease and anxiety that caused them to question continued membership of the party:

There were people who left over it. I had a wobble myself…just lost all interest. And then, I sort of thought about it.[126]

I remember well, when they [Sinn Féin] first went into government, I felt a real pull and I did have two minds on whether to stay or not. I talked it over with my colleagues and I have to say, whenever you look at it in the cool light of day, we really didn't have an alternative to this. If we didn't go forward with the Assembly, with all the pain with all the anxiety, with all the hassle, then the British Government could have imposed some form of power-sharing between

Dublin and here and we would have had, from a unionist perspective, a greener tinge of it than what we have today.[127]

While accepting the new pragmatism discourse of the party leadership as the way forward, the consequences were far from desirable, as articulated, in a typical response, by one councillor:

> You can see the outcome of that now, where you have a shared government. But there are still terrorists in government. We have to go with it now, that is the best thing for Northern Ireland, but if someone would say to me, 'did you want that?' I would say 'no'.[128]

Across the party membership, there remain underlying senses of mistrust of, and sometimes continued defiance to, the involvement of Sinn Féin in government, as expressed in the following comments:

> I wouldn't trust Sinn Féin from here to the window. Their political ideology is what drives them every day, but they recognize and they realized that their people need jobs, their people need health, they don't want any more of their soldiers in prison, they don't want to go through what they have gone through, but they will use every method, every means in this place to still give the perception that the war is still going on, but in different methods and in different ways. They are not the organization they were ten or fifteen years ago in terms of the murders and the bombings and the terrorist campaign. I try and keep it in that context. I don't trust them any more, they don't trust me any more [than in the past].[129]
>
> I followed the DUP from when they started and I went to most of the rallies...and followed Dr Paisley. Whenever the DUP went into partnership...with Sinn Féin/IRA, I was totally disgusted at that because those IRA/Sinn Féin are murderers, and in that chamber sits the Army Council of the IRA and that disgusted me to the last letter. To see those murderers sitting up there in Stormont and them making rules and regulations and trying to run a country, and telling me, as a British subject, what I should be doing...personally, I'm thinking I can't wait for the day they are dumped out.[130]

Such views were particularly strongly expressed by those who felt they had suffered directly during the IRA military campaign:

> I was a part-time soldier in the UDR as well and I was shot going to my work in 1981. Some of the boys that would have done it would be in Sinn Féin. It is not too nice working with some of them.[131]
>
> ...if you want my personal view on the Assembly and going into the Assembly then, I had reservations, I had massive reservations because the Provos a number of years ago shot four of my family, so I think, from a victim's perspective, if your family are shot or murdered, you had a different outlook. Maybe some of the younger MLAs coming into the Assembly would not have had the same deep rooted contacts with the Troubles. Some would have accepted it easier; I felt it was difficult.[132]

While there is clear support for the leadership of Peter Robinson across the DUP membership, and a strong belief within the party that 'the constitutional debate has been won',[133] there remains work to be done to convince the wider membership that, in order for unionism to control its own destiny[134] and secure Northern Ireland's position in the United Kingdom, 'everyone [must be] seen to have a real say in how we are governed'.[135]

Conclusion

This chapter has identified some of the overarching discourses that have helped structure political direction and policy formation within the DUP. Over four decades, dialogues that highlight the centrality of (Protestant) faith in politics and place the DUP in the frontline of Ulster's defence from attacks by republicans, and from those unionists identified as weak or liberal enough to concede to betrayal from Westminster, have driven the DUP political project. Some of these discourses have remained stubbornly consistent since the formation of the party. Even though the party moved republicans to the positions the DUP demanded, the party's members remain cautious.

Perpetual vigilance is still required, as republicans in government cannot be trusted and republican militants beyond Sinn Féin are still seen as an armed threat. However, DUP discourses have not remained static. The party has witnessed the transition from populist rhetoric located in Free Presbyterian ideas to those espousing political pragmatism in a new era involving engagement in working relationships with Sinn Féin and the identification of a 'new political space developing in Northern Ireland'.[136] If such space is to be created, it will involve an altered understanding of unionism, and changes to the senses of unionist identity and belonging within the DUP membership.

Notes

1. I. Paisley (2001) 'Statement by Party Leader', DUP 30th Anniversary Conference, Newcastle, County Down, Nov.
2. Peter Robinson (2012) Leader's Speech, DUP Annual Conference, Belfast, Nov.
3. See e.g. DUP Conference Booklet 2012, branded under 'My Council; My Assembly; My Westminster; My Europe; My Party; My Future. Let's Keep Northern Ireland Moving Forward; DUP—The Party for Northern Ireland', Belfast: DUP.
4. See S. Wilson (no date) *The Carson Trail*, Belfast: Crown Publications.
5. See e.g. W. McCrea (1980) *In his Pathway: The Story of the Reverend William McCrea*, London: Letterworth Press; I. Paisley (1999) *Grow Old along with Me*, Belfast: Ambassador.

6. S. Hall (1997) 'Introduction', in S. Hall (ed.), *Representation: Cultural Representations and Signifying Practices*, London: Sage, 6.

7. K. Hayward (2008) 'The Role of Political Discourse in Conflict Transformation: Evidence from Northern Ireland', in K. Hayward and C. O'Donnell (eds), *Journal of Peace and Conflict Studies*, 15/1, Special Issue on Political Discourse as an Instrument of Conflict and Peace: Lessons from Northern Ireland, 1–20; See also various in K. Hayward and C. O'Donnell (eds) (2011) *Political Discourse and Conflict Resolution: Debating Peace in Northern Ireland*, London: Routledge.

8. See S. Hall (2006) 'The Rediscovery of Ideology: The Return of the Repressed in Media Studies', in J. Storey (ed.), *Cultural Theory and Popular Culture: A Reader*, London: Pearson, 101.

9. P. Schnapper (2011) *British Political Parties and National Identity: A Changing Discourse, 1997–2010*, Newcastle upon Tyne: Cambridge Scholars Publishing, 2.

10. S. Bruce (1996) 'Paisley: Politician, Preacher, Prophet', *Irish Times*, 30 Nov.

11. M. A. MacIver (1987) 'Ian Paisley and the Reformed Tradition', *Political Studies*, 35/3, 359–78.

12. G. Ganiel (2004) *Evangelical Political Identity in Transition: Mapping the Intersections of Religion, Politics, and Change in Post-Belfast Agreement Northern Ireland*, Geary Institute Discussion Paper Series, WP 2004/01, 1, Dublin: University College Dublin.

13. Ian Paisley's reading of his life through evangelical texts can be seen in works such as I. R. K. Paisley (1999) *Grow Old along with Me*, Belfast: Ambassador Publications, or I. R. K. Paisley (1999) *For Such a Time as This: Recollections, Reflections, Recognitions*, Belfast: Ambassador Publications.

14. See D. Cooke (1996), *Persecuting Zeal*, Dingle: Brandon, 41–57.

15. F. E. Scott (1976) 'The Political Preaching Tradition in Ulster: Prelude to Paisley', *Western Speech Communication*, 40/4: 249–59.

16. See R. L. Jordan (2013) *The Second Coming of Paisley: Militant Fundamentalism and Ulster Politics*, New York: Syracuse University Press.

17. D. McKittrick (1981) 'The Class Structure of Unionism', *The Crane Bag*, 4/2, 28.

18. Interview with Lord Maurice Morrow, DUP party chair, Stormont, 10 Jan. 2013.

19. Lord Maurice Morrow, cited in D. Gordon (2009) *The Fall of the House of Paisley*, Dublin: Gill & Macmillan, 205.

20. M. O'Callaghan and C. O'Donnell (2006) 'The Northern Ireland Government, the "Paisleyite Movement" and Ulster Unionism in 1966', *Irish Political Studies*, 21/2, 203–22.

21. O'Callaghan and O'Donnell, 'The Northern Ireland Government', 207.

22. Wilson, *Carson Trail*, 11.

23. T. Gallagher (1981) 'Religion, Reaction, and Revolt in Northern Ireland: The Impact of Paisleyism in Ulster', *Journal of Church and State*, 23/3, 423.

24. The Scarman Tribunal (1972) *Violence and Civil Disturbances in Northern Ireland in 1969*, available at: <http://cain.ulst.ac.uk/hmso/scarman.htm>, accessed July 2013.

25. C. Smyth (1987) *Ian Paisley: Voice of Protestant Ulster*, Edinburgh: Scottish Academic Press, 55.

26. Smyth, *Ian Paisley*, 57.
27. MacIver, 'Ian Paisley and the Reformed Tradition', 361.
28. Interview with Fermanagh councillor, 15 Mar. 2013.
29. Interview with Edwin Poots MLA, Lisburn, 10 Jan. 2013.
30. See S. Bruce (1986) *God Save Ulster! The Religion and Politics of Paisleyism*, Oxford: Oxford University Press; Smyth, *Ian Paisley*.
31. Smyth, *Ian Paisley*, 36, argues that by the spring of 1973, Paisley had lost political confidence in Boal and that only the overt promoting of 'Paisleyism' was capable of lifting loyalism 'out of the quicksand and back on to the commanding heights'.
32. P. Mitchel (2003) *Evangelicalism and National Identity in Ulster, 1921–1998*, Oxford: Oxford University Press.
33. See D. F. Taylor (1983) 'The Lords of Battle: An Ethnographic and Social Study of "Paisleyism", in N. Ireland', Ph.D. thesis, Queen's University Belfast.
34. E. Moloney and A. Pollak (1986) *Paisley*, Dublin: Poolbeg, 216.
35. Interview with Dungannon councillor, 27 Nov. 2012.
36. Interview with Craigavon councillor, 5 Nov. 2012.
37. Interview with Lisburn councillor, 3 Dec. 2012.
38. Interview with Mervyn Storey MLA, Stormont, 8 Jan. 2013.
39. Interview with Belfast councillor, 27 Sept. 2012.
40. Interview with Craigavon councillor, 5 Nov. 2012.
41. Interview with Coleraine councillor, 5 Oct. 2012.
42. Interview with Nelson McCausland MLA, Belfast, 9 Jan. 2013.
43. Interview with Nelson McCausland, 9 Jan. 2013.
44. C. Mitchell (2006) 'The Religious Content of Ethnic Identities', *Sociology*, 40/6, 1135–52.
45. J. Bell (2013) *For God, Ulster, or Ireland? Religion, Identity, and Security in Northern Ireland*, Belfast: Institute for Conflict Research, 21.
46. C. Mitchell (2005) *Religion, Identity, and Politics in Northern Ireland*, Aldershot: Ashgate, 138.
47. S. Farrell (2006) Review of Mitchel, Patrick, *Evangelicalism and National Identity in Ulster, 1921–1998*. H-Albion, H-Net Reviews, Jan. Available at: <http://www.h-net.org/reviews/showrev.php?id=11376>, accessed June 2011.
48. Interview with Strangford MLA, 9 Jan. 2013.
49. Interview with Edwin Poots MLA, 10 Jan. 2013.
50. Interview with Mervyn Storey MLA, 8 Jan. 2013.
51. Interview with Coleraine councillor, 5 Oct. 2012.
52. Former member of the Free Presbyterian Church, cited in D. H. Akenson (1992) *God's Peoples: Covenant and Land in South Africa, Israel, and Ulster*, New York: Cornell University Press, 99–100.
53. *The Voice of Ulster*, Oct. 1982, 8.
54. For elaborations of this position within DUP literature, see e.g. DUP (1996) *Our Covenant with the Ulster People: Manifesto for the Forum Election*, DUP: Belfast and Democratic Unionist Party, (1995) *The Framework of Shame and Sham: Yes, the Framework Document is a One-way Road to Dublin*, DUP: Belfast.

55. Interview with Councillor Alan Graham, North Down, 25 Nov. 2012

56. Interview with Lisburn councillor, 3 Dec. 2012.

57. J. Cusack and H. McDonald (1997) *UVF,* Dublin: Poolbeg, 325.

58. *Irish News,* 26 Jan. 1998.

59. I. Paisley (1998) Leader's Speech to the DUP Annual Conference, Omagh, 28 Nov.

60. Paisley, Speech to the DUP Annual Conference, 1998.

61. I. Paisley (2004) Leader's Speech to the DUP Annual Conference, Belfast, 8 May.

62. See Ian Paisley, cited in J. W. McAuley (2001) *Redefining Loyalism: An Academic Perspective,* Institute for British-Irish Studies, paper 4, Dublin: University College Dublin.

63. W. McCrea (2002) 'DUP Give the Lead, Now the UUP Must Follow', DUP press release, 8 Oct.

64. I. Paisley (2001) 'Vote DUP: Eve of Poll Message', available at: <http://www.dup. org.uk>, accessed Nov. 2012.

65. I. Paisley, Leader's Speech to the DUP Annual Conference, 2004.

66. I. Paisley (1998) 'The Fruits of Appeasement', DUP press release, 3 Sept.

67. I. Paisley (2001) Leader's Speech to the DUP Annual Conference, Newcastle, County Down, Nov.

68. *New Protestant Telegraph,* June 1995.

69. Paisley, writing in the Free Presbyterian Church magazine, *The Revivalist,* at the start of 1998, cited in 'Ian Paisley in his own words—Democratic Unionist MP who is to stand down after 40 years representing North Antrim', *Guardian,* 2 Mar. 2010.

70. *Irish News,* 26 Jan. 1998.

71. I. Paisley, Leader's Speech to the DUP Annual Conference, 2001.

72. Ian Paisley (jun.) cited in *Observer,* 11 Jan. 1998.

73. L. Dowds and B. Lynn, *The Changing Face of Unionism: Evidence from Public Attitude Surveys,* Belfast: ESRC Devolution and Constitutional Change Programme, Research Briefing, 32, Aug. 2005.

74. *Shankill Mirror,* Nov. 2002.

75. J. W. McAuley (2005) 'Whither New Loyalism—Changing Politics After the Belfast Agreement', *Irish Political Studies,* 20/3, 323–40.

76. Interview with DUP MLA, North Down, 4 Dec. 2012.

77. Interview with Adrian McQuillan MLA, Londonderry East, 4 Dec. 2012.

78. Independent Commission on Policing (1999) *A New Beginning: Policing in Northern Ireland* (the Patten Commission Report), available at <http://cain.ulst. ac.uk/issues/police/patten/patten99.pdf>, accessed Sept. 2013.

79. McCrea, 'DUP Give the Lead'.

80. Interview with Coleraine councillor, 4 Oct. 2013.

81. Interview with Pam Brown MLA, Stormont, 2 Oct. 2013.

82. Interview with Ards borough councillor, Newtownards, 16 Oct. 2013.

83. Interview with Craigavon councillor, 5 Nov. 2012.

84. Interview with Fermanagh councillor, 15 Mar. 2013.

85. Interview with Jim Allister MLA, leader, TUV, North Antrim, 18 Apr. 2013.

86. Police Service of Northern Ireland Security Situation Statistics, available at <http://www.psni.police.uk/annual_security_situation_statistics_report_2011.12.pdf>, accessed Sept. 2013.

87. Interview with Peter Robinson MLA, DUP leader, Stormont, 25 June 2013.

88. Interview with Lisburn councillor, 3 Dec. 2012.

89. Interview with North Antrim MLA, Ballymena, 30 Nov. 2012.

90. Interview with David Simpson MP, Westminster, 3 July 2013.

91. Interview with Fermanagh councillor, 15 Mar. 2013.

92. Interview with Lord Maurice Morrow MLA, DUP chairman, Stormont, 10 Jan. 2013.

93. Interview with Carrickfergus councillor, 27 Feb. 2013.

94. Interview with Strabane councillor, 16 Apr. 2013.

95. Interview with William Hay, Speaker, Northern Ireland Assembly, Stormont, 8 Jan. 2013.

96. Interview with Peter Robinson, 25 June 2013

97. Interview with Belfast councillor, 9 Oct. 2012.

98. Interview with South Antrim MLA, Ballyclare, 7 Jan. 2013.

99. Belfast councillor, Belfast focus group, Belfast city hall, 26 Feb. 2013.

100. Interview with Peter Robinson, 25 June 2013.

101. Interview with Strabane councillor, 16 Apr. 2013.

102. Interview with Mervyn Storey MLA, 8 Jan. 2013.

103. Interview with Londonderry (Rural) councillor, 26 Mar. 2013.

104. Interview with Newtownabbey councillor, 11 Sept. 2012.

105. Interview with Craigavon councillor, 5 Nov. 2012.

106. Interview with Strangford MLA, 9 Jan. 2013.

107. Interview with Fermanagh councillor, 15 Mar. 2013.

108. Interview with Newry and Armagh MLA, Stormont, 19 Nov. 2012.

109. Interview with Gregory Campbell MP, MLA for East Londonderry, Stormont, 22 Oct. 2012.

110. Interview with Arlene Foster MLA, Netherleigh House Belfast, 8 Feb. 2013.

111. Interview with Paul Givan MLA, Lisburn, 11 Jan. 2013.

112. Interview with Antrim councillor, 2 Oct. 2012.

113. Interview with North Down MLA, Stormont, 4 Dec. 2012.

114. Interview with Councillor Roy Young, Lisburn, 3 Dec. 2012.

115. Interview with Adrian McQuillan MLA, 4 Dec. 2012.

116. Interview with DUP MLA, 4 Dec. 2012.

117. J. Caldwell, 'No Alternative to Deal—Paisley', BBC News website, 4 Apr. 2007, available at <http://news.bbc.co.uk/1/hi/northern_ireland/6527333.stm>, accessed Sept. 2013.

118. Interview with Craigavon councillor, 5 Nov. 2012.

119. Interview with North Antrim councillor, 4 Oct. 2012.

120. Speech by Peter Robinson to DUP Spring Conference, Enniskillen, 27 Apr. 2013, available at <http://www.mydup.com/news/article/spring-policy-conference-leaders-speech>, accessed June 2013.

121. P. Robinson (2011) John Kennedy Lecture, Institute of Irish Studies, University of Liverpool, Oct.
122. J. W. McAuley (2010) *Ulster's Last Stand?* Dublin: Irish Academic Press.
123. B. White (2007) 'You may Not have Noticed, But it's the End of Paisleyism', *Belfast Telegraph*, 19 Sept.
124. Speech by Peter Robinson to DUP Spring Conference, 2013.
125. Interview with North Antrim councillor, 4 Oct. 2012.
126. Interview with Craigavon councillor, 5 Nov. 2012.
127. Interview with David Simpson, 3 July 2013.
128. Interview with Castlereagh councillor, 3 Jan. 2013.
129. Interview with Mervyn Storey, 8 Jan. 2013.
130. Member of DUP Fermanagh focus group, 26 Apr. 2013.
131. Interview with Councillor Allan Bresland, Strabane, 16 Apr. 2013.
132. Interview with Mid-Ulster MLA, 4 Dec. 2012.
133. Peter Robinson (2012) Leader's Speech to DUP Annual Conference, Belfast, Nov.
134. Peter Robinson (2007) 'Unionists are in Control Says Deputy Leader', available at: <http://groups.yahoo.com/group/scotch-irish/message/23579?var=1>, accessed Apr. 2013.
135. Speech by Peter Robinson to DUP Spring Conference, 2013.
136. Peter Robinson, cited in *News Letter*, 2 Dec. 2012.

5

Britishness, Identity, and Belonging

> Democratic Unionism has defended the Union at a time when other unionists were prepared to sell the Union. Like the gallant thirteen apprentice boys in Londonderry who shut the gates on the coming enemy, so the DUP has prevented the destruction of the Union.
>
> (Ian Paisley, DUP Leader, 1996[1])

> The old Orange-Green, British-Irish dichotomy no longer adequately sums up the myriad of shades of identity here. Old-style unionist majority is a thing of the past.
>
> (Peter Robinson, DUP Party Leader, 2013[2])

An essential aspect of the DUP has always been the expression of identity politics. Since its formation, the party has claimed that it offers the most direct and legitimate conduit for the political representation of a distinct ethno-cultural identity within the Protestant community. It has constantly maintained that the DUP offers the securest form of unionism and the strongest guarantee of the continuance of the Union. Moreover, as previous chapters have indicated, in the period following the Belfast Agreement, the DUP convinced an increasing number of unionists that, due to its actions, the political settlement was renegotiated to ensure both the long-term security of Union and the endurance of Protestant Britishness on the island. One of Ian Paisley's parting claims when stepping down as party leader was that the DUP had 'smashed Sinn Féin', which had been forced to accept 'the right of Britain to govern this country'.[3]

This chapter examines in detail the validity of the DUP claim to be 'the protector of British identity and culture'[4] and the political exhibition of this as expressed by DUP members and activists. Central to this are several forms of identification with Britishness or a British identity. Across the party, understandings differ and the membership offers a wider understanding of British identity than many would imagine. Essentially, however, Britishness, as understood by members of the DUP, remains more Protestant, more homogeneous, and more socially conservative than senses of Britishness found elsewhere in the UK.

The chapter identifies the rival pulls of national British versus regional Northern Irish identities at both the leadership and grassroots levels of the party. It highlights the exclusiveness of the DUP sense of identity in the continued outright rejection by its members of any sense of Irishness. It further explores the different ways in which members seek to express their sense of Britishness, drawing on social and political markers from past, present, and future to construct a seamless narrative placing the DUP as the key organization to defend British identity in Northern Ireland. Finally, the chapter considers what DUP members regard as some of the main sources of threat to their core senses of self, and what they perceive as the central challenges to their identity.

Identity and Belonging

As Stuart Hall[5] suggests, identity is best understood as a rendezvous between those subjective processes surrounding the way in which people live their lives and the broader social and political discourses that situate individuals in society (see Chapter 4). In Northern Ireland, the depth of competing group-based social identities goes some way to explaining the intensity of the conflict and the continuance of deep social and political divisions. The strength of these collective identities rests in shared common interests and political understandings that are made meaningful through everyday group experiences. These processes distinguish social categories and groups, simultaneously enhancing uniformity and cohesion within the group and setting boundaries between in-groups and out-groups. This sense of identity is bonded through shared icons and finds expression through mutually understood discourses and representation through various organizations, including political parties.

The construction of a political identity within the DUP has always included expressions of Protestantism and cultural separateness, alongside elements of social and political dissent and an overt commitment to Britishness. Most common throughout its existence have been statements of political dedication to the British Crown, an emotional attachment to 'Ulster', and claims to give political representation to the democratic will of 'the people of Ulster' (a phrase regularly used by Ian Paisley). For the DUP (and sections of loyalism more broadly), these have often been given a hierarchal position over any idea of subjection to the will of the UK parliament or of the wider demands of the British state. Thus, as William Hazleton once so clearly pointed out, the essence of the conflict is 'Northern Ireland's relationship with the rest of the

United Kingdom, not an anachronistic seventeenth-century religious battle between Protestants and Catholics.'[6]

Britishness and Cultural Unionism

For the DUP, the essence of the relationship with other parts of the UK has been encapsulated by robust claims to British identity and expressed through the values of cultural unionism,[7] celebrating the virtues of Protestantism and the Union within a discrete ethnic identity. In so doing, the DUP constantly recreates a self-defined party that places the defence of a Protestant/British way of life at the core of its political values.

Further, the DUP often gives primacy to those aspects of culture, social relations, and religion within unionism[8] that accent the distinctiveness and historical separation of Northern Ireland.[9] While this understanding of unionism remains central to the DUP, it also finds clear expression in other groupings, such as large sections of the Orange Order, which is still regarded by many across unionism as being at the nucleus of cultural opposition to Irish unity.[10]

Senses of Britishness

As can be seen in Figure 5.1, almost 80 per cent of DUP members see their primary national identity as 'British'. As we might expect, this identification is much more extensive than that found amongst the broader population, where, in the 2011 census, 40 per cent described their principal national identity as British, while 48 per cent included some sense of British in their national identity.[11] Attachment to Britishness is expressed through geography, national symbols, people, values and attitudes, cultural habits and behaviour, citizenship, language, and achievements.[12] DUP members draw from across these identifiers to construct their major sense of identity. As we shall see, however, this does not mean that there is a uniform understanding across the party of what British identity is, or an agreed understanding of what comprises Britishness.

For some within the DUP, the association with Britishness is simply seen as innate and natural. As MP Gregory Campbell put it, 'I instinctively describe myself as British'.[13] Another leading figure, Sammy Wilson, expressed a similar sense of intuitive belonging when he said: 'I would describe myself as British. I have just always regarded myself as British and that is the way it is.'[14] One councillor simply stated, 'I see the United Kingdom as my home and I feel British,[15] while another claimed, 'I know we're British, like, and

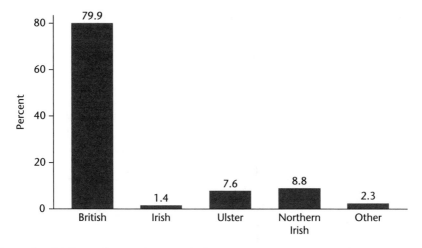

Figure 5.1 DUP members and national identity

that's it'.[16] Another put it straightforwardly when he said, 'I would just call myself British, I really, to be honest, hate to be called Irish or Northern Irish.'[17] Expressions of Britishness, community, and national identity indicators are articulated though a series of often routine symbols, habits, and language,[18] and reinforced by some of the central discourses and political actions identified throughout the book.

For others, their sense of Britishness was best expressed through a strong sense of cultural attachment and a feeling of belonging to a wider British community. As Nelson McCausland put it:

> Britishness... is a sense of belonging to the United Kingdom and all the things it has achieved... essentially, it is that a common sense of belonging to all of that history and culture, those are the things that I think shape it. That sort of liberal parliamentary democracy.[19]

Another leading party member sought to explain his sense of being British as follows:

> I think it is a sort of level of national pride, a certain element of monarchy, a sense of history, certain sorts of British characteristics, whether defending the underdog, supporting a British team, standing patiently in a queue. I think it is a constantly evolving process.[20]

Peter Weir expressed the view that primarily 'Britishness... is a sense of national identity, [a] sense of cultural linkage with Britain',[21] while Arlene Foster expanded on her sense of belonging as follows:

> It means having that connection with the UK. I think last year... was actually a very good example of what it meant to be British in Northern Ireland. The visit of

Her Majesty the Queen to Enniskillen...the Olympic torch coming to the whole of the UK, including Northern Ireland, to watch the Olympics and to see merchandise for sale in Northern Ireland that was very openly British.[22]

A common point of reference is the monarchy, of which these comments from a range of DUP elected representatives are typical:

Britishness to me? Well, it is just being part of the Union. I think a lot of it comes back to the Royal family for me, the Queen. I am very proud of the Royal family and the Queen. That is what keeps me British, more than saying I am Northern Irish.[23]

I think it is a certain sense of history. I think it is linked in to some extent with pride in the monarchy, pride in British institutions.[24]

[Britishness] means having the Queen as my monarch; having my flag.[25]

Beyond the monarchy, many of the broad reference points upon which DUP members drew to express their sense of Britishness were framed in terms of cultural and religious freedom, sometimes posited in an oppositional sense to the Irish Republic. As a prominent MLA put it:

Britishness...it's an attachment [at] many, many levels. It is historical, it's very much political because I believe being in a political system with the United Kingdom makes us stronger, and its where I want to be politically...socially it is good for me, economically it is good for me, culturally I feel an attachment to the rest of the UK, as opposed to the Republic of Ireland. I don't feel comfortable with the culture of the Republic of Ireland, but I feel very comfortable with the culture of the UK. I suppose the protection of religious freedom in Northern Ireland is very important and I see that as being attached the UK because of the history of what happened with Protestantism in the Republic of Ireland, particularly after partition.[26]

For some, the attachment to Britishness is located in direct political interest or perceived economic benefit of the Union. A Castlereagh councillor couched her response in economic terms:

I just identify myself as British...when you are looking at it economically, I wouldn't want to be ever part of the Republic of Ireland. Obviously, the block grant that we get from Westminster, stuff like that, helps. We are a lot better off in Britain.[27]

As others have observed, however, it would be incorrect to suggest that unionists stress common links with Britain simply to serve their own political and economic interests.[28] DUP members and elected representatives often expressed their affiliation to Britishness in ways that stretched far beyond any rational explanation, as an allegiance also fulfilling emotional needs. For some, what matters is the connection to a British 'way of life'. Ian Paisley (jun.) insists: 'I don't look to see what is happening in the Irish exchequer.

I am interested in what is happening in the British budget...interested in English football teams, in television, such as British soap operas, all those things.'[29] Another put it this way:

> Britishness—you can tick all the boxes, the Queen, the flag, the economy...parliament, everything about it....We are brought up in the British way of life and not the Irish way of life.[30]

As one delegate at the annual conference in 2013 put it, 'it's not that we feel British...we are British'.[31]

The DUP and Regional Identities

Within these expressions of Britishness from the DUP, there is strong support for devolution. Amongst the Protestant population, in general, those with pro-devolution views are largely supportive of the DUP. In contrast, Protestants who favour direct rule are much more evenly split between the UUP and the DUP.[32] Within the DUP membership there is overwhelming support for a devolved administration as the best long-term policy for government in Northern Ireland, as Figure 5.2 indicates.

The percentage of Northern Ireland's population claiming a Northern Irish identity has varied between slightly more than one-in-five[33] to nearly one-in-three,[34] according to recent census and survey evidence, with

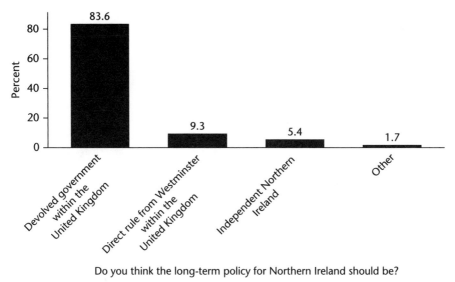

Do you think the long-term policy for Northern Ireland should be?

Figure 5.2 DUP members' views on the best long-term policy for Northern Ireland

Protestants, especially younger ones, slightly more likely to identify as such than Catholics. Those actively promoting Northern Irishness often suggest that it offers a mutual sense of identity to both unionists and nationalists, alongside those who define themselves as neither, and even that it may provide for the 'beating heart of a shared future'.[35]

Expressions of Northern Irish identity are evident, but not particularly commonplace, within the DUP. For the small number claiming their identification as Northern Irish, the label is worn with considerable pride, as one adherent explains:

> I would actually view myself as being from Northern Ireland. First and foremost, I'm from Northern Ireland. I'm proud to be from Northern Ireland. I do write 'British' as my nationality in various forms because there is no other box to tick. I wish there was, so I could put down 'Northern Irish'. I suppose it's a bit odd. But I'm from Northern Ireland and I take great pride in it....I am probably loyalist rather than Unionist, and loyalist in the sense that I am loyal to our wee country.[36]

There are also those who express some limited or qualified support:

> I don't see any harm in Northern Irish. I can definitely identify with [Northern Irish]. I think we are proud of our wee country. I don't have any problem with people describing themselves as Northern Irish. I personally describe myself as British, but if somebody told me I was Northern Irish, I would have no issue with that whatsoever. It shows they are proud...I think you have to be saying I am really proud of where I am from.[37]

Many, however, are resistant to the idea of Northern Irishness as a central point of identity:

> Northern Irish is not a term I use. I always say British. I might say I am an Ulsterman, but never Northern Irish.[38]
>
> If someone asked my nationality, I would say British. I don't have a strong sense of Northern Ireland.[39]
>
> To describe myself as Northern Irish...I always think it shows less of a commitment to...the Union. I would describe myself as part of that British unit.[40]
>
> We are part of the United Kingdom, we are British. We are not Northern Irish and we are definitely not Irish. We are all British and we are Ulster men and women.[41]
>
> Northern Irish in any way? No, I suppose we are different, but to create a false identity of Northern Irish—to stand there alone. We are aligned to the mainland, we aren't so different.[42]

Among our respondents, there is little sense of Northern Irishness being regarded as a new sanctuary for Protestant unionist identity, or that there is any positive shift from within the DUP membership towards Northern Irishness as a more regional sense of belonging. There was some awareness of Northern Irishness being adopted as a prime expression of identity across Northern Ireland by growing numbers in a new post-conflict generation. One councillor set this out in personal terms:

> My husband would say he was British, but my daughter would say she was Northern Irish. She attends the Tech [Technical College] in Omagh and she has both Protestant and Roman Catholic friends. Her attitude has changed because she is the younger generation. We were brought up with being British, because of the troubles and all you are more staunch. I would always associate myself with being British, but the younger generation wouldn't....I would never call myself Northern Irish. Never. My daughter would say I should and I would get very cross at that.[43]

Her broad understanding found support with Arlene Foster, who expressed the following view:

> Northern Irish...means the region that I live in...this was a very interesting thing about the census...there were twenty-five per cent [the actual figure was 29 per cent] of the people who were quite comfortable with it and picked Northern Irish as their first identity. That says to me, I think, a different generation to mine. The generation below mine are quite comfortable with their identity.[44]

So is there evidence to suggest within the DUP membership that a Northern Irish identity is closely dependent on age, in a similar pattern to that seen in the broader population? The short answer is 'no'. As Table 5.1 indicates, although the percentage of those considering themselves to be Northern Irish is, in general, lower among those over 60 years old, the category identifying most extensively as Northern Irish is not younger people, but amongst middle-aged members (those aged 41–50)—the only group where the percentage within reaches double figures in terms of such identification. There is no evidence to suggest a linear relationship within the membership, indicating that identification with Northern Irishness increases with age. This lack of identification with Northern Irishness amongst the DUP is noteworthy, given the party's long-term support for regional devolution, and clearly distinct from those patterns found in the overall population.

Some within the party saw the upturn in Northern Irish identity as a direct challenge to their existing sense of identity, one MLA claiming that: '[Northern

Table 5.1 DUP members' identification with Northern Irish identity, by age (as a percentage of members in each category)

	17–30	31–40	41–50	51–60	61–70	70
N. Irish	8.5	8.8	17.3	8.9	4.2	4.5
	Chi-sq p = .113 (not significant)					

Irish] is a play with words to antagonize unionism. I don't recognize Northern Irishness.'[45] For another, the recent prominence of Northern Irishness was seen as part of a deliberate strategy to undermine a Protestant British identity, and they claimed to 'feel uneasy about a lot of these terms, for the reason that a lot of people are using them for political advantage'.[46]

This view found agreement with Nelson McCausland, who argued that:

> Northern Irishness was deliberately pushed by the government because the term was that ambiguous. It was generating and creates that middle ground. I found it interesting because people would refer to the Northern Ireland weather, the media will refer to it now as the Northern Irish weather. There are all sorts of phrases. It is almost as if there is a policy of pushing that terminology...I think that the term Northern Irish was quite deliberately developed by officials over the years, going way back to direct rule. To have that flexibility can mean I am a resident of Northern Ireland or I am a northern form of Irishness. So whether it is Northern Ireland or north of Ireland you can have, it is a bit ambiguous as a term. It is a term I don't particularly like because of that ambiguity. I don't see myself as Irish or Northern or any other type of Irish. I live in Northern Ireland, but I don't see myself as Irish.[47]

Irishness

Nelson McCausland is far from alone in his unconcealed rejection of any sense of an Irish identity. Fundamental to DUP identity is the belief that 'Ulster has always had a distinct and separate identity from the rest of Ireland' and that the entire 'history of Ulster has...shown marked differences from that of the rest of the island'.[48] This often manifests in an outright rebuff of anything seen as Irish in any way and certainly any notion of an Irish identity. The following quotations are representative of the views of many members:

> I don't have any sense of an Irish identity. No, I never see that. But then that's how we were brought up.[49]
>
> I am British. I support the UK and Northern Ireland being part of it. I don't like being called Irish. It's a different country.[50]
>
> Do I have a sense of Irish identity? We live on the island of Ireland but that is it.[51]
>
> I'm under the umbrella of British, but I'm Northern Irish...Ulster-Scots, because that's where my family came from a few generations back. Irish is a different thing. There are no Irish descendants in my roots.[52]
>
> I'm British...I don't see myself as Irish at all, culturally, and socially. My allegiance is entirely with the United Kingdom. I speak in the Ulster Scots when the opportunity arises.[53]

I am part of the UK and Northern Ireland. I'm always British, not Northern Irish. I don't feel Irish.[54]

Gregory Campbell expanded his thinking as follows:

If you look to America and ask the average Canadian if he or she is American, if you say to them, is there not a bit of you that is American, they will say 'no I am a Canadian'. I may be in the landmass that is North America, but Americanism to a Canadian is the USA. To them, if you want to describe the American flag, the American way of life, anything that has the word America in it, that means the USA. That might not be right but that's the way it is, that is the way they look at it. Every Canadian I have ever asked, that is what they say, and that is what happens to me when you say Irish.[55]

Even those cognizant of the multidimensional aspects of their identity refused to recognize Irishness as a possible component. Take the following from William Humphrey:

I'm British [but] my identity is multi-layered. When I'm at football I'm Northern Irish, when I'm on the mainland I say I'm from Northern Ireland. That is in a British context. Then in Europe, I'm from the UK, when in America I'm from the UK. I'm British, I'm an Orangeman. I'm an Ulster Scot. I'm not Irish in any way.[56]

Arlene Foster elaborates:

There are so many layers to identity. You can't just say that you are one thing and I think that's true no matter where you come from. I could identify myself as a Fermanagh person, or I could identify myself by religion. What am I comfortable with? I am comfortable with being called British; I am comfortable being called Northern Irish. I am not comfortable being called Irish because it associates with everything green and Gaelic and everything from the Republic of Ireland.[57]

The tendency has long been noted amongst some Protestants to define their identity negatively, in terms of what they are not, as opposed to positively stating what they are.[58] While it is clear that many members do have strong feelings of Britishness, and this finds expression in a variety of ways, for many, an awareness of 'not being Irish' remains core in the construction of identity.

Defending Britishness: 'Culture Wars'

Given the strength of the attachment expressed by its members, it is little wonder that the contemporary period for the DUP has been dominated by the theme of the overt defence of Britishness in face of what many have seen as 'the destruction agenda of Ulster within the Union' set in place by the Belfast Agreement.[59] In this context, the focal point of the Provisional IRA campaign was regarded as more than military in its direction and sought to 'attack every...aspect of...[the] Protestant and British way of life'.[60] Alongside was a belief that the UK Government was increasingly engaged in agreeing to a resolution that would sacrifice British identity in Northern Ireland.[61]

Thus, at the twenty-fifth anniversary of the party, Ian Paisley claimed that a central task for the party was to 'save our heritage and keep Ulster British', and that the DUP had turned the tide on militant Republicanism and intended to go on turning that tide.[62] The DUP has extended its interpretation to argue that unionists have regained ground to the point where the most recent phase of republicanism has been defeated. Further, the DUP believe that it is because of the resilience of the stance they have taken that the DUP 'sets the political agenda in Northern Ireland'.[63]

While many outside the party presented the view that the Belfast Agreement was virtually a panacea for the Northern Ireland conflict, the DUP formulated a coherent (and eventually successful) opposition. Members believe the current political consensus has been arrived at, 'not because we [the DUP] were weak, but because we were firm; not because we caved in under pressure, but because we stood up for what was right; not because we accepted other people's deadlines and diktats, but because we insisted our own requirements be met'.[64] Part of the response from the DUP has rested on the unequivocal assertion that unionists 'are British and intend to stay that way'.[65]

In 2008, the DUP responded directly to what the party claimed was a coherent and sustained attack on their British identity by announcing it would form an 'Academy for Britishness'[66] as a think-tank to undertake research on themes related to British identity. At the same time, it announced the formation of a 'British Cultural and Equality Unit' to 'monitor and respond to attacks on unionist culture'.[67] However, little has been heard of either body since and there remains concern over the best methods of defending British culture, given the problems of parades and flags. As one MLA put it, 'there is a specific campaign to erode our culture and wind our community up',[68] while a North Belfast councillor suggested 'there is a step up from republicans to try and marginalize Britishness'.[69]

This idea, that British culture in Northern Ireland is constantly contested and in peril, encourages a siege mentality amongst some Ulster Protestants, many viewing themselves as part of a 'threatened community'.[70] Throughout the contemporary period, the DUP has always demanded continual vigilance against any 'hollowing out (of) Ulster's Britishness'.[71] Even given the ending of the Provisional IRA's armed campaign and Sinn Féin's transfer into constitutional politics, many unionists perceive that their core identity of Britishness continues to be threatened,[72] and that Sinn Féin 'can't get away from...opposing Britishness'.[73]

The perceived battleground for this clash is extensive. The DUP MLA George Robinson, for example, recently claimed that all symbols of Britishness, 'even a Princess Diana mug', were being removed from the Limavady council building, as part of a campaign to remove 'all vestiges of Britishness' in the area.[74] Elsewhere, the DUP members of Lisburn's district council have consistently resisted demands for street names to be written in both Irish and English.[75] Belfast's Deputy Lord Mayor, Christopher Stalford, encapsulated such issues:

> I think the constitutional question is settled. Northern Ireland has now moved into relative peace and normality, but there are cultural issues that become a new outlet for conflict or disagreement. Now, obviously, it is disagreement in a way that doesn't manifest itself in violence—but there are issues around Britishness, and the ethos of Northern Ireland as a part of the United Kingdom, where there is a battle to be won.[76]

Another put it even more directly when he insisted that 'we've won the political war, but we haven't won the cultural or ethnic war. We have plenty of work to do there.'[77]

The idea that the DUP are engaged in a 'culture war' has been given further momentum by perceptions that attacks on Orange Order halls are not just sectarian, but also politically inspired. This understanding is also applied to other issues, such as restrictions placed on Orange marches, or the limiting of the flying of the Union Flag on Belfast City Hall to designated days. Such actions are interpreted by the DUP as evidence of a broader campaign of 'anti-British bigotry'[78] waged by Irish republicans.

Many members offered examples of this perspective, typified by the views of MLA Sydney Anderson, who suggested 'what you find in politics is...Sinn Féin...coming along and anything that's anti-British, they do it'.[79] As the culture war intensifies, Sinn Féin 'artificially creates an objection to parades as part of their attack on the Protestant identity'.[80]

The range of engagements in the culture war is seen as wide. Hence, continuing debates about the existence of the grammar school system are viewed not in educational terms, but as part of the culture wars. As this member argued:

> They [Sinn Féin] see the grammar school system as being British-orientated. They feel that because it is British-orientated, it has to go and become something comprehensive. I feel we have very good grammar schools in Northern Ireland. They perform very well, preparing young people for going out to get good academic qualifications and for going to university. [Sinn Féin]...are too blinkered in their notion that everything British has to go and they tend to work toward that agenda.[81]

Hence, pressure mounts on the DUP to respond, in the context of cultural unionism and the protection of Britishness, as this member made clear:

I feel that our politicians are not saying enough and warning the British government that this here is the British country. We see the Orange Order being re-routed, Sinn Féin and the republicans seem to be getting their way. Our flags have been taken down and our heritage in the council chamber is being removed out. To me, we need our politicians for the way forward, to stand up and say, the British government has to recognize that we are British and our flag should never be in question by republicans or council chambers.[82]

A major part of the engagement in the culture war involves interpretation and control of the past, and an awareness by the DUP that 'the efforts of some to rewrite the history of Northern Ireland will not go unchecked and that the actions of those who inflicted so much suffering upon the people of our Province will not be airbrushed from the record'.[83]

Peter Robinson has directly addressed what he identified as the attempt by Sinn Féin to rewrite history, in saying:

We will not permit Sinn Féin to erase those parts of history that are inconvenient. We will not allow them to engage in revisionism . . . to airbrush the evil acts of republican terrorists from the history books. It would be a betrayal of the legacy of all who have suffered if history were to be rewritten to salve the consciences of the perpetrators. . . . we will not allow history to be re-written! I seek true and genuine reconciliation, but it will not happen by trying to spin a false or sanitised version of the past.[84]

The future, according to Robinson, will also be one of contestation and battles, albeit of the constitutional variety:

While there is good reason to be optimistic that after nearly forty years of terrorism, the military conflict in Northern Ireland is over, the political battle between unionism and nationalism goes on. Republicans have not called a halt to aspiring to a United Ireland and we as unionists will tenaciously hold on to the Union with Great Britain.[85]

Hence, 'the past' becomes central to issues surrounding victims,[86] and in DUP objections, after significant internal debate, to the building of a historical project, or, to critics, 'terrorist shrine', on the site of the old Maze prison.[87]

The Contemporary Defence

Britishness remains the core signifier for large sections of the DUP membership and the 'ownership' of Britishness remains a site of contestation across the broader discourses and politics of Unionism. Britishness is, of course, a 'variable ideology', and the competing definitions of contemporary Britishness throw into relief 'a central dilemma about how to combine the past and the future'[88] in order to continue the constuction of an imagined or mythical British community.[89]

Britishness, as understood by large sections of the DUP membership, is constructed as homogeneous and unproblematic. It is distant and non-commensurate with what many would regard as the realities of life in contemporary multicultural Britain.[90] The understanding of Britishness, for many within the DUP, is seemingly unchallenged by patterns of globalization, the loss of empire, immigration, and so on. This does not, however, in any way weaken its salience to DUP members. As the MLA Jonathan Craig explained, central to the identity of the DUP remains its 'strong pro-British stance', which for him meant 'not giving in to someone diminishing my right to be British. That is at the core of what we stand for.'[91]

Defining and defending 'Britishness' are core to DUP party politics, as is resolution. Ian Paisley outlined the key rules of politics as 'stick to your policy and never deviate' and 'stay on message and stay united'.[92] Given that the DUP's defence of Britishness endorsed, from 2006, power-sharing with the 'enemy', Paisley had to rely upon personal kudos to sell the changed methodology:

> I have not failed the Ulster people since I first took up the reins in 1969. There is nothing to suggest I will fail you by 2009. My trust has been earned the hard way, and through thick and thin I have always sought to advance the interests of the people of our province. I am not about to betray that trust.[93]

The seeming transformation of Paisley, from a 'malign colossus'[94] into a peacemaker and statesman, astonished many observers. Despite much speculation in the media and beyond, even for party members, the reasons why someone who throughout most of his political career had been characterized as a 'man of wrath'[95] and who built his political reputation on 'Bible-and-brimstone rhetoric'[96] should have so openly and copiously accepted power-sharing remain fairly opaque. Indeed, the processes of transition following St Andrews and the subsequent public image of his cordial relationship with Martin McGuinness led one leading commentator to suggest that 'even Paisley has given up on Paisleyism, in which no offensive holds or words were barred'.[97] The 'new Paisleyism' quickly precipitated his stepping down as moderator-for-life of Free Presbyterianism and as leader of the DUP. Paisley's position was threatening to bring about further splits in the party, beyond resignations and defections to the TUV. For many, the position was 'hopelessly incompatible, denouncing Rome and the IRA on a Sunday and doing business with all manner of representative Catholics, and ex-terrorists, on the other days of the week'.[98] The resignation of Ian Paisley reinvigorated long-standing debates about the religious balance within the DUP and the future identity of the party.

It was within this context that Peter Robinson's influence grew within the party, as he became the focal point for changes bringing about a more professional structure and organization to the DUP. Much of this was driven by Robinson's tactical and administrative skills, which quickly made him indispensable to Paisley and the party leadership. Indeed, it has been claimed that Robinson was responsible

> as much as any other factor for transforming the DUP into a coherent, well organised political party with a ruthless commitment to winning votes. Robinson set about regularising and centralising the DUP's affairs...a party constitution creating new party structures...would help to co-ordinate the DUP's membership and election efforts.[99]

Moreover, Robinson's growing prominence involved gradual separation of the DUP from the Free Presbyterian Church and, amid growing graduate recruitment, the emergence of[100]

> two distinct strands in the DUP. The contrast with the older, traditional DUP member was striking. Most of the old guard had only the most basic education, a simple unquestioning faith in fundamental Protestantism, and an equal faith in the infallibility of Ian Paisley. Invariably, their route into the DUP was via the Free Presbyterian Church. The new breed were different. Some were Free Presbyterians, but many were not.[101]

It is important to note that this trend began long before the Belfast and St Andrews Agreements. The competing tendencies brought about by the influx of new members into the DUP have been described in different ways, such as rivalry between militants and moderates, or between fundamentalists and pragmatists.[102] The tensions were between those emphasizing an overtly political platform and those continuing to accentuate religious and moral agendas within the party, the former largely feeling that the party's expansion and political advancement was being inhibited by its public face of fundamental religious-moral discourse.

Although the DUP remains a disciplined top–down party, Ian Paisley's departure opened up political and ideological space within it. As one elected representative put it:

> People are making their own minds up; it's like an evolutionary process rather than being told. There is good and bad come from that. People are more inclined to think for themselves, whereas before, it was the defined line and people followed Ian Paisley and agreed with him, people put their total faith and trust in him.[103]

Certainly, in recent times, much of the public face of the party has changed. Moloney and Pollak record, for example, that throughout the 1980s, the following was a typical opening to a DUP conference:

A Free Presbyterian minister, usually the ever-popular Revd William McCrea MP, is invited to the platform to say a few words. His 'few words' last for the best part of five minutes. First, he takes the delegates through a reading from the Bible and then he prays—in passionately archaic language—for Ulster, for Protestantism, and for the Democratic Unionist Party.[104]

The highlight of such conferences was always the speech by the Reverend Ian Paisley, during which he took his audience 'through a litany of their fears and hates' and reinforced how numerous and dangerous were the many enemies of Protestant Ulster.[105]

Today, the feel of the DUP conference and the image it seeks to project is very different. With the exception of opening prayers (and the near-absence of alcohol on its fringe), the overall structure and texture of the conference is akin to that of any other modern political party. In part, this rests in the confidence which comes from the belief that the constitutional debate has been 'won', whereby DUP members speak with confidence of the nature of the second century of unionism[106] and what that will mean for Northern Irish society. It also flows from the leadership style of Peter Robinson and the influence of party modernizers. Indeed, following the Assembly elections in May 2011, it was claimed that, under the leadership and political persona of Peter Robinson, the direction and political identity had altered dramatically, taking the party 'on a long march from Protestant extremism towards the middle ground of unionism'.[107]

Overall, the willingness of the DUP leadership to reposition the party draws assurance from their belief that Northern Ireland's progress is irreversible. At times, the new thinking within the DUP even seems to draw on expressions of civic unionism and to promote the development of pluralist institutions to which all can give allegiance. Frequently, the political agenda set by the contemporary DUP leadership resembles some of the key facets of European Christian democracy, with its strong emphasis on the linking of social issues to traditional moral values, emphasis on law and order, and assertion of the Christian (in DUP terms, Protestant) heritage of their country. This also involves constructing a positive new symbolism and structures that move away from traditional communal loyalties, clearly seen, for example, in recent efforts of the DUP to attract more Roman Catholics to the party.

In emphasizing the creation of institutions that can be acceptable across the population, and 'practices that...are regarded as the common possession of all, rather than the exclusive preserve of one group, tribe, or tradition',[108] Robinson draws upon a vision of a more civic form of unionism that develops shared ground beyond existing communal divisions and acknowledges new groupings:[109]

> Ours is a nation that is made up not just of those from England, Scotland, Wales, or Northern Ireland, or those for whom English is the language of their birth, but of those who have come to live here and who share our values and ideals. I'm proud that Britishness is about diversity and inclusivity.[110]

While this may not go as far as the much criticized vision of 'inclusive Britishness' once projected by the UUP,[111] it is a different sense of citizenship from that referred to Ian Paisley when he spoke of 'the people of Ulster'.

Almost all individuals are, at any given time, members of several different social groups and hold multiple reference points of identity,[112] and at certain points in time and space, some identities hold more salience than others. In all societies undergoing transition from violent conflict to political engagement, public political discourse has particular importance and resonance. In their study of the impact of devolution on identity in devolved regions of the United Kingdom, Wilson and Stapleton highlight the interrelationship of discursive and institutional change, whereby the 'new political structures and changing public discourses (of nation, state, culture, and citizenship) provide new categories of membership, belonging, and allegiance, while simultaneously closing off others or altering others'.[113]

Throughout most of its history, the DUP has presented a strong sense of British identity, broadly characterized by the signifiers of religious fundamentalism and political conservatism cast in the image of the party and, for many years, in the image of its leader, Ian Paisley. For many from the Protestant unionist tradition and certainly for DUP members, it is Britishness that continues to hold the most relevance as a primary point of identity. In the past, the DUP consistently articulated a concept of Britishness that was both exclusive and homogenized. It proved profoundly divisive, in erecting political frontiers to actively exclude the 'other'. Today, the message from the DUP is somewhat different. Its public discourse is that politics is about accommodating difference so that everyone in Northern Ireland 'can enjoy the fruits of peace'.[114]

This is not to suggest that the current DUP leadership is any less forthright in its belief in the Union. The sense of political identity currently offered by the leadership of the DUP reflects a change of emphasis away from cultural unionism and towards an agenda drawing on more civic understandings of politics. That said, although the DUP membership and leadership clearly remain unified around a sense of Britishness and British identity, the contemporary party is not without its contradictions and internal anxieties surrounding the expression of that Britishness.

The move away from cultural unionism, perhaps to the centre ground of unionism, does not necessarily represent a sense of identity or belonging shared by the entire membership. The modernizing agenda of the leadership presents a challenge to sections of the membership who are fearful that the current repositioning by the DUP may mark a weakening of its core identity and disrupt what many members, talking about the party, referred to as 'the family'. There is also a concern amongst some members that DUP moves towards cultural pluralism and accommodation of the 'other' community could represent a further hollowing of Britishness in a Union which, according to these Fermanagh members, is 'far from safe'; one in which

> the siege is on. We are going to lose the majority very soon, once they get the majority in Belfast and the majority in Londonderry, Northern Ireland is finished. There is only one part of Belfast that is safely in Protestant hands and that is East Belfast. East Belfast is the last resort and fighting for the flag. Once the flag leaves Belfast, Northern Ireland is finished...Sinn Féin got a lot of what they are enjoying, but we seem to be on the losing side.... what have they [Sinn Féin] lost? What have they sacrificed?[115]

For these members, recent shifts in emphasis from the DUP leadership have led to a concern that the DUP risks being out-manœuvred. Some are even concerned that the DUP may no longer effectively defend their 'Britishness' in the face of a legacy of demise and constant challenge in the culture wars. This position is made overt by the following:

> If you go back fifteen or twenty years ago, Ian Paisley was leading the so-called Protestant community in a direction that we all believed in. Then, when the Good Friday Agreement came, the direction had changed an awful lot. It changed too much for us. We have only one concession left to give away and that is the flag issue. Once the flag issue goes away, there is nothing to fight for, there is nothing left for us. We have lost the B Specials, the UDR, the reserve police, we have lost the RUC, we have one thing left and that is the flag.[116]

The task for Robinson and his successor as party leader will be to balance the competing forces of modernization and change evident within the DUP. This is no different from the role of any party leader, but the difference within unionism historically is that it has been infested by cries of Lundyism and resistance to 'sell-out' or betrayal. For years, the DUP joined in that chorus. Now it is required to manage those processes of accommodation, albeit in a far more promising political environment which it helped to shape.

Conclusion

Core to the identity of the DUP is its representation as a party that guarantees to act as a firewall against Irish unity, a claimed bulwark for the protection of the Union and the guardians of British identity in Northern Ireland. For much of its existence, the core appeal of the party has rested in its articulation of Protestantism within a distinct ethnic identity; a form of cultural unionism manifest in expressions of a constant fear of those enemies seeking to weaken or destroy the constitutional link. The oppositional politics of the DUP was firmly grounded in self-perceptions based upon common religious and cultural practices and a Protestant British way of life. Many members believe that it was only by buttressing Protestant unionist identity and the values of cultural unionism that the DUP was able to force the republican movement to accept partitionist institutions within a devolved administration.

While there are long-standing debates inside the party concerning its focus and direction, these have taken on a new meaning following the demise of Ian Paisley as party leader. As it has set about further modernizing the party, the DUP leadership continues to highlight the existence of an enemy that is always untrustworthy, albeit one that has largely moved its point of attack from the military to the cultural. The sense of political identity currently offered by the DUP leadership reflects a change of emphasis away from cultural unionism and towards an agenda drawing on more civic understandings of politics. For some within the party who continue to frame their understanding within the parameters of cultural unionism, this has raised concerns regarding the core messages emanating from the DUP.

Notes

1. Ian Paisley, Leader's Speech, DUP 25th Anniversary Conference, 1996, Broughshane.
2. Cited in R. Edwards (2013) 'Peter Robinson: "Old-Style Unionist Majority is a Thing of the Past"', *The Impartial Reporter*, 27 Apr.
3. I. Paisley. (2008) 'I Did Smash Sinn Féin', <http://news.bbc.co.uk/1/hi/uk_politics/7285912.stm>, 16 Sept. 2008, accessed Oct. 2013.
4. S. Dempster (2008) 'DUP Issues Leaflet on its Achievements', *News Letter*, 14 July.
5. S. Hall (1996) 'Introduction: Who Needs Identity?' in S. Hall and P. du Gay (eds), *Questions of Cultural Identity*, London: Sage, 1–17.
6. W. Hazleton (1993) 'Constitutional Uncertainty and Political Deadlock: Overcoming Unionist Intransigence in Northern Ireland', *Journal of Conflict Studies*, 13/3, 24–41.
7. N. Porter (1996) *Rethinking Unionism: An Alternative Vision for Northern Ireland*, Belfast: Blackstaff.
8. Porter, *Rethinking Unionism*, 166.
9. B. Graham (2004) 'The Past in the Present: The Shaping of Identity in Loyalist Ulster', *Terrorism and Political Violence*, 16/3, 493.
10. J. W. McAuley, J. Tonge, and A. Mycock (2011) *Loyal to the Core: Orangeism and Britishness in Northern Ireland*, Dublin: Irish Academic Press.

11. Northern Ireland 2011 Census, available at <http://www.nisra.gov.uk/Census/2011_results_detailed_characteristics.html>, accessed Oct. 2013.
12. Commission for Racial Equality (2005) *The Decline of Britishness: A Research Study*, London: CRE.
13. Interview with Gregory Campbell, MP, East Londonderry, 18 Oct. 2012.
14. Interview with Sammy Wilson, MLA, East Antrim, 25 Jan. 2013.
15. Interview with Coleraine councillor, 5 Oct. 2012.
16. Interview with Councillor Mark Baxter, Craigavon, 5 Nov. 2012.
17. Interview with Strangford councillor, 11 Sept. 2012.
18. M. Billig (1995) *Banal Nationalism*, London: Sage.
19. Interview with Nelson McCausland, MLA, Belfast North, 9 Jan. 2013.
20. Interview with Peter Weir, MLA, North Down, 9 Nov. 2012.
21. Interview with Peter Weir, 9 Nov. 2012.
22. Interview with Arlene Foster, MLA, 24 Jan. 2013.
23. Interview with Fermanagh councillor, 15 Mar. 2013.
24. Interview with Peter Weir, 9 Nov. 2012.
25. Interview with DUP MLA, 4 Dec. 2012.
26. Interview with Arlene Foster, 24 Jan. 2013.
27. Interview with Councillor Sharon Skillen, Castlereagh, 28 Feb. 2013.
28. See F. Cochrane (1997) *Unionist Politics and the Politics of Unionism*, Cork: Cork University Press, 70.
29. T. Hennessey and R. Wilson (1997) *With All Due Respect: Pluralism and Parity of Esteem*, Democratic Dialogue, report no. 7, Belfast: Democratic Dialogue.
30. Interview with Councillor Alan Leslie, Bangor, 20 Sept. 2012.
31. Conversation with delegate, DUP Annual Conference, Belfast, Nov. 2012.
32. J. Garry (2011) 'Report for the Electoral Reform Society on the Northern Ireland 2011 Assembly Election and AV Referendum', School of Politics, International Studies and Philosophy, Queen's University Belfast, unpublished.
33. The Northern Ireland Life and Times 2012 Survey showed 22% adopting a Northern Irish identity, <http://www.nilt.ac.uk>, accessed Oct. 2013. See also D. Morrow (2013) 'Northern Ireland Remains Sharply Divided over National Identity But with No Strong Desire for Irish Unity', *Belfast Telegraph*, 10 June.
34. 'Census 2011: Northern Ireland', suggested 29% held a Northern Irish identity. Available at <http://www.theguardian.com/news/datablog/2012/dec/11/2011-census-northern-ireland-religion-identity>, accessed Sept. 2013.
35. J. McCallister (2013) Unionism and a Shared Future', *News Letter*, 18 Jan.
36. Interview with Paula Bradley MLA, Newtownabbey, 20 Sept. 2012.
37. Interview with Fermanagh councillor, 15 Mar. 2013.
38. Interview with Strangford councillor, 11 Sept. 2012.
39. Interview with Peter Weir, 9 Nov. 2012.
40. Interview with Sammy Wilson MLA, East Antrim, 25 Jan. 2013.
41. Fermanagh focus group, 26 Apr. 2013.
42. Interview with Trevor Clarke MLA, South Antrim, 22 Jan. 2013.
43. Interview with Strabane councillor, 16 Apr. 2013.
44. Interview with Arlene Foster, 24 Jan. 2013.

45. Interview with DUP MLA, 4 Dec. 2012.
46. Interview with Sydney Anderson MLA, Craigavon, 5 Nov. 2012.
47. Interview with Nelson McCausland MLA, Belfast North, 9 Jan. 2013.
48. Peter Robinson 'A Separate Identity', available at: <http://www.dup.org.uk/identity.htm>, accessed Feb. 2001.
49. Interview with Paula Bradley MLA, Newtownabbey, 20 Sept. 2012.
50. Interview with Belfast councillor, 27 Sept. 2012.
51. Interview with Craigavon councillor, 5 Nov. 2012.
52. Interview with Craigavon councillor, 5 Nov. 2012.
53. Interview with Jim Shannon MP, Strangford, 3 Oct. 2012.
54. Interview with Dungannon councillor, 27 Nov. 2012.
55. Interview with Gregory Campbell MP, Stormont, 18 Oct. 2012.
56. Interview with William Humphrey MLA, Belfast, 9 Jan. 2013.
57. Interview with Arlene Foster, 24 Jan. 2013.
58. See e.g. R. Wallis, S. Bruce, and D. Taylor (1987) 'Ethnicity and Evangelicalism: Ian Paisley and Protestant Politics in Ulster', *Comparative Studies in Society and History*, 29/2, 293–313.
59. Ian Paisley, 'Address to the Centenary Demonstration of the Independent Orange Institution, Ballymoney, 12th July 2003'. Archived at <http://www.dup.org.uk>, accessed Aug. 2003.
60. Peter Robinson (1996) Speech to a 'Right to March' rally in Portadown, DUP press release, 31 July.
61. *News Letter,* 31 Oct. 1997.
62. Ian Paisley, Leader's Speech, DUP 25th Anniversary Conference, 1996.
63. Peter Robinson, Leader's Speech to DUP Annual Conference, 2008, Armagh.
64. Peter Robinson, Leader's Speech to DUP Annual Conference, 2008, Armagh.
65. *Belfast Telegraph,* 25 June 2008.
66. 'DUP Fights Back Against "Erosion of Britishness"', *News Letter,* 25 June 2008.
67. In a leaflet, 'DUP Delivering', published in July 2008, the party claimed that these two new bodies were originated to fight back against those attempting 'to erode our British identity' and to resist 'those who wage an anti-British agenda'.
68. Interview with DUP MLA, 4 Dec. 2012.
69. Interview with North Belfast councillor, 30 Nov. 2012.
70. D. G. Boyce (1995) 'The Suffering People and the Threatened Community: Two Traditions of Political Violence in Ireland', in A. O'Day (ed.), *Terrorism's Laboratory: The Case of Northern Ireland*, Aldershot: Dartmouth, 11–25.
71. G. Lucy and E. McClure (eds) (1999) *Cool Britannia? What Britishness Means to Me*, Lurgan: Ulster Society.
72. See K. Brown and R. MacGinty (2003) 'Public Attitudes toward Partisan and Neutral Symbols in Post-Agreement Northern Ireland', *Identities: Global Studies in Culture and Power*, 10, 83–108.
73. Interview with Coleraine councillor, 5 Oct. 2012.
74. 'Unionist anger is Growing in Limavady Claims Politicians', *Londonderry Sentinel*, 9 Mar. 2013.
75. 'DUP Rejects Irish Street Naming', *Irish News*, 6 Sept. 2005.

76. Interview with Councillor and Deputy Mayor Christopher Stalford, Belfast, 9 Oct. 2012.
77. Interview with William Humphrey, 9 Jan. 2013.
78. Nigel Dodds MP (2008) 'Address to DUP Annual Conference', Armagh, Nov.
79. Interview with Sydney Anderson, 5 Nov. 2012.
80. Interview with Jonathan Craig MLA, Lisburn, 11 Jan. 2013.
81. Interview with Coleraine councillor, 5 Oct. 2012.
82. Fermanagh focus group discussion, 26 Apr. 2013.
83. Nigel Dodds (2012), *Leading at Westminster*, DUP annual conference booklet, Belfast: DUP.
84. Peter Robinson (2012) Leader's Speech to DUP Annual Conference, Belfast, Nov.
85. Peter Robinson, 'Unionists are in Control Says Deputy Leader'. Archived at: <http://www.dup.org.uk/Articles.asp?Article_ID=2732>, accessed July 2007.
86. DUP (2003) *A Voice for Victims*, Policy Paper, Belfast: DUP.
87. See M. Davenport (2013) 'DUP Caught up in Maze', available at: <http://www.bbc.co.uk/news/uk-northern-ireland-23716157>, and P. Robinson (2013) 'Leaders Letter on Maze Development', available at: <http://www.mydup.com/news/article/leaders-letter-on-maze-development>, both downloaded Sept. 2013.
88. D. Morley and K. Robins (2001) *British Cultural Studies: Geography, Nationality, and Identity*, Oxford: Oxford University Press, 4.
89. We use this term in the widely understood sense developed by B. Anderson (1991) *Imagined Communities: Reflections on the Origin and Spread of Nationalism*, London: Verso.
90. F. Cochrane (1997) *Unionist Politics and the Politics of Unionism since the Anglo-Irish Agreement*, Cork: Cork University Press, 70.
91. Interview with Jonathan Craig, MLA, Lagan Valley, 11 Jan. 2013.
92. *Irish Times*, 9 Dec. 2006, 10.
93. Ian Paisley, cited in the *Irish Times*, 9 Dec. 2006.
94. E. Moloney and A. Pollak (1986) *Paisley*, Dublin: Poolbeg.
95. P. Marrinan (1973) *Paisley: Man of Wrath*, Tralee: Anvil Books.
96. E. McCann (2013) 'Real Reason DUP's Ian Paisley Decided to Strike Deal with Sinn Féin', *Belfast Telegraph*, 12 Apr.
97. B. White (2007) 'You may Not have Noticed, But it's the End of Paisleyism', *Belfast Telegraph*, 19 Sept.
98. White, 'End of Paisleyism'.
99. Moloney and Pollak, *Paisley*, 289–90.
100. Moloney and Pollak, *Paisley*, 293.
101. Moloney and Pollak, *Paisley*, 295.
102. D. McKittrick (2004) 'Will the Fundamentalist Paisley Prevail over the Moderates within his Ranks?' *Independent*, 17 Sept..
103. Interview with North Antrim councillor, 4 Oct. 2012.
104. Moloney and Pollak, *Paisley*, 262.
105. Moloney and Pollak, *Paisley*, 263.
106. See e.g. Peter Robinson, Leader's Speech to DUP Annual Conference, 2012.

107. E. Curran (2011) 'How Peter Robinson has Morphed to Fully Occupy the Middle Ground', *Belfast Telegraph*, 10 May.
108. Porter, *Rethinking Unionism,* 163.
109. Porter, *Rethinking Unionism,* 180.
110. Peter Robinson, Leader's Speech to DUP Annual Conference, 2012.
111. D. Godson (2004) *Himself Alone: David Trimble and the Ordeal of Unionism,* London: Harper Collins.
112. See e.g. M. J. Hornsey (2008) 'Social Identity Theory and Self-Categorization Theory: A Historical Review', *Social and Personality Psychology Compass,* 2/1, 204–22; S. Stryker and A. Statham (1985) 'Symbolic Interaction and Role Theory', in G. Lindzey and E. Aronson (eds), *Handbook of Social Psychology,* New York: Random House, 311–78.
113. J. Wilson and K. Stapleton (2006) 'Identity Categories in Use: Britishness, Devolution, and the Ulster Scots Identity in Northern Ireland', in J. Wilson and K. Stapleton (eds), *Devolution and identity,* Aldershot: Ashgate, 28.
114. Peter Robinson (2013) 'Huge Job to Keep Northern Ireland Moving Forward', available at: <http://www.mydup.com>, accessed Sept. 2013.
115. Interview with Fermanagh focus group, 26 Apr. 2013.
116. Interview with Fermanagh focus group, 26 Apr. 2013.

6

Still for God and Ulster? Religion and Faith

The DUP has long been viewed as an ethno-religious organization, fusing a stout defence of a particular (Ulster-Scots) people with support for the Protestant religion. Ian Paisley's formation of his own Free Presbyterian Church in 1951, prior to the emergence of his own political party, led to common assumptions that the politics of the DUP were a derivative of what remained a very small but religiously intense church. Religion and policy were seen as inextricably linked within the party. The DUP's moral and political agendas appeared largely indistinguishable, influenced by a fundamentalist version of Protestantism eschewed by the larger Protestant Presbyterian and Church of Ireland denominations. For Free Presbyterian DUP members, there was a clear link between the need to hold steadfast to a particular austere version of the Reformed faith and the requirement to resist an expansionist Roman Catholic and republican project to take Northern Ireland out of the United Kingdom.

Yet the DUP's support base always extended beyond a fervent, often rural, evangelical core to embrace much more nominally religious, even secular, loyalists, whose own God-fearing was far more marginal and for whom church attendance was, at most, episodic. Whilst anti-Catholicism may have held some appeal for urban loyalists, the DUP's perceived stoutness on the constitutional question may have been of greater significance. This chapter examines the extent to which Free Presbyterianism dominated the DUP and assesses the degree to which that church may still influence the party. The chapter concentrates particularly upon the broader degree of religious influence—not necessarily Free Presbyterian, but certainly conservatively Protestant—which underpins aspects of party policy and outlook.

Paisleyism and the Fusion of Religion and Politics

There is insufficient space for a detailed history of the influence of the Free Presbyterian Church upon the DUP in the 1970s and 1980s, but the analyses of Bruce[1] and Smyth,[2] more particularly the latter's insider view, suggest it was very considerable. Similar space constraints preclude deep analysis of the theological stances of the Free Presbyterian Church and evangelical Protestantism more broadly, and readers are directed elsewhere.[3] What can be asserted is that, from its inception, the DUP fused a defence of the Union with a particular religious approach. That the DUP emerged from Paisley's Protestant Unionist Party of the late 1960s with a modified name indicated cognizance that it needed a secular as well as religious appeal to flourish. This concession did not dilute the fundamentalist Protestantism which infused the DUP in its early years. That the Protestant Unionist Party was the parent of the DUP was obvious. The name change did not greatly alter the membership from the old party, each of whose branches 'were advised to organise themselves within the new Party'.[4] The DUP would be guided by God in its operation, Paisley insisted: 'We look to the God of our Fathers to guide and direct our paths. He did not fail them. He will not fail us.'[5] The DUP was to represent a loyalism underwritten by Protestantism, but whose constitutional vehemence would give it appeal beyond the narrow confines of uber-religious Protestants.

DUP branch meetings began with prayers, a practice still continued in most branches, especially those in rural areas. Church and party matters were formally separate, but the bulk of the party's elected representatives were drawn from the Free Presbyterian Church, which, in the very early years of the party, influenced decisions over which election candidates were fielded by the DUP.[6] This relationship between church and party offered considerable strength, an activist base dedicated in its commitments to faith and politics. Association with a particular sect was also a weakness, eliciting suspicion from moderate Protestants, wary of the perceived demagoguery of Ian Paisley, as leader of church and party. A Craigavon councillor asserted (erroneously, but indicative of perceptions of the DUP) that 'when the party was formed and in the Seventies and Eighties, you couldn't join if you weren't Free Presbyterian'.[7] The DUP Deputy Leader, Nigel Dodds, acknowledged the Free Presbyterian influence in the party as 'very strong in rural areas west of the Bann, less strong East of the Bann',[8] whereas his fellow DUP MP David Simpson believed that the links were country-wide and would 'certainly say in Belfast the church would be aligned with the party'.[9] The former DUP member, Clifford Smyth, once claimed of the DUP that 'the whole edifice is cemented together through a sense of loyalty to the leader and a religious affiliation to Free Presbyterianism'.[10]

Part of the necessary broadening of the DUP's appeal has involved the conveying of the message that all strands of Protestantism (and beyond) are welcome. According to a male Ballymoney councillor, there was insufficient previous separation of church and party:

The Free [Presbyterian] Church played too big a role within the party. The DUP was known as the Free Church...that was bad for the party. I'm a great lover of the Doctor (Paisley), but I think that the leader isn't a member of the [Free Presbyterian] Church is a big asset to the party. The Doc in North Antrim is a legend, but it's good to get away from that within the more liberal Northern Ireland.[11]

For most early joiners, the overt fusion of religion with politics formed part of the DUP's appeal. Nelson McCausland, decades later to become a minister in the Northern Ireland Executive, joined in 1972 when the DUP was 'very much a Protestant party. That was reflected in the terminology, in the policies, in a whole range of things.'[12] The party was dominated by its leader—a 'Protestant Pope', as the Strangford MLA Jonathan Bell[13] (affectionately) described Ian Paisley, heavily influenced initially by that leader's church.

The Free Presbyterian Church has been summarized as 'fundamental in doctrine, evangelical in outreach, sanctified in behaviour, Presbyterian in government, Protestant in conviction, and separatist in practice'.[14] Free Presbyterianism offers one of the most literal interpretations of scripture, believing that the Bible is the true word of God. To be saved, individuals, as sinners, have to adhere rigidly to scripture and, in effect, 'present' themselves to God—the idea of being 'born again'. Living as a true Christian to please the Saviour requires abstinence from a wide range of humanly vices, including drinking alcohol, gambling, and even dancing. Free Presbyterians are encouraged to steer clear of these vices or risk the wrath of God. Given the importance placed upon good *individual* conduct in order to be saved, it is not necessarily clear how Protestants in Northern Ireland, as a *collective*, might possibly constitute a chosen people, whom God has saved politically from incorporation into a Catholic Ireland, preventing betrayal by other clergy and politicians.[15] The issue of individual versus collective paths to salvation is not easily resolved. Paisley insisted that 'God will deliver Ulster. The salt of the earth, God's people, are in this country. No matter how dark the hour, how terrible the foe, how awful the betrayal, and no matter what voices are raised...God will give us deliverance.'[16]

Active Protestants of different denominations would accept much of the above, if eschewing the stricter prohibitions, but Free Presbyterians offer greater zeal in their religious interpretations and observance. Free Presbyterians tend to be critical of the supposed apostasy of other Reformed Church denominations. Even the Presbyterian Church is seen as too liberal. Paisley cited the 1926 acquittal of a Presbyterian cleric on charges of heresy and theological liberalism as part of the origins of the Free Presbyterian Church.[17] Presbyterians are viewed by Free Presbyterians as insufficiently dedicated to following the call of Christ via the Gospels and as lacklustre in their religious mission. Moderate Protestant churches, most particularly the somewhat more 'High' Church of Ireland, are perceived as dangerously ecumenical.

Free Presbyterians have always regarded Roman Catholicism as a bogus religion. The Free Church denies the credibility of priests, arguing that such mediators between God and people are superfluous. All that is required are ministers to assist in the people's knowledge and interpretation of the Bible. Priests celebrating Mass and claiming to facilitate transubstantiation (the Roman Catholic belief that the body and blood of Christ are literally present via via the host and wine at Communion) are viewed as false prophets. Idolatry, such as the worshipping of Mary, the use of religious statues, and the intercession of saints, is equally repudiated by Free Presbyterians. The Catholic Church is also seen as undemocratic and hierarchical, charges which might be more readily accepted by some Catholics.

Most sections of the Reformed faith would not necessarily disagree with these stances and the supposedly false doctrines of Rome are indeed listed in the Articles of the Church of England, headed by the Queen. This allows Free Presbyterians to highlight links between church, faith, monarchy, and Northern Ireland's place in the United Kingdom, given the monarch's sovereign position as head of state.[18] However, whilst mainstream Protestant churches moderated their stance towards the Roman Catholic Church, denunciations of Rome formed a regular part of the Paisley repertoire. Of course, Paisley's criticisms of sympathy towards Roman Catholicism long predated his formation of the DUP. The UUP Prime Minister Terence O'Neill was lambasted by Paisley for having the temerity to offer condolences on behalf of the government of Northern Ireland to Cardinal Conway, the leader of Ireland's Catholics, following the death of Pope John XXIII in 1963. Paisley demonstrated against Pope John Paul's visit to Britain in 1982 and six years later was ejected from the European Parliament after denouncing the Pope as the 'Anti-Christ'. He maintained his steadfast opposition to the papacy, opposing Pope Benedict's visit to Britain in 2010.

Opposition to the 'false doctrines' of the Roman Church does not equate to automatic hostility to Roman Catholics as office bearers. Free Presbyterians are not jihadists, wishing to crush unbelievers. Moreover, elected Free Presbyterian DUP members have always been conscious of their responsibilities to look after Roman Catholic constituents. Repudiation of their faith was not rejection of the individual. Yet Paisley's position as leader of a church so hostile to Roman Catholicism bolstered Catholic perceptions that the DUP was not a party for them. Receptiveness to Roman Catholics as people amongst DUP elected representatives was overshadowed by the anti-Roman Church outlook of the church with which people closely associated the DUP. Paisley's anti-Catholicism adopted conspiratorial tones, his belief that the Roman Catholic Church supported Irish republicans set against considerable evidence. Pope John Paul II appealed for an end to violence during his visit to Ireland in 1979 and IRA violence was regularly denounced from Catholic pulpits. The refusal of the Catholic Church to excommunicate IRA members or label the deaths of the republican hunger strikers as suicides owed far more to a desire to maintain pastoral care than it did to any endorsement of republicanism. Indeed, the Catholic hierarchy and the IRA were regularly at odds, a pattern of enmity seemingly overlooked by Paisley. Paisley's religiosity ensured his repudiation of violence as the means to defend Northern Ireland's position in the United Kingdom. Occasional flirtations with extra-constitutionalism, most notably via the Ulster Protestant Volunteers of the late 1960s and Ulster Resistance (the so-called 'Third Force') during the 1980s, proved short-lived and he consistently condemned sectarian attacks upon Catholics.

Religious Affiliations: How Free Presbyterian is the Modern DUP?

The Free Presbyterian Church has always been tiny. It represented only 0.7 per cent of Protestants at the time of the formation of the DUP and this figure had risen to a mere 1.1 per cent by 2001. Free Presbyterian total membership across Northern Ireland was only 10,068, according to the 2011 census.[19] The 1991 census figure of 12,314 members may have been a peak. Free Presbyterian membership in 2011 amounted to 3 three per cent of the 345,101 Presbyterians and 4 per cent of the 248,821 Church of Ireland identifiers in the same census. By 2011, the number of Free Presbyterians was slightly less than the number of Baptist and Pentecostal church members, whereas in the 1990s, the Free Presbyterian Church was the fourth-largest Protestant denomination.[20] The Roman Catholic Church, with 738,033 members, had a higher membership in Northern Ireland than the Presbyterians and Church of Ireland combined. The DUP has done far better in attracting voters than the Free Presbyterian Church has managed in gaining religious adherents. The Free Presbyterian 10,000 core membership is nonetheless a figure far higher than the number of Northern Ireland electors belonging to the DUP. Moreover, the church has been highly successful in raising funds from its devotees, despite a very restrictive set of rules on how money has to be raised which prohibit even raffles, dinner dances, and jumble sales.[21] This fund-raising has been sufficient to build a small number of Free Presbyterian schools.

Despite its tiny size, the Free Presbyterian Church remains the largest single denominational provider of DUP members. It is remarkable that so many members of a single, tiny church can populate a political party. Table 6.1

Table 6.1 Religious denominations of DUP members, by upbringing and contemporary affiliation (%)

Denomination	Brought up in	Belong to now
Free Presbyterian	13.3	30.5
Presbyterian	39.2	29.1
Church of Ireland/Episcopal	29.8	17.7
Baptist	3.9	4.2
Methodist	4.7	4.2
Protestant-no denomination	1.9	2.5
Christian-no denomination	0.6	1.9
Pentecostal	0.6	1.4
Elim Pentecostal	0.6	1.1
Brethren	1.1	0.8
United Reformed Church	0.6	0.8
Roman Catholic	0.3	0.6
Other	1.7	3.0
Not religious	1.9	2.2

shows denominational affiliations within the DUP, indicating not only that Free Presbyterian membership is very large, but also that a sizeable number of DUP members who switched to Free Presbyterianism were brought up in another Protestant denomination.

It is apparent from Table 6.1 that a large number of Free Presbyterians within the DUP joined the church as well as the party, rather than simply being born into their religious organization. Many were 'born again', in most cases, undergoing conversion from the Presbyterian Church or the Church of Ireland. The number of DUP members raised as Free Presbyterian is high, given the small size of the church, but this represents less than half the picture. The party remains heavily populated with converts to that church.

The non-Free Presbyterian denominational figures in Table 6.1 indicate that DUP membership is otherwise broadly in line with the percentages of the broader Protestant population. Thus, the proportion of DUP Presbyterians, at 29 per cent, nearly tallies with the 32 per cent across Northern Ireland, whilst the Church of Ireland is slightly, but not hugely, under-represented within the DUP, at 18 per cent, compared to the overall 20 per cent amongst Northern Ireland Protestants. Methodists are marginally under-represented in the DUP, the figure of just over 4 per cent being 1 per cent lower than amongst the wider Protestant population. Roman Catholics form 41 per cent of Northern Ireland's population, but their numbers in the DUP are lower than even the smallest Protestant denomination. Equally unsurprising is that the proportion of non-religious members of the DUP is tiny.

As Bruce has demonstrated,[22] Free Presbyterians have been present in large numbers amongst the elected representatives of the DUP. Between 1973 and

Table 6.2 Free Presbyterian and Orange Order affiliation within the DUP, according to type of member

Category	Free Presbyterian	Orange Order
MPs (2010 election)	62.5	75.0
Assembly Members (2011 election)	36.8	50.0
Councillors (2011 election)	39.7	54.2
Ordinary members (2012)	30.5	34.6

2005, nearly two-thirds of DUP members elected to councils or assemblies belonged to the Free Presbyterian Church.[23] Free Presbyterians continued to be present in sizeable numbers in the post-2011 Assembly. Fourteen of the thirty-eight DUP MLAs belonged to the church, whilst Free Presbyterians formed a majority (five of the eight members) of the DUP's 2010–15 Westminster contingent. The percentage figures for Free Presbyterian membership for different levels of the party are summarized in Table 6.2, with membership percentages of the Orange Order (the relationship with which is discussed separately below) also provided as a comparison.

Free Presbyterians remain hugely over-represented, relative to their church's size, at all levels of the DUP, but more significantly amongst its elected representatives, especially in the top tier of Westminster. Nonetheless, Free Presbyterians are no longer an outright majority of the party's elected wing within the Northern Ireland polity, and its former numerical overall dominance is unlikely to be recovered. Amongst the DUP membership as a whole, 70 per cent are outside the Free Presbyterian Church. As a Carrickfergus councillor put it: 'When I joined the party I felt a bit of an outcast because I wasn't part of the church. Now it is accepted that most members of the party aren't part of the church.'[24] One female non-Free Presbyterian DUP councillor in Ballymena recalled, upon election, 'people asking me, "have you left your church"?...they thought it was only the Free Presbyterians' who could represent the party.[25]

The Protestant denominational composition of the DUP alters according to date of joining, with a very significant diminution in the percentage of Free Presbyterians signing up in more recent times. Indeed, it seems certain that Free Presbyterians will soon no longer be the largest denomination. Prior to the 1998 Belfast Agreement, 56 per cent of DUP members were Free Presbyterians. During the period of DUP opposition to the 1998 deal, Free Presbyterian membership still ran at one in five of new members (well down on the early days), but declined to a mere 13 per cent after the 2006 St Andrews Agreement. That some Free Presbyterians still wished to join the party after St Andrews might be seen as remarkable, given their church's unease with the deal, but what the trends show is the DUP becoming a broad

Protestant party, whose future membership will no longer be heavily skewed towards Free Presbyterianism.

Following the Belfast Agreement, the percentage of DUP joiners citing how the party 'suited my Protestant values', as a reason for joining, did not decline markedly (14 per cent, compared to 17 per cent pre-Agreement) and this religiously oriented reason remained the second most frequent explanation for joining, but there was less evidence of a particularly vigorous and exclusivist brand of Protestantism infusing the organization. UUP defectors to the DUP, such as Peter Weir, acknowledged that their original perception of the DUP was that it was 'very narrowly based around the Free Presbyterian Church', but that this was no longer the case, Weir highlighting that in former UUP strongholds such as his Assembly constituency of North Down, 'the vast bulk of DUP members were not from a Free Presbyterian background'.[26] Another UUP defector, now a North Belfast councillor, insisted that he 'never got the sense being in the DUP that it is a political wing of the Free Ps...there was a disconnect between the two even before St Andrews and those who were Free P and DUP were starting to draw the distinction between the two'.[27] Occasional incidences of interdenominational rivalry were evident. A former DUP Lord Mayor of Belfast recalled being asked by a fellow DUP councillor what church he attended and being surprised, after replying 'Stormont Presbyterian', to be told: 'You haven't found freedom yet'. His retort 'I have as many freedoms as I like actually. How many do you have?' 'didn't go down very well'. The former mayor is nonetheless very comfortable with the overall 'strong influence of evangelical Christian faith' within the party, which 'spans a wide spectrum'.[28]

Non-Christians in the DUP are rare. One, a Ballymena councillor, admitted 'on occasions I would be made to feel like an outsider...I would like to see a bit more openness in the members, who are there with strong beliefs, to the likes of me. I am not a disease coming in the midst of them.' This 'outsider' accepted that 'the DUP was built on a strong Christian faith and...is a party that will go forward on its Christian faith'.[29]

The diminution in Free Presbyterian entrants to the DUP is likely to continue. The ending of Ian Paisley's lengthy tenures as the head of both church and party heralded a new era and terminated the obvious link. In a party where rejection of the Belfast Agreement was pervasive, Free Presbyterians were still significantly more likely to have voted no to the 1998 deal. Other (non-Free Presbyterian) very regular church attendees and Orange Order members were also significantly more likely to have voted no to the Belfast Agreement, but Free Presbyterianism was the most significant variable of all, the deal rejected as morally repugnant. Given this, it is perhaps not surprising that a significant proportion of the Free Presbyterian wing of the DUP appeared to be less than enamoured by the Belfast Agreement's 2006 successor. Indeed, some Free

Presbyterians were so offended by the St Andrews power-sharing deal with Sinn Féin that they exited the party, but it is their declining rate of entrance relative to other denominations that is making the DUP now more representative of the broader Protestant population. This diminished velocity of entrance relative to other Protestant church members *preceded* the St Andrews Agreement, as disaffected unionists unconnected to Free Presbyterianism joined the party after the Belfast Agreement.

In January 2008, Paisley stepped down as the leader of the Free Presbyterian Church, quitting as his own church considered whether to stand him down. A commission of the church was undecided whether Paisley should remain as moderator after he had assumed the post of First Minister, following the St Andrews Agreement and restoration of the devolved executive, now headed by the DUP and Sinn Féin. The large number of Free Presbyterians opposed to what Paisley had done meant that his church was irreparably damaged and his own position difficult to maintain. There was considerable hostility, sadness, and a sense of betrayal felt by many church members that Paisley had agreed to share power with people most regarded as unrepentant terrorists, the previous 'enemies of Ulster'. Although Paisley still had majority support for his position at the head of the church he founded, the backing was far from overwhelming. Paisley decided to remove himself from the post, to avoid the considerable risk of humiliation in being pushed.[30] There was a general view that it was impossible for Dr Paisley to maintain both leadership roles, partly because of the physical demands, but also because the inevitable compromises involved in government impinged upon the religious 'purity' of Free Presbyterian positions. Paisley nonetheless felt betrayed, a feeling exacerbated three years later when he was removed as a minister from the Martyrs Memorial Church he established in East Belfast. This sense of betrayal, athough disguised for several years, had extended into the political sphere when Paisley stepped down as DUP leader in May 2008, replaced by the obvious successor, the Elimite Pentecostalist Peter Robinson. Other than in aspects of spiritualism and Pentecostalism (although these are significant), the doctrines of the Elim Pentecostal Church are not markedly different from those of the Free Presbyterian Church.

In shock, the Free Presbyterian Church struggled to recover from the impact of the St Andrews deal, members quitting or engaging in public criticism of some of its political figures. There was talk of 'DUP and TUV churches now...some people disagreed [with St Andrews] and some people agreed, and you found there were some people who didn't like the attitudes of people in church and they left'.[31] Nelson McCausland acknowledged the impact of the St Andrews deal regarding relations with the Free Presbyterian Church. Asked whether that church remained as an organizational point for the party in rural areas, he responded:

No, I think the Free Church has changed markedly, particularly when Dr Paisley retired as moderator and the issues around that. You saw some churches where you had very strong TUV sympathies. In some cases, it has created bitterness between people, which shouldn't happen in a church, but it does.[32]

A further perception was that the division was another stage in the shift in DUP membership, part of a 'deliberate move to bring through people who weren't necessarily traditionally DUP. That includes people who aren't necessarily Free P…there has been an attempt to move away from being too outwardly and overtly fundamentalist. I think there is still a Christian core to the party.'[33]

Levels of Religiosity

Most DUP members are highly religious. Almost all identify with a religion, with only 2 per cent declining to do so, compared to one in five not identifying with a social class. Fifty-nine per cent claim to attend church once a week or more. Table 6.3 measures the avowed church attendance of DUP members, for many of whom the Sabbath remains a crucial day set aside for religious observance, one on which work should not normally be conducted.

Table 6.3 Frequency of church attendance of DUP members

Frequency of church attendance	%
Once a week or more	59
Two or three times per month	16
Once per month	6
Several times per year	8
Less frequently than above	5
Never/no religion	6

Yet the stated level of church attendance is only one indicator of the level of religious observance. The term 'Massing Catholic' once commonly described those Catholics who attended Sunday Mass, but engaged in little or no religious worship for the remainder of the week. If there are equivalents on the Protestant side, perhaps the DUP is not the best place to start searching. The largest category of religious observers within the party is of those claiming to be 'very religious'. Table 6.4 indicates the level of religiosity of DUP members, according to their own evaluation.

DUP members may be somewhat self-effacing. One suspects many offering the self-ascription of 'somewhat religious', the second largest category, might be viewed as very religious in other parts of the UK. There is the suspicion, however, that the DUP membership, although still religious, is less

Table 6.4 Self-evaluation of religiosity by DUP members

	%
Very religious	45
Somewhat religious	39
Not very religious	12
Not at all religious	4

fervent than might have once been the case. To test this, we looked at the importance of the date of joining and also tested for differences in church attendance between pre- and post-Belfast Agreement party joiners. More religious members, as measured by regularity of church attendance ('not religious' categorized as those who never attend services or don't have a religion; 'somewhat religious' as those who attend services once a month or less; and the 'very religious' are members who attend services more than once a month), are clearly found among those who joined the party earlier. This is not merely a consequence of older members being more religious, as when age is also controlled, year of joining the party is still significant. When, instead of the date of joining being deployed as a continuous variable, we looked at members who joined before and after the Belfast Agreement, we found that those who joined after the Belfast Agreement tended to be less religious. Age matters as one might expect, but again, controlling for this variable, we can see a clear difference between levels of church attendance between pre- and post-1998 DUP members. We also found similar effects when the obvious alternative measures, of self-identified level of religiosity—'very', 'somewhat', 'not very', or 'not'—were used.

Even more importantly for an analysis of the DUP, the party's members believe that their party is influenced by religious principles and want the party's outlook to be conditioned in that way. Members were asked, first, 'on a scale of zero to ten, with zero meaning no influence and ten meaning maximum influence, how much influence do you think Faith and Church have upon the DUP?' The response averaged at 7.3, a high figure and one surely marking the DUP as more distinctively religious than most Western political parties. Utilizing the same scale, members were also asked how much influence faith and church *should* have upon the DUP. Whilst the average figure was slightly lower, 6.8 still amounts to a considerable desire for a religious infusion to party ideas. Many members desire that a broad Protestant-Christian ethos should pervade their party, but do not feel that a particular denomination or group should wield exclusive influence. The Creationist Bible group, the Caleb Foundation, attracts the sympathy of some senior DUP members and lobbies for the party to adopt strong moral stances conditioned by a literal biblical interpretation.[34] Yet the foundation's influence is played down by adherents and non-adherents: 'It's not that Caleb has an over influence [sic]; it's just that the DUP has the same views as Caleb', claimed one Coleraine councillor.[35]

Many younger members do not want a departure from the Christian ethos and were content for practices, such as prayers at the start of branch meetings, to continue, whilst acknowledging there was some local variation in whether this is normal.[36] North Belfast members said that prayers preceded meetings 'sometimes but not always' and stressed that 'we wouldn't treat it [a branch gathering] as a religious meeting'.[37] Elected representatives elsewhere in the UK may be uneasy over admitting that faith shapes and maintains their politics; not so in the DUP. This is logical, given the deep religious convictions of many elected members. The party leader, Peter Robinson, argued that the influence of faith 'should be ten',[38] but that a single church should not dominate, a point reiterated by the (Free Presbyterian) Nigel Dodds, who placed the DUP 'in the great tradition of the European parties where Christian Democracy is a mainstream political view'.[39] Newtownabbey councillor Paul Girvan argued: 'Some people say religion and politics should never really mix. I am a total disbeliever in that aspect because I believe politics came about through religion. If you use the Ten Commandments, you can formulate almost every law that you need.'[40] A Belfast city councillor, Christopher Stafford, opined: 'You can't expect them [elected representatives] to simply become irreligious or to leave their personal views to one side because they put their name on a ballot paper, because they are elected.'[41] Whilst distinguishing between party and church, the MLA Jim Wells views the DUP as a bulwark against a Northern Ireland that is 'becoming less and less evangelical, less Christian'.

Those who joined the DUP between the Belfast and St Andrews Agreements, the 1998–2006 period, are the least likely to think that faith and church have maximum (i.e. ten out of ten on the scale) influence within the party. Only 8 per cent of those joining during this period believed that the DUP is dominated by faith and church to the highest possible degree, half the percentage figure recorded for those who joined the party at other times. This is significant in indicating that the religious aspects of the DUP were not seen as extreme by those looking for a new political home as support for the pro-Belfast Agreement UUP slumped after that deal was struck. The 1998–2006 period saw a large influx of former UUP members and supporters, alongside political novices, into the DUP, many due to bitter opposition to the Belfast Agreement. It appears that former UUP supporters did not perceive Paisley's party as an excessively religious vehicle, which may explain why they have felt so comfortable in the DUP since joining. In terms of the perceived level of faith and church influences, denominational and demographic variables are not statistically significant.

In comparing those members who think that faith and church *should* have a very large amount of influence within the party (i.e. those who responded with a 10, on the 0 to 10 scale of desirability) with those who think faith and church should have less influence, there are significant differences between older members and those who joined the party amid the sharp switch in unionist party support during the extraordinary 1998–2006 era. Those most desirous of maximum religious influence upon the DUP are mostly found among 1971–97 joiners (38 per cent). Very few—a mere 14 per cent—of those who joined the DUP between 1998 and 2006 would like faith and church to have such a large degree of influence within the party. This again indicates that the 1998–2006 period of intra-unionist turmoil heralded the arrival of a different type of DUP member, one angered by aspects of the Belfast Agreement and keen to find a superior substitute, but also one less concerned with—or desirous of—the deeply religious ethos which once pervaded the party they now joined. Yet, perhaps surprisingly, this diminished desire for a deeply religiously conditioned party does not necessarily signal the beginning of the end of religious influence within the DUP, in that amongst post-St Andrews DUP joiners, there is a higher number of people believing that religion should have maximum influence, compared to the 1998–2006 intake. However, this is well below the 1971–97 figure.

Free Presbyterianism is a significant factor in shaping views as to the desirability of maximum faith and church influence upon the DUP. Amongst Free Presbyterians, the percentage scoring the desired level of influence as 10 out of 10 was 48 per cent, compared to only 18 per cent of non-Free Presbyterians. Table 6.5 outlines the relative importance of several key variables, including Free Presbyterianism, in the view of the degree of influence that faith and church should have upon the DUP. The desired degree of influence is higher for Free Presbyterian members of the party, the first coefficient in Models 1 to 3. This effect does not disappear when other variables are added in Models 2 and 3. As can be seen in Model 2, sex, age, and social class do not seem to have a significant effect upon the perceptions of desirability of religious influence. In contrast, the year of joining does have a (weakly) significant effect, as the desired level of influence is higher among those who joined the party earlier. The effect of the year of joining is nonetheless slight and disappears when religiosity (as measured by church attendance) is introduced (Model 3). This is because the wave of members who joined more recently, in the immediate post-Belfast Agreement the years, tend to be less religious, and these somewhat less religious, members think that faith and church should have less influence.

In assessing religious influence upon the DUP, it is necessary to assess whether the party is a product of the historical institutional religious affiliations of many of its members, or whether its policies merely reflect a conglomeration of personal beliefs, an aggregation of individual faith held by

Table 6.5 Multivariate model of DUP members' views on the desirability of faith and church influence upon their party

How much influence do you think faith and church should have?	(1)	(2)	(3)
VARIABLES	Faith and church should have maximum influence	Faith and church should have maximum influence	Faith and church should have maximum influence
Free Presbyterian	2.214***	1.765***	0.786**
	(0.342)	(0.378)	(0.368)
Year of joining		0.102*	0.0292
(length of membership)		(0.0591)	(0.0549)
Age		0.00279	0.00260
		(0.0109)	(0.00976)
Male		0.107	0.0598
		(0.364)	(0.326)
Working class		-0.0319	0.000712
		(0.327)	(0.291)
Church attendance			-0.965***
(from more to less)			(0.111)
Constant	6.104***	5.572***	8.199***
	(0.190)	(0.630)	(0.659)
R^2	0.108	0.112	0.317

Standard errors in parentheses
*** $p<0.01$, ** $p<0.05$, * $p<0.1$

its adherents. Clearly, the DUP's Christian ethos and outlook remains. As a female County Down councillor put it: 'I'm a Christian and that is why I am in the DUP. I'm not sure if I wasn't a Christian that I would be in the DUP.'[42] The party leader is in no doubt that individual faith, not institutional church loyalty, should hold sway:

> I don't think that the church should have any influence on it [DUP policy]. People's own faith will guide them in terms of their outlook on life and therefore, from a structural institutional point of view, it [the score] should be a zero, but from a personal point of view, it should be ten...Individuals are what they are because of the beliefs that they hold and nothing will be held more sincerely than whatever their religious beliefs are.[43]

A minority of members are concerned about the risk of dilution of the party's Christian ethos. A Lisburn councillor declared: 'Out of all my concerns, this is my main one. There would be more of a liberal wing coming in.... There is a lot of watering down and liberalization of some members which will impact the party. We can be a broad church, but we cannot take our eyes off the Christian values.' Overall though, members are sanguine over prospects for the continuation of the party's Christian-based outlook.[44]

Inter-Community Relations

Most DUP members believe that there is discrimination against Protestants in Northern Ireland, differing only over its extent. Half think that there is 'a lot' of prejudice and a further 42 per cent think there is a 'little'. Only 9 per cent declare 'hardly any' prejudice exists and the percentage stating 'none' was below 1 per cent. Despite these perceptions, there is optimism over Protestant–Catholic relations. Only 8 per cent thought they had worsened over the previous five years, whereas 59 per cent felt that they had improved.

Ninety-one per cent of spouses of DUP members are also Protestants (if not necessarily belonging to the same denomination as their husband or wife), although this exclusivity is unexceptional by Northern Ireland standards, and the surprise is perhaps that 7 per cent have married outside their own religion (a further 2 per cent of members claimed no religious affiliation). Prominent DUP members have also adjusted to family marriages to partners beyond the Reformed faith. A senior elected party representative commented: 'My son is married to a Roman Catholic. Do I love him any less? No. I had to go on that journey, an acceptance of how I was going to deal with this. They love each other and that is all that matters.'[45] On the issue of 'mixed marriages', party members are frank in their concerns, as Table 6.6 indicates. Acceptance of inter-faith marriages is significantly lower among Free Presbyterians, compared to other DUP members, who overall are not enamoured of such unions.

There is also considerable caution evident over educational integration, as evidenced in Table 6.7. The segregationist attitudes are surprising, given that the party leadership has regularly called for greater educational integration in recent times. Peter Robinson's pleas that Northern Ireland needs such integration were reinforced by US President Obama on his visit to Northern Ireland in 2013, when he questioned the continuation of religiously segregated schools. In terms of wider society, the DUP-Sinn Féin-led executive produced Shared Future plans in 2013, calling for a removal of the

Table 6.6 DUP members' attitudes to 'mixed marriages'

Would you yourself mind or not mind if one of your close relatives were to marry someone of a different religion?	%
Would mind a lot	54
Would mind a little	21
Would not mind	22
Don't know	3

Table 6.7 DUP members' attitudes to integrated education

If you were deciding where to send your children to school, would you prefer a school with children of only your own religion, or a mixed-religion school?	%
Own religion	58
Mixed religion	34
Don't Know	8

Table 6.8 The significance of Free Presbyterianism and social class in attitudes to mixed marriages and mixed schooling

	(1) Would mind a lot if close relative married someone from another religion	(2) Would prefer a school with children only of own religion
Free Presbyterian	1.497***	1.157***
	(0.286)	(0.300)
Working class	0.113	0.737***
	(0.243)	(0.261)
Constant	–0.190	–0.0187
	(0.165)	(0.168)
Pseudo R^2	0.075	0.068

Standard errors in parentheses
*** $p<0.01$, ** $p<0.05$, * $p<0.1$

most visible physical symbols of division, the so-called peace walls, within ten years.

Free Presbyterian hostility to 'mixed' marriages and educational integration is stronger than that found elsewhere in the DUP. This is shown in Table 6.8. Model 1 in the table looks at those who would mind a lot if a family member married someone of a different religion, versus those who answered 'would not mind' or 'would mind a little'. In addition to the Free Presbyterian test, we also look for class effects, based upon the self-ascribed social class reported by members, but these are not significant. With regard to schooling, however, reported in Model 2, working-class DUP members are, along with Free Presbyterians, significantly more likely to favour separate schools. This may reflect the acute patterns of residential segregation evident in working-class areas. Integrated schools are rarer in such areas and travel across urban areas to other schools that are not overwhelmingly Protestant in composition may still be an unattractive option. For Free Presbyterian members, scepticism towards mixed-religion schools is more religiously based.

Although not shown in Table 6.8 and with a weaker effect than Free Presbyterian membership, older people tend to be significantly less prone than young people to accept inter-faith marriages. However, when it comes to attitudes to mixed schooling, age does not have a significant effect.

The DUP and the Orange Order

As could be seen from Table 6.2 earlier, Free Presbyterianism is not the only common characteristic of DUP members. More than one-third belongs to the Orange Order, double the percentage holding trade union membership, as one comparison. Some members were frank in interviews in asserting that Orange Order membership meant more to them than their party membership as, despite scepticism over whether the Order held much contemporary influence, they felt particularly valued within its ranks. Historically, such claims might have come from UUP members. Asked how they felt about the Orange Order, 51 per cent of DUP members declared they 'strongly like' the organization, with a further 26 per cent expressing a liking. Only 7 per cent of DUP members said they were against the Order.

The level of Orangeism increases in the upper echelons of the party. Three-quarters of the party's Westminster elected representatives elected in 2010 were members of the Orange Order and half of the party's thirty-eight Assembly members elected in 2011 also belonged. Eleven were members of the separate Apprentice Boys of Derry. A very slight majority of DUP councillors are also Orange Order members. This very sizeable Orange representation amongst DUP elected members has tended to be overlooked amid the concentration upon the party's Free Presbyterians.

Some of these Orange Order members are also Free Presbyterians and the onetime suspicion between the Free Presbyterian Church and the Orange Order appears to have dissipated. Previously, several of the most religiously observant Free Presbyterians believed that the Orange Order was overly cultural and insufficiently religious in outlook, a number claiming it was unchristian to belong to the Order. Ian Paisley eschewed membership of the Loyal Orders throughout his leadership of the DUP and a small number of DUP Free Presbyterians preferred membership of the Apprentice Boys of Derry. Indeed, it was claimed of Paisley that he 'always maintained an adversarial, obstructionist stance towards the Order and UUP'.[46] Some DUP members favoured the Independent Orange Order and preferred its stricter emphasis upon religious observance, notably, respect for the Sabbath and for its strict prohibitions on alcohol.[47] DUP members disdained the formal association between the Grand Lodge at the head of the Order and the UUP, a link finally ended in 2005.

For its part, the Grand Lodge refused to recognize the Free Presbyterian Church as an 'official' Protestant denomination until 1998, meaning that Free Presbyterian ministers could not become chaplains of local lodges or hold events in Orange halls.[48] In more recent times, the coexistence of Orange and Free Presbyterian affiliation has become more normalized and Free Presbyterians form 4 per cent of the Order's 30,000+ membership, not far

Table 6.9 The significance of Free Presbyterian and Orange Order membership in levels of activity within the DUP

VARIABLES	(1) Level of activity	(2) Level of activity
Free Presbyterian	0.554***	0.380***
	(0.132)	(0.136)
OO member	0.283**	0.234*
	(0.131)	(0.130)
Age		−0.00443
		(0.00506)
Joining date		0.0811***
(length of membership)		(0.0239)
Constant	−0.255***	−0.309
	(0.0975)	(0.221)
R^2	0.091	0.148

Robust standard errors in parentheses
*** p<0.01, ** p<0.05, * p<0.1

off the percentage provided by Methodists, with Presbyterians of the non-Free hue forming half of the entire membership total.[49]

The importance of Free Presbyterian and Orange Order membership within the DUP does not lie merely in percentages. Those individuals tend to be the most active within the party. We show this in the models in Table 6.9. Free Presbyterians and Orange Order members are more likely than other members to declare themselves 'very active', claims that can hardly be written off as mere bragging. In the case of the Orange Order, the activity effect is especially significant. It is the Orange contingent not, contrary to popular myth, the Free Presbyterians, who really count as the most active. However, when taking into account the different degrees of activity (from 'not at all active' to 'very active'), rather than just those self-reporting as 'very active', Free Presbyterians and Orange Order members stand out as above average, in terms of level of activity.

It is nonetheless necessary to move beyond subjective levels of involvement and create a more objective measure of activity, by employing five different indicators of how often members have participated in the following activities: leaflet delivery, doorstep canvassing, canvassing by phone, branch meetings, and annual conference attendance. A composite measure was created, using principal component analysis. The measure takes higher values the more active the members, in terms of their self-reporting of participation in these activities. Table 6.9 reports the findings. Using this more objective measure, albeit one still constructed from self-reported levels of activities, Free Presbyterians and Orange Order members again appear involved in party activities significantly more often than other members (Model 1). The effect is very strong for both groups. It is also necessary to control for age and length of membership, as palpably these may affect the level of activity. Free Presbyterians are more likely to be older members. Model 2 controls for the date of joining, because longer term members have had more chances to participate in activities. Indeed, the positive coefficient indicates that those who joined the party earlier have been involved in party activities more often. The model also controls for age, in case younger members are more active, but this does not seem to be the case. Once these variables are controlled for, the significance of being an Orange Order member declines slightly, but Orange Order members remain significantly more active than the rest of the party, even more so than Free Presbyterians, who are, in turn, significantly more active than other DUP members.

Shared hostility towards the Belfast Agreement and associated political changes brought the Free Presbyterian Church, DUP, and Orange Order together far more than alterations in religious positions. The DUP appealed to the Orange Order in criticizing the 'scandalous denial of civil and religious liberties to the Loyal Orders', insisting that the Parades Commission 'has failed in its operation'.[50] The Grand Master of the Orange Order from 1996 to 2010, Robert Saulters, declined to support the UUP and severed his organization's link to the UUP (the Order jumped first, before it was pushed). It became almost routine for DUP elected representatives to also belong to the Orange Order. The DUP became the 'go-to' party for the Order, the party instrumental in, as examples, delivering community space funding schemes to help improve Orange halls and in exempting Orange halls from rates.

As parading controversies increased during the 1990s, the DUP stoutly defended the right of the Orange Order to march along its 'traditional routes'. Famously, Ian Paisley linked arms with the UUP leader, David Trimble, in 1995 after completing a parade along the Garvaghy Road contested by republicans. The victory proved pyrrhic as, from 1998 onwards, the Orange parade along the same stretch of road was banned and a Parades Commission was established to regulate routes and the timings of marches. Opposed by the DUP as an affront to Protestant-Orange cultural traditions, the Parades Commission has long been the subject of party ire. In findings not dissimilar to the survey of Orange Order members conducted by McAuley et al.,[51] a majority of DUP members advocate unfettered marching rights for the Orange Order, as Table 6.10 indicates.

Unsurprisingly, Orange Order membership is a significant variable, in terms of those with a propensity to support unfettered parading rights, whilst long-standing DUP members are also significantly more insistent that there should be no nationalist restrictions.

In 2010, however, the Grand Lodge declined the DUP's proposals for the replacement of the Parades Commission by a less prescriptive code of conduct,

Table 6.10 DUP members' views on Orange Order parading rights

	%
The Orange Order should be able to march wherever it wants, without restrictions	58.3
The Orange Order should be able to march through mainly nationalist areas only if there is prior agreement with nationalist residents	31.6
The Orange Order should not be allowed to march through mainly nationalist areas	5.2
Other views	4.9

but one with some pressure upon the Order to engage in local dialogue. The refusal angered the DUP and emphasized that, despite the considerable overlap of membership, institutional relations between the party and the Order would never be as cosy as those between the UUP and the Orange Institution in the first half-century of Northern Ireland's existence. The Order's rejection of the DUP proposals frustrated party leader Robinson:

> The Grand Lodge is of course a very diverse organization. It also has people who are from the PUP/UVF end and people from the TUV and from the Ulster Unionist Party. Sadly, when it came to this kind of issue, for political reasons, many of these people ganged up. I think they did a disservice to the organization that they were voting within by carrying their party politics with them. I think we have seen some of the outcome of the mistakes that they made in not accepting the proposal that was put.[52]

At the 2013 talks on parades, flags, and the past, brokered by the US diplomat, Richard Haass, the Reverend Mervyn Gibson, the Orange Order's Chaplain, acted as a negotiator for the DUP to ensure that there would be no repetition of the 2010 problems. Any replacement of the Parades Commission would need to be acceptable not merely to the DUP, but most crucially, to the Order's representative on the DUP's talks team. The Haass talks concluded without agreement at the end of 2013.

Morality and Modernization

Given its church influence, it is scarcely surprising that the DUP has been involved in high-profile campaigns on moral issues. However, the distance between political and religious matters has widened. As one example, the party was obliged to drop opposition to infringements of the Sabbath, such as the Sunday opening of shops and bars, in favour of allowing people local choices.[53] It would have been politically unpopular with its much less religious urban loyalist support base for the DUP to have maintained diehard opposition to 'breaches' of the Sabbath, such as drinking, gambling, and other forms of entertainment. Although the DUP membership is largely socially conservative and greatly influenced by Christian belief, the party does not necessarily impose its religiously derived views upon the electorate. The nature of the DUP's Protestant influence is that it permits individual choice. If electors wish to behave in a 'sinful' way, that is their choosing.[54] There is also recognition of the limits to what can be imposed. As Nigel Dodds put it, 'I think there is a greater recognition that in a modern pluralist society you simply cannot impose your views on everyone else regardless of how they feel.'[55]

Nonetheless, the bulk of the DUP has remained opposed to some significant societal changes introduced by the Westminster government, two examples being opposition to gay marriage and rejection of calls to extend the 1967 Abortion Act to Northern Ireland. Ian Paisley's 'Save Ulster from Sodomy' campaign of the late 1970s was not run by the DUP, although it naturally became closely associated with the party. The DUP was powerless in opposing the decriminalization of homosexual acts in 1982, undertaken by a British Government administering direct rule over the region. Since the replacement of direct rule by devolution, the party has jealously guarded its regional opt-outs from UK legislation on some social issues. The South Down MLA Jim Wells claimed that 'if we had the 1967 Abortion Act in Northern Ireland, 91,000 people, precious human beings, would have been murdered, killed through abortion', and he was proud that 'the overwhelming majority in the Party would be anti-abortion, anti-gay marriage, anti- so much of what is happening in our society that worries me intensely'.[56]

The DUP membership profile offers a picture of a traditionalist outlook on marriage. Almost two-thirds are in (heterosexual) marriage; one-quarter are single. Only 4 per cent are divorced or separated (6 per cent are widowed) and a mere 1 per cent state they are 'living as married', a cohabitation without marriage rate surely below what would be found in surveys of British political parties. An often religiously derived conservatism runs through the party. During the 1990s, Peter Robinson made clear his view that homosexuality was 'unnatural':

> Of course it is. There can't be the slightest doubt that it isn't a natural act. I take it ill that these people set themselves up as being the arbiters of these matters. The Supreme Moral Arbiter is Almighty God. And he has decreed that homosexuality is unnatural. That's the end of the matter. It's not open to discussion.[57]

Robinson's wife, Iris, spoke out very strongly against homosexuality when DUP MP for Strangford. In June 2008, she described it as an abomination and recommended homosexuals seek psychiatric counselling,[58] before telling a Northern Ireland Grand Committee meeting at Westminster later that month that 'there can be no viler act, apart from homosexuality and sodomy, than sexually abusing innocent children'.[59]

Yet Northern Ireland, having been the last part of the UK to decriminalize homosexuality became, in 2004, the first region where a gay civil partnership was registered, both measures introduced under British direct rule. Rather than attacking homosexuality outright, the DUP has tended to concentrate upon particular aspects of related legislation when Northern Ireland may be affected and stressing the need for regional autonomy on such issues. Thus, the party's 1998 Assembly election manifesto argued:

> In many regards, the law in Northern Ireland recognises the Christian ethos of the province.
>
> The DUP has opposed plans to allow homosexual couples to adopt children in Northern Ireland. The vast majority of people in the province are totally opposed to this measure.
>
> For such an emotive issue, changes should only be made where it is clear that there is overwhelming public support or through a local Assembly.
>
> A mountain of social science, the world's major religions, common sense, and observation tell us that children have the best chance to thrive in married mother and father-based families.[60]

In 2013, the DUP tabled a Petition of Concern to prevent nationalist and non-aligned MLAs introducing same-sex marriage in Northern Ireland. Whilst this stance is vulnerable to challenges via human rights courts, for so long as the DUP (and other unionists) have a veto, it is unlikely to change.

DUP members remain robust in their views on abortion and homosexuality, and these issues remain of considerable concern to many. The strident denunciation of gay marriage as 'wrong, anti-biblical, and against common decency', to cite a Strabane DUP councillor's comments, was common amongst interviewees.[61] A Coleraine councillor described homosexuality as 'unnatural', 'a deviation', 'an insult to your own nature', and opined that 'legalizing it opens up a whole new dimension in morality', whilst insisting that 'People who have those tendencies...one should have sympathy for them rather than bringing a big rod down on them'.[62]

An Ards councillor offered similarly typical thoughts:

> I believe scripturally it is wrong. I would be against same sex marriage and civil partnerships as well. I believe that with the Word of God it's wrong. But I also know people who are homosexual and as a councillor I have worked for homosexuals. I don't discriminate against anybody who comes to me for help. I believe to love the sinner and not the sin. But I believe that marriage between one man and one woman was ordained by God. [63]

The DUP MP for North Antrim, Ian Paisley, Jr., insisted that his constituency correspondence had been 'overwhelmingly' against gay marriage.[64] The Lagan

Table 6.11 DUP members' views on homosexuality

Proposition: 'Homosexuality is wrong'	%
Strongly agree	53.6
Agree	12.6
Neither Agree nor Disagree	11.0
Disagree	6.6
Strongly Disagree	16.2

Table 6.12 DUP members' views on whether abortion should be legalized in Northern Ireland

	%
Strongly agree	6.0
Agree	9.3
Neither Agree nor Disagree	11.5
Disagree	13.9
Strongly Disagree	59.3

Valley MLA and executive minister, Edwin Poots, argued that gay campaigners 'won't leave it alone until they are demanding marriage within churches and that would be something that would cause a huge amount of damage'.[65]

Table 6.11 shows that almost two-thirds of DUP members believe that homosexuality is wrong, with a majority strongly believing this. Although a liberal wing does exist within the DUP, it is very much outnumbered by those members with traditional, hardline moral views. Conservatism is usually religiously derived.

Similar religiously inspired conservatism is also evident on the abortion issue. Table 6.12 indicates that nearly three-quarters of members are opposed to the legalization of abortion in Northern Ireland.

On abortion, Edwin Poots, appointed Health Minister in 2011, asserted:

> We would look on abortion very negatively, in that it is being used as a form of contraception. There are myriad methods of not getting pregnant. You can engage in sexual activity and not get pregnant...we do see that a person's life does not begin whenever they leave the womb. It starts before that...It is somewhat farcical that they [elsewhere in the UK] are trying to save babies at 24 weeks of age, but that at 23 weeks [the foetus] can be aborted.

The DUP does not impose its social and moral conservatism upon a hostile electorate demanding progressive change; rather, it tends to reflect the cautious, religiously influenced conservatism of electors, which may be waning, but is still very significant. Only a minority of Northern Ireland's electors support a woman's right to choose on abortion, with this figure as low as one in five amongst the over-65s.[66] On same-sex marriage, one relatively youthful and liberal DUP MLA argued:

> I certainly don't believe that the majority of people in Northern Ireland are in favour of it. I certainly don't believe anywhere close to the majority of my voters are in favour of that. It would be suicidal for me to get up and say I am in favour of this if I was. I'm not, but if I was.[67]

Several interviewees claimed that support for the St Andrews Agreement was influenced by the threats of the British Government to extend the 1967 Abortion Act to Northern Ireland if a devolved power-sharing deal could not be reached. This may be a further attempt at justification of a controversial deal by DUP representatives. No mention of abortion legislation appears in the accounts of the St Andrews talks provided by Tony Blair's Chief of Staff, Jonathan Powell, or the Secretary of State, Peter Hain, and, even if it had been a threat, it may have been a bluff.[68] Whilst Blair, Powell, and Hain were determined to concentrate DUP minds, the threat of direct rule and the ending of Assembly member salaries might have been sufficient. Direct rule with a greener tinge would not automatically have led to an agenda of social liberalism, given the conservatism of northern nationalists and the Irish Government. Nonetheless, that DUP elected members highlighted fears over abortion liberalization in respect of a deal concerned entirely with other matters indicates how the issue has salience for the party. The near-uniformity of DUP views on issues such as same-sex marriage and abortion means that unity holds, regardless of whether a party whipping operation was deployed or a free vote permitted in the Assembly. The party leader declared:

> I am fairly relaxed. You will get the same result, whichever route you take. It wouldn't matter in the DUP if it was a free vote. People would be freely voting the way they always have. I think the very fact everybody knows what everyone else's views in the party would be on these kinds of issues makes it comfortable for us to organize ourselves within the party for them.[69]

Non-religious DUP members often agree with the wider party on social and moral issues. As one example, a female Castlereagh councillor declared: 'I wouldn't class myself as religious, but I don't agree with abortion. I don't agree with gay marriage either...abortion I see more as a moral issue than a religious issue.'[70] The thrust of party attitudes on such issues is unlikely to alter dramatically, even if the DUP does become more secular in composition.

Liberal voices on social and moral issues can occasionally be heard. They tend to be muted and grounded in the personal choices domain. On homosexuality, they argue that what occurs in the private domain is up to individuals. On abortion, a Carrickfergus elected representative proclaimed that, 'unless you walk a mile in their shoes, I don't think you can judge. It is not for me to go around and tell some young girl there, who is pregnant, who doesn't want to be pregnant, that it [abortion] is the wrong thing to do.'[71] One MLA said that 'privately' she believed that abortion should be legalized. Whilst not agreeing with 'abortion on demand' or it 'being used as a form of contraception', the Assembly member argued that 'it's a very sensitive issue and one on which we should be free to vote'.[72]

To what extent are there internal differences within the DUP on issues such as homosexuality and abortion, according to age, gender, or religious denomination? The percentage of women stating that homosexuality is wrong is lower than that of men, but only slightly, at 60 per cent compared to 68 per cent. Age is a more important variable, based upon raw percentages. The proportion of members that think homosexuality is wrong increases with age (Table 6.13). About half of those aged 17–35 agree with the statement, but this rises to 70 per cent amongst those aged 56 or older.

The multivariate analysis in Table 6.13 provides an outline of which aspects of membership really matter. Once the year of joining is introduced, age ceases to be significant (Model 1). Importantly, negative attitudes towards homosexuality are significantly reduced among those who joined the party more recently, regardless of the age of those joiners. However, it is difficult to separate both effects, as most of the recent joiners are fairly young. What can be said for certain is that early joiners of the DUP, regardless of their age, display more negative attitudes towards homosexuality. The gender of members does not have a significant effect on this and neither does social class.

Model 2 introduces another variable, Free Presbyterianism, which is highly significant. Negative attitudes towards homosexuality are more, prevalent among Free Presbyterians. When this variable is added to the model, the effect of the year of joining vanishes. So the main reason why we found older people, who joined the party at an earlier stage, have a more negative opinion about homosexuality, at this stage of the model, lies in the fact that there are many more Free Presbyterians among them. However, it is important not to simply assume that Free Presbyterianism is the defining religious aspect of negative attitudes towards homosexuality. Model 3 refines the previous model by introducing religiosity as a variable, measured by regularity of church attendance. Religiosity is highly significant, with members who are highly religious people even likelier to hold negative attitudes towards homosexuality. Indeed, general religiosity is sufficiently significant to absorb the effect of Free Presbyterianism. So, it is not age, the year of joining, or even Free Presbyterianism that principally explains attitudes towards homosexuality, although they are all factors in their own right. Controlling for those factors, it is religiosity, regardless of Protestant denomination. In summary, the key to explaining attitudes towards homosexuality within the DUP is the presence of very religious members, often, but not exclusively,

Table 6.13 Multivariate model of types of DUP members and attitudes to homosexuality ('homosexuality is wrong': 1 = strongly agree; 5 = strongly disagree)

VARIABLES	(1)	(2)	(3)
Year of joining	−0.0983***	−0.0380	−0.00246
(length of membership)	(0.0371)	(0.0421)	(0.0442)
Age	−0.00428	−0.00754	−0.00652
	(0.00700)	(0.0071)	(0.00744)
Male	−0.271	−0.310	−0.350
	(0.243)	(0.247)	(0.251)
Working class	0.157	0.190	0.154
	(0.215)	(0.220)	(0.226)
Free Presbyterian		−0.839***	−0.348
		(0.285)	(0.302)
Church attendance			0.418***
(more to less)			(0.0765)
Cut1	−0.661	−0.810*	0.386
	(0.414)	(0.420)	(0.476)
Cut2	−0.105	−0.221	1.047**
	(0.412)	(0.416)	(0.480)
Cut3	0.400	0.297	1.633***
	(0.411)	(0.415)	(0.485)
Cut4	0.827**	0.744*	2.097***
	(0.414)	(0.418)	(0.490)
Pseudo R^2	0.014	0.025	0.062

Standard errors in parentheses
*** $p<0.01$, ** $p<0.05$, * $p<0.1$

Free Presbyterians, who joined the party earlier and therefore tend to be older, displaying very conservative attitudes.

On the legalization of abortion, there are scant differences between men and women, the latter less than 1 per cent more likely to support the lifting of the current prohibition. Age differences are slightly greater but still fail to reach statistical significance. One-third of those aged 17–35 believe that abortion should be legalized, compared to one-quarter of the members above that age range, but differences are not significant.

Table 6.14 explores key variables on attitudes towards abortion. Those joining the DUP earlier exhibit more negative attitudes towards abortion, offering stronger disagreement with its possible legalization in Northern Ireland. Age, sex, and social class do not have a significant effect. However, Free Presbyterians exhibit significantly more negative attitudes than other members (Model 2). When religiosity is introduced, again, based upon frequency of church attendance (Model 3), the effect of year of joining vanishes. The reason is probably the same as explained in previous models regarding homosexuality, namely, that the very religious within the DUP are so against

Table 6.14 Multivariate model of types of DUP members and attitudes to the legalization of abortion (negative attitudes towards abortion, ordinal logit)

VARIABLES	(1)	(2)	(3)	
Year of joining	0.166***	0.0872**	0.0465	
(length of membership)	(0.0425)	(0.0439)	(0.0447)	
Age	−3.58e−05	0.00148	0.00327	
	(0.00757)	(0.00757)	(0.00767)	
Male	0.0666	0.0295	−0.0264	
	(0.269)	(0.273)	(0.279)	
Working class	−0.0692	−0.165	−0.236	
	(0.226)	(0.233)	(0.237)	
Free Presbyterian		1.536***	1.037***	
		(0.330)	(0.350)	
Church attendance			−0.480***	
(from more to less)			(0.0753)	
Cut1	−1.982***	−1.983***	−3.587***	
	(0.481)	(0.479)	(0.570)	
Cut2	−0.949**	−0.934**	−2.464***	
	(0.463)	(0.462)	(0.517)	
Cut3	−0.265	−0.219	−1.618***	
	(0.443)	(0.443)	(0.485)	
Cut4	0.324	0.422	−0.873*	
	(0.442)	(0.439)	(0.468)	
Pseudo R^2	0.0268	0.0592	0.113	0.124

Robust standard errors in parentheses
*** p<0.01, ** p<0.05, * p<0.1

abortion that it usurps in importance the period when a member joined the party. However, this time, the effect of Free Presbyterianism continues to be significant. Thus, whilst negative attitudes towards abortion are significantly stronger among more religious members, Free Presbyterians exhibit even more negative attitudes than very religious members of other denominations.

Conclusion

The DUP remains a party comprising a mainly deeply religious membership, whose political outlook is very markedly and unashamedly influenced by their faith. Free Presbyterianism is no longer the dominant force it was within the DUP and the party has seen an influx of a different type of member since the 1998 Belfast Agreement—one decidedly less likely to be Free Presbyterian and less socially conservative than the type who joined the DUP in earlier years. Yet, as one of the party's elected representatives put it, the DUP 'does have some way to go in terms of being seen to dispel perceptions of being very socially conservative and a party which would have affiliations to certain brands of Protestant Christianity'.[73] The party is nonetheless moving at a significant pace towards a less skewed denominational composition, in terms of its Protestant make-up. It is now more Orange than Free Presbyterian.

Given that Free Presbyterianism is a highly significant variable, in terms of hardline attitudes to the contemporary social and moral issues of homosexuality and abortion analysed here, it might be tempting to conclude that the diminution of Free Presbyterian representation within DUP ranks might shift party attitudes. After all, denomination matters, whereas gender and social class barely matter attitudinally on these issues and age does not matter much. The temptation to assume the subsiding of the Free Presbyterian contingent will elicit rapid internal change ought to be resisted. It is worth recalling that religiosity was an even more significant attitudinal variable than membership of a particular denomination. For the DUP to change its attitudes on these key questions would require the party membership to become substantially less religious. There is some evidence of dilution in terms of the post-1998 joiners, but a more secular DUP is a long way off, the maximum influence of faith upon outlook endorsed from the party leader downwards. The DUP has become a broader party, its religious ferocity now far less overt, but it remains resolutely and unashamedly guided by points of Protestant and Christian principle.

Notes

1. S. Bruce (1986) *God Save Ulster! The Religion and Politics of Paisleyism*, Oxford: Oxford University Press.
2. C. Smyth (1987) *Ian Paisley: Voice of Protestant Ulster*, Edinburgh: Edinburgh University Press.
3. See as examples, Bruce (1986) *God Save Ulster!* S. Bruce (2009) *Paisley: Religion and Politics in Northern Ireland*, Oxford, Oxford University Press; G. Ganiel (2008) *Evangelicalism and Conflict in Northern Ireland*, Basingstoke: Palgrave Macmillan; J. MacLeod (2000) *The Second Disruption: the Free Church in Scotland and the Origins of the Free Presbyterian Church*, Edinburgh: Tuckwell; N. Southern (2005) 'Ian Paisley and Evangelical Democratic Unionists: An Analysis of the Role of Evangelical Protestantism within the Democratic Unionist Party', *Irish Political Studies*, 20/2, 127–45.
4. D. Calvert (1981) *A Decade of the DUP*, Crown: Belfast, 6.
5. D. Paisley, 'Foreword', in Calvert, *Decade of the DUP*, 3.
6. C. Smyth (1986) 'The DUP as a Politico-Religious Organisation', *Irish Political Studies*, 1/1, 33–43.
7. Interview with Craigavon councillor, 5 Nov. 2012.
8. Interview with Nigel Dodds MP, DUP deputy leader, 3 July 2013.

9. Interview with David Simpson MP, 3 July 2013.

10. Smyth, *Ian Paisley*, 68.

11. Interview with Ballymoney councillor, 4 Oct. 2012.

12. Interview with Nelson McCausland MLA, Belfast, 9 Jan. 2013.

13. Interview with Jonathan Bell MLA, Strangford, 9 Nov. 2012.

14. G. Spencer, *Protestant Identity and Peace in Northern Ireland*, Basingstoke: Palgrave Macmillan.

15. D. Cooke (1997) *Persecuting Zeal: A Portrait of Ian Paisley*, Dublin: Brandon.

16. Revd Ian Paisley (1994) 'The Ulster Crisis! The Bible Way Forward', speech at Martyrs Memorial Free Presbyterian Church, Belfast, 4 Sept.

17. F. Holmes (2000) *The Presbyterian Church in Ireland*, Dublin: Columba.

18. See Bruce, *Paisley: Religion and Politics*, 73–4.

19. Northern Ireland 2011 Census, Religion Report, QS218NI, <http://www.nini s2.nisra.gov.uk/public/Theme.aspx>, accessed July 2013.

20. S. Bruce (1994) *The Edge of the Union*, Oxford: Oxford University Press, 19.

21. Bruce, *Paisley: Religion and Politics*, 142.

22. Bruce, *God Save Ulster!* and *Paisley: Religion and Politics*.

23. Bruce, *Paisley: Religion and Politics*, 207.

24. Interview with Carrickfergus councillor, 27 Feb. 2013.

25. Interview with Ballymena councillor, 4 Oct. 2012.

26. Interview with Peter Weir MLA, 9 Nov. 2012.

27. Interview with Belfast councillor, 16 Oct. 2012.

28. Interview with Councillor Gavin Robinson, 11 Jan. 2013.

29. Interview with Ballymena councillor, 10 Oct. 2012.

30. E. Moloney (2008) *Paisley: From Demagogue to Democrat*, Dublin: Poolbeg.

31. This split was highlighted by DUP student members. DUP student focus group, Belfast, 22 Jan. 2013.

32. Interview with Nelson McCausland MLA, Belfast, 9 Jan. 2013.

33. DUP student focus group, Belfast, 22 Jan. 2013.

34. *Belfast Telegraph*, 1 Sept. 2012: 'Creationist Bible Group and its Web of Influence at Stormont', <http://www.belfasttelegraph.co.uk/news/politics/creationist-bible-gr oup-and-its-web-of-influence-at-stormont-28787760.html>, accessed July 2013.

35. Interview with Coleraine councillor, 4 Oct. 2012.

36. Interview with Coleraine councillor, 4 Oct. 2012.

37. North Belfast focus group, Belfast, 26 Feb. 2013.

38. Interview with First Minister Peter Robinson MLA, Stormont, 25 June 2013.

39. Interview with Nigel Dodds, 3 July 2013.

40. Interview with Paul Girvan MLA, Ballyclare, 7 Jan. 2013.

41. Interview with Belfast councillor, Belfast, 9 Oct. 2012.

42. Interview with Banbridge councillor, 19 Sept. 2012.

43. Interview with Peter Robinson, 25 June 2013.

44. Interview with Lisburn councillor, 19 Sept. 2012.

45. Interview with senior elected representative, 3 Oct. 2012.

46. E. Kaufmann (2007) *The Orange Order: A Contemporary Northern Irish History*, Oxford: Oxford University Press, 84.

47. D. Bryan (2000) *Orange Parades: The Politics of Ritual, Tradition, and Control*, London: Pluto, 115–16.
48. J. McAuley, J. Tonge, and A. Mycock (2011) *Loyal to the Core? Orangeism and Britishness in Northern Ireland*, Dublin: Irish Academic Press, 162–4.
49. McAuley et al., *Loyal to the Core?* 161.
50. Democratic Unionist Party (2003) *The DUP's Vision for Devolution: Northern Ireland Assembly Election Manifesto*, Belfast: DUP, 29.
51. McAuley et al., *Loyal to the Core.*
52. Interview with Peter Robinson, 25 June 2013.
53. Southern, 'Ian Paisley and Evangelical Democratic Unionists'.
54. Bruce, *Paisley: Religion and Politics.*
55. Interview with Nigel Dodds, 3 July 2013.
56. Interview with Jim Wells MLA, Stormont, 9 Jan. 2013.
57. Peter Robinson, DUP leader: interview with Joe Jackson, *Hot Press*, 24 Aug. 1994.
58. BBC Radio Ulster, Stephen Nolan Show, 6 June 2008.
59. Minutes of the Northern Ireland Grand Committee, 17 June 2008, available at <http://www.publications.parliament.uk/pa/cm200708/cmgeneral/nigc/080617/80617s02.htm>, accessed 4 July 2013.
60. DUP (1998) *Your Best Guarantee for the Future of Northern Ireland: Assembly Election Manifesto 1998*, Belfast: DUP, 4.
61. Interview with Strabane councillor, 16 Apr. 2013.
62. Interview with Coleraine councillor, 4 Oct. 2012.
63. Interview with Ards councillor, 11 Sept. 2012.
64. *BBC Question Time*, 23 May 2013.
65. Interview with Edwin Poots MLA, Lisburn, 10 Jan. 2013.
66. *Belfast Telegraph*, 30 Nov. 2012, <http://www.belfasttelegraph.co.uk/news/local-national/northern-ireland/abortion-45-want-a-liberalisation-of-the-law-in-northern-ireland-28999931.html>, accessed July 2012.
67. Interview with County Down MLA, Stormont, 9 Jan. 2013.
68. P. Hain (2012) *Outside In*, London: Biteback; J. Powell (2009) *Great Hatred, Little Room: Making Peace in Northern Ireland*, London: Vintage.
69. Interview with Peter Robinson, 25 June 2013.
70. Interview with Castlereagh councillor, 28 Feb. 2013.
71. Interview with Carrickfergus councillor, 27 Feb. 2013.
72. Interview with County Antrim MLA, 2 Oct. 2012.
73. Interview with Newtownabbey councillor, 11 Sept. 2012.

7

Electoral Politics

The electoral rise of the DUP was far from inevitable. DUP members who joined the party before the Belfast Agreement were frank in interviews about never expecting their party to become the dominant force within unionism. This section does not dwell on the near three decades the DUP endured in the electoral doldrums, but instead concentrates upon the dramatic realignment in unionism after the 1998 Agreement. That deal was constructed amid the expectation that the UUP and SDLP would be the dominant communal forces. Yet within a decade the DUP had seen off the UUP to assume a hegemonic role within unionist politics, acquiring members and support from unionism's historically dominant force. The DUP picked off the UUP's talent, outwitting its rival as it strove for a better deal than the 1998 version and offered impressive internal discipline, which contrasted sharply with the rudderless chaos engulfing the UUP. The chapter analyses the data on the views of members on electoral consolidation, exploring whether tactical alliances, or full distancing from the UUP, are seen as the most appropriate way forward. The section assesses the willingness of DUP members to offer lower preference votes to other unionist parties. It also considers whether it is possible for the DUP to extend its support base beyond the sectarian divide and attract backing from Catholics.

This chapter also considers how the DUP saw off a challenge from hardliners, who defected from the party arguing that its compromises in the 2006 St Andrews Agreement betrayed unionism in a manner similar to the concessions to republicans offered by David Trimble's UUP in 1998. Not everyone was impressed by the sharing of power with republicans, given previous rejectionist DUP utterances. Opposition largely coalesced around Traditional Unionist Voice (TUV), under the leadership of former DUP MEP Jim Allister, which was highly critical of the DUP's willingness to operate joint rule with the 'unrepentant terrorists'. Internal DUP discipline, the improved terms of the 2006 deal, and the new stability of power-sharing all helped to ensure that the DUP leadership avoided the earlier fate of its UUP counterparts.

Overtaking the UUP: Responses to the Belfast Agreement

Prior to the Belfast Agreement, even many staunch members of the DUP expected to remain members of an oppositionist party, not one of government. Although relations with the UUP varied greatly according to locality, the DUP were often treated with a combination of scepticism and scorn by the dominant party. A founder of the DUP recalled that 'when I was on Omagh council, I was a pariah—they [the UUP] wouldn't even shake hands with me...we were detested'.[1] Oliver Gibson's description of the UUP as 'dumb', 'steeped in nepotism', and with a 'terrible degree of incompetence', is stronger than that offered by most DUP activists, but there is little doubt that there was strong mutual antipathy between the two main unionist parties, not fully glossed over by elite-level cooperation against unpopular measures, notably the 1985 Anglo-Irish Agreement.

Although support for the DUP was substantial, the UUP's electoral hegemony appeared unchallengeable. The Deputy Leader of the DUP, Nigel Dodds, acknowledged that when he joined the party in the late 1970s 'there was absolutely no prospect of the DUP at that stage coming anywhere near power, not only because the DUP was where it was at that stage, but because the idea there would be stable workable devolution in Northern Ireland in the '70s was a pipedream'.[2]

Only in European elections was the DUP the persistent victor over the UUP, as Table 7.1 shows. Those 'beauty contests', not regarded as of major import by many electors, saw the personal charisma of Paisley triumph amid the sure knowledge that two unionist candidates, in addition to one nationalist, would be returned anyway, given the three-member Single Transferable Vote system utilized in Northern Ireland. Otherwise, only in the 1981 local elections, conducted at a time of acute crisis amid republican hunger strikes, did the DUP beat the UUP. UUP dominance was invariably exaggerated at elections, in that the DUP did not contest some UUP-held seats, either due to holding no hope, or for fear of allowing a nationalist victory. Nonetheless, the overall picture was very much one of the UUP as the natural repository of the Protestant vote.

Table 7.2 shows how electoral fortunes changed dramatically in the aftermath of the Belfast Agreement. Unionist reaction to the Belfast Agreement proved fatal for the UUP, the old party of unionism polling only half of the DUP's vote by the second decade of the twenty-first century. Beset by crisis, the UUP underwent regular changes of leadership, as the DUP, in contrast, maintained an upward trajectory, other than during a brief wobble after the party concluded the St Andrews Agreement.

The orthodoxy at the time of the Belfast Agreement was to write the DUP's political obituary, as the defeated party's leaders were jeered out of the May

1998 referendum count by a variety of shades of unionist opinion, ranging from UUP moderates to loyalist paramilitaries. Seventy-one per cent
of Northern Ireland's population had backed the deal, including an admittedly uncomfortably low proportion (57 to 43 per cent) of Protestants.[3] The
assumption of the British and Irish Governments was that a UUP-SDLP axis
would dominate Northern Ireland's new devolved arrangements. It was an
assumption widely and understandably shared in academia. The DUP had,
after all, lost the referendum, Northern Ireland was making political progress,
paramilitary ceasefires were in place, and the DUP, as a militant party of 'no'
unionism, looked dated. Few academics (and we do not claim to have fore-
seen the rapid rise of the DUP either) would have profoundly dissented from
the assessment at the onset of the ceasefires that 'the party most threatened
by long-term peace is the DUP...its leadership derives almost exclusively
from evangelical Protestants who have thrived on a politics of fear. In conditions of peace and if proportional representation applies in all elections, there
is no compelling reason why the DUP's electoral bloc should hold together.'[4]
Such predictions underestimated the capacity of the DUP to tap into continuing unionist fears, amid imperfect peace and resentment over aspects of
the peace deal. Tapping into such concerns was juxtaposed with the DUP's
increasing (but far from transparent) hints that it would not oppose a deal
with republicans, provided that the terms were right.

The DUP's electoral rise was derived from its capacity to act as an ethnic
tribune party, articulating the perceived interests of a particular community
more effectively than any rival.[5] The interests of that community were in local
self-government and acceptance of power-sharing. Thus, the DUP needed to
offer the prospect of the realization of secure devolved government (quietly
abandoning the party's earlier commitment to majoritarian government as
unrealistic), but on better terms than those achieved by the UUP the first time
around. That the DUP waited until Sinn Féin had moved away from the IRA
and obliged that party to support Northern Ireland's police force represented
significant advances on the 1998 deal agreed by Trimble. The thesis offered
by some commentators, that what emerged was a triumph of the extremes,
ignored the centripetal tendencies being displayed by the emergent onetime

Table 7.1 DUP-UUP electoral competition, 1973–2011,
by type of election

Contest	DUP % vote	UUP % vote
Westminster	16.7	30.4
Local	19.7	27.1
Assembly (1998-2011)	25.7	18.0
European	28.7	20.0

Table **7.2** DUP-UUP electoral competition,
1973–2011: percentage vote share by decade

	DUP	UUP
1970s	12.5	31.7
1980s	23.4	29.0
1990s	19.2	26.4
2000s	26.7	19.6
2010s (to 2011)	27.2	14.5

hardline representatives of the unionist and nationalist communities. The DUP was cognizant that support for *aspects* of the Belfast Agreement, such as the Assembly, power-sharing, and even North–South bodies, increased amongst its voters from 1998 to 2003.[6] Yet those voters disliked the continuing presence of the IRA, the non-completion of decommissioning, and the refusal of Sinn Féin to back the state's police force. Attention to those details by the DUP would bear even greater electoral fruit than that gathered in the first (1998–2003) phase of the post-Belfast Agreement era.

The inner confidence of DUP members that their party would benefit from exposing the weaknesses of the deal was unshaken. Nigel Dodds claims to have taken 'enormous reassurance from the vote at the referendum: what it showed was a substantial number of people who opposed the Belfast Agreement and virtually all of them would be our voters'.[7] Naturally, those 'no' voters also included DUP members. A minority, 16 per cent, did vote yes in May 1998, but 68 per cent of current DUP members voted no, resistant to the considerable television and press coverage in favour of the deal. As the somewhat Belfast Agreement-sceptic *News Letter* is the only newspaper read regularly by a majority (62 per cent) of members, (followed by the one-third who read the *Belfast Telegraph*, with no British-wide newspaper having a regular DUP readership above 19 per cent of members) it is perhaps understandable that many were impervious to external pressure to back the Agreement. Of the other 16 per cent of the membership, most were ineligible to vote (too young in most cases), with a small number choosing not to participate in the referendum. Asked how they would vote today on the Belfast Agreement, only 22 per cent say they would vote yes, confirming the long-held DUP view that it was a bad deal for unionism.

Although the DUP led the opposition to the Belfast Agreement on a political basis, there was a quasi-religious dimension to the no campaign, based around the claimed immorality of the deal. The Orange Order was more explicit than the DUP on this theme, insisting that the Agreement was one which 'no Protestant in good conscience could support'.[8] There were strong religious and denominational effects in how DUP members voted in the referendum on the 1998 deal. Table 7.3 examines the impact of some of those key variables. The reference category is 'voted against', so the models try to elucidate three behaviours: didn't vote, voted against the Belfast Agreement, and voted in favour.

The first model looks at whether DUP members belonging to the Church of Ireland voted differently to the rest of the DUP, to test for a more moderate wing, but they did not. The second model adds several other variables. DUP members that used to belong to the UUP are significantly more likely to have abstained rather than voted against the Belfast Agreement, but they are not significantly more likely to have voted yes. At first glance, this may surprise, given the large influx of former UUP members joining the DUP due to hostility to aspects of the Belfast Agreement, and it should be noted that most did indeed vote no. Those who did abstain were wrestling with conflicting loyalties in 1998, torn between fidelity to a UUP party leadership backing the deal, but unable themselves to declare outright support given its troubling aspects. Such UUP members, soon to defect, would have readily supported the constitutional apparatus of the Belfast Agreement, but struggled with its other aspects, such as prisoner releases and Sinn Féin in government without prior or even parallel IRA decommissioning guaranteed. They became increasingly unhappy with the failure of their party leadership to 'nail down' those difficult issues, but in 1998 a greater propensity to abstain was understandable.

Model 2 also shows that Free Presbyterians are significantly less likely to have voted yes (i.e. more likely to have voted against), as also were Orange Order members. The third model adds religiosity to the equation, based upon self-reported regularity of church attendance, from weekly to never. More religious members are more likely to have voted against the Belfast Agreement. Significantly, the effects of Free Presbyterianism and Orange Order membership do not vanish after adding religiosity. This suggests that Free Presbyterians and Orange brethren had a particularly negative opinion towards the Belfast Agreement, compared even to other very religious members of the DUP. Some struggled to adjust their mindset when the time came for the DUP to act as midwife to the St Andrews successor deal in 2006, treating the revised package with similar hostility.

At the Assembly election held in June 1998, already there were clear signs that DUP optimism might be fulfilled, as the party narrowed the gap on the UUP to a mere 3 per cent vote share. Largely unnoticed at the time and admittedly partly explained by vote management, the average vote for the DUP's thirty-four Assembly candidates *exceeded* that for the forty-eight fielded by the UUP by 704 votes, the DUP average first preference vote being 4,292 (bettered only by the SDLP), compared to 3,588 for the UUP.[9] From thereon, the DUP's support rose dramatically. The growth of the DUP between 1998 and 2003

Table 7.3 Multivariate analysis of DUP members' voting on the Belfast Agreement, May 1998 Referendum

	Model 1		Model 2		Model 3	
Vote Belfast Agreement:	Abstention (v voted no)	Yes (v no)	Abstention (v voted no)	Yes (v no)	Abstention (v voted no)	Yes (v no)
Free Presbyterian			−15.16	−1.436***	−14.40	−1.029**
			(974.3)	(0.443)	(669.5)	(0.472)
Church of Ireland	0.942	0.161	0.228	−0.152	0.308	−0.133
	(0.728)	(0.377)	(0.774)	(0.419)	(0.778)	(0.440)
Ex-UUP			2.268***	0.0194	2.274***	−0.102
			(0.836)	(0.365)	(0.839)	(0.380)
Orange Order			−1.329	−1.257***	−1.386	−1.063***
			(0.853)	(0.384)	(0.888)	(0.390)
Church attendance (from more to less)					−0.000361	0.269***
					(0.230)	(0.096)
Constant	−3.507***	−1.427***	−3.618***	−0.675***	−3.616***	−1.429***
	(0.414)	(0.161)	(0.747)	(0.224)	(0.928)	(0.371)
Pseudo R^2	0.004		0.130		0.152	

Dependent variable: vote on the referendum on the Belfast Agreement (those ineligible to vote in 1998 are excluded). Standard errors in parentheses.

*** $p<0.01$, ** $p<0.05$, * $p<0.1$

did not derive from a collapse of UUP support. The UUP's percentage first preference vote share *increased* marginally between those elections. However, the DUP's share grew much more substantially to overtake the UUP, rising from 18 per cent to 26 per cent between the two elections, as the party captured the votes of fringe unionist parties, who virtually disappeared. Added to skilful constituency targeting, the DUP Assembly total exceeded that of the UUP. Collapse for the UUP came after the 2003 Assembly election as, with the Assembly already suspended indefinitely since October 2002, its section of the unionist electorate gave up on the prospect of a restoration of political institutions under the worthy but often chaotic UUP leadership of Trimble, some abandoning voting outright. Trimble's ousting at the 2005 general election was the most visible manifestation of a humiliating performance, which saw the UUP lose all bar one of its seats (with the one successful candidate, Lady Sylvia Hermon, later to leave the party).

The DUP was always careful not to block off the possibility of a renegotiated deal, even at the height of its attacks upon the Belfast Agreement. Nonetheless, the initial focus was more upon the ills of the Agreement rather than a clear indication of what might constitute a satisfactory replacement. The party's 1998 Assembly manifesto fed upon fears amongst a wide unionist constituency of hostile or merely uncertain unionists, without directly pledging to reverse what had happened, which would have been a feat beyond the party's gift. Electors were told:

> Whether you are one of the majority of Unionists who voted 'No' or someone who voted 'Yes' with reservations, we share your concerns about:
> Unreconstructed terrorists in government
> The retention of illegal weapons by terrorists
> The plans for the destruction of the RUC
> All-Ireland bodies with executive powers
> The mass release of terrorists
> British sovereignty being eroded[10]

At the 2003 phantom Assembly election—to an institution which had not sat for the previous thirteen months and would not resume until 2007—the DUP was even more strident in its denunciation of the 1998 deal, confident that the arguments against the Belfast Agreement had gained further traction. Electors were asked whether they wanted Sinn Féin/IRA 'appointing High Court judges', 'to control public appointments', 'to run policing', and 'to control Criminal Justice', the DUP claiming that, with the UUP leading unionism, 'all of this will happen'.[11] Nonetheless, the party stressed its positive credentials, the title of its manifesto referring to the party's 'vision for devolution', and indicated that it sought a mandate for a new agreement, not a permanent absence of a deal. Negativity towards what the UUP had negotiated was tempered by an outline of what might replace the Belfast Agreement—a more satisfactory arrangement which did not involve terrorists in government—even if there was again a lack of precision over what might follow. The DUP tactics worked, the party gaining 26 per cent of the vote, beating the UUP by 3 per cent and gaining three more Assembly seats than its rival.

Having overhauled the UUP at the previous Assembly contest and made huge advances at the 2005 General Election, the DUP entered the May 2007 Assembly election confident of further gains—one reason the party was so keen to proceed. Yet there was some risk to the party, as the unionist electorate realized that the DUP was about to embark on a route not exactly highlighted as the basis of the party during the previous thirty-six years of its existence: running a government of Northern Ireland with Sinn Féin. The DUP leadership had long signalled that it had no intention of pulling the entire edifice down and, more mutedly, hinted that the size of Sinn Féin's mandate would need to be recognized. Nonetheless, the appearance of Paisley and Adams together in March 2007, as the visible beginning of the outworking of the agreement reached at St Andrews five months earlier, had startled. Until St Andrews, the DUP's public line to its electorate had been that a deal could not happen, as Sinn Féin would never change. As deputy leader, Peter Robinson had insisted in 2005:

> If you ask us, 'What if, at some later stage, republicans meet your requirements and do become involved in exclusively democratic politics, will you join them in government?' we say to respond to that question would require us to contemplate a hypothesis which is not simply suspect and implausible, but quite frankly, requires us to suspend intellect, judgement, and logic.[12]

The party leader had also offered the public message that no deal would be possible, telling his party conference that autumn that 'any man that talks to Sinn Féin or the Dublin government about the internal affairs of Northern Ireland is a traitor'.[13]

Having engaged in precisely such talks and cognizant of the need to now reassure the unionist base in a potentially tricky contest, the DUP sensibly highlighted how the party had forced Sinn Féin ministers to support policing and the courts. With some chutzpah, given the solo runs and rotation of its own ministers from 1998–2002, the DUP also stressed that 'all ministers will be bound by decisions of the Executive, allowing a more coherent administration. Ministers will no longer be able to act alone, in narrow party interests.'[14] The DUP used the St Andrews Agreement revisions to the Belfast Agreement as a rallying call for a maximum DUP vote. The party's 2007 Assembly election manifesto emphasized the headcount aspect of the contest:

> The new arrangements also mean that the large political party in the Assembly will be entitled to nominate a First Minister. The DUP is the only political party which can keep Sinn Féin from holding this position. At the last Assembly, the DUP was only 15,000 votes ahead of Sinn Féin, so it is vital for unionists to unite behind the DUP.[15]

Post-St Andrews, the DUP continued to advocate, if not particularly loudly or convincingly, given what had been agreed, for the replacing of mandatory coalition by a voluntary partnership in the executive. The party also advocated for the replacement of the Unionist, Nationalist, or Other designation system in the Assembly by weighted majority voting, claiming that 'we do not envisage the present arrangements as anything other than short-term',[16] although the length of 'short-term' was, understandably, not defined. In terms of 'normal' politics, the DUP was conscious of the need for cross-class appeal. The party's strong support for academic selection played well with middle-class beneficiaries, precisely those former UUP supporters whose backing the DUP now needed to retain. Cognizant of the need to maintain its loyalist working-class base, however, the DUP policy was tempered by acknowledgement of the need to revise the eleven plus transfer test, often failed by working-class Protestants, to diminish its stresses and make it less vulnerable to social-class effects, in terms of the pass rate. Anxious to stress the economic dividends of peace, the party also pledged to cut the costs of politics and bureaucracy, via populist plans to cut the number of government departments and the size of the Assembly.

It is possible to pick holes in the DUP's electoral performance. Abstention has been a common response of the unionist middle classes. Turnout in unionist-held constituencies by the time of the DUP's spectacular 2005 General Election win, in which the party captured half of Northern Ireland's parliamentary seats, was 60 per cent, 11 per cent lower than in nationalist-held seats. The DUP performed best in areas of low turnout, whereas Sinn Féin's vote was positively correlated to high turnout.[17] Whilst turnout in nationalist areas was falling more sharply than in unionist constituencies by 2010, there remained a substantial differential. Only a slight majority (55 per cent) of voters bothered to go to the polls in unionist-held constituencies in that year's General Election. The DUP were winning big and had a vibrant party, but amongst Protestants more generally, the enthusiasm was hardly overwhelming, if judged on the admittedly reductionist measure of propensity to vote. Whilst it would be absurd to speak of a DUP victory by default, the success of the party was enhanced by the turning away of many unionists, hitherto UUP supporters, from the electoral process altogether. Based on its vote shares, the DUP is slightly over-represented in political institutions, other than on local councils. At the 2011 Assembly election, under the proportional STV system, the party emerged with 35 per cent of the seats on 30 per cent of the vote. In the 2009 European election, the DUP won one of the three seats with less than one in five of first preference votes, and following the first-past-the-post 2010 Westminster election, the DUP held 44 per cent of the parliamentary seats on a 25 per cent vote share. [18]

The Brief Electoral Threat from Traditional Unionist Voice

A brief threat to the DUP emerged in the immediate aftermath of the St Andrews Agreement. Having rejected the 2006 deal, Jim Allister formed the Traditional Unionist Voice (TUV) in December 2007, claiming his new party represented all that the DUP had stood for prior to what was concluded on Scotland's east coast. Although the DUP performed well in the 2007 Assembly election, increasing its vote share by over 4 per cent and gaining six seats, the unionist electorate did not have any significant organizational repository for its disaffection at that stage. Moreover, the DUP's impressive performance owed much to the unionist electorate's determination to remove any slight risk (and the threat was indeed small) of Sinn Féin becoming the largest Assembly party and thus providing the First Minister.

As the electorate saw the outworking of the St Andrews deal—the DUP sitting alongside the republicans they had denounced for so long, at the head of the Northern Ireland Executive—there was considerable disquiet. The DUP's base, in the words of its soon-to-be leader Peter Robinson, had been underprepared, as the party 'wasn't travelling at the same pace' as its leadership, and there was a need for a 'clearer view beforehand of what we were prepared to settle for'.[19] After all, the party had contested the 2005 general election arguing that mandatory coalition was wrong, yet now readily acknowledged Sinn Féin's place as the joint head of precisely such an arrangement. Meanwhile, the TUV promoted the message from Sinn Féin's Martin McGuinness that the First and Deputy First Minister were equals, to foment unionist discomfort. Dr Paisley had apparently dedicated his career to making a former IRA man his equal in government. That McGuinness declared, six months into the arrangement, that there 'had not been one angry word' between him and Paisley merely added to Allister's wrath—and opportunity to promote discontent.[20]

The consequence of the lack of DUP preparation of its supporters was a short-lived threat from the TUV. At the Dromore by-election in 2008, the DUP lost 40 per cent of its support, some of which defected to the TUV. With the TUV capturing 20 per cent of first preference votes, a DUP electoral strategist acknowledged that 'the TUV and Jim Allister challenge has not been well managed'.[21] On a rising tide and with a strong incumbency factor, as a sitting MEP, Allister polled 66,000 votes, almost 14 per cent of the total, in the 2009 European election. Although the DUP's Diane Dodds was elected and Allister lost his seat, her party lost almost half of the 175,761 cast for Allister as DUP representative in the previous European contest and trailed Sinn Féin by nearly 8 per cent, in a contest which had always previously seen the DUP comfortably topping the poll.

However, as power-sharing embedded, the DUP's support stabilized, whilst the TUV failed to build on its initial promise, increasingly seen as a one-man band. Although the party leader, Peter Robinson, surprisingly lost his East Belfast Westminster seat to the Alliance Party in 2010, this was due to non-related financial and personal issues, rather than a wider disaffection with his party. At that General Election, the TUV amassed only 26,000 of the 66,000 votes gathered just one year earlier. It was apparent that the only person likely to be elected to the Northern Ireland Assembly in the 2011 election was Allister himself. This duly came to pass, as the TUV took less than 3 per cent of the vote, and Allister was only elected for the sixth North Antrim seat on the final count, after polling 10 per cent of first preference votes. The

TUV acquired six seats in the accompanying council elections. According to Peter Robinson:

> None of us ever believed that the TUV would surpass the DUP. We knew they had the ability to damage us and maybe damage us to an extent that would allow the Ulster Unionist Party to come back into some credible position. I think there was an acceptance by most of us who would have looked strategically at it that there was going to be damage, but bit by bit our support base was going to come back when all the scaremongering was seen to be fairly hollow.[22]

Many DUP interviewees look more in sorrow than anger at Allister, acknowledging his forensic debating capabilities. The DUP leader adopts a less sanguine take, eschewing rapprochement and insisting, 'I don't think there is room for Jim Allister in any party. He is extremely negative and nit-picking. There isn't a positive bone in his body. He was born for opposition. He is not born to be in a party of government.'[23] DUP MLA Paul Givan argued:

> I didn't think it [the TUV] would be a serious threat, more because the individuals that formed the TUV were people that we were quite happy to get rid of. Some of them were problematic for us within the party and therefore, put them together in one group and they inevitably would be problematic with each other. Really, they weren't going to present a serious political threat to us: also, as far as I am concerned, we have the evangelical fundamentalist base still with us.[24]

For his part, Allister is scathing about even those DUP MLAs who might be considered most sympathetic to his own organization, referring sarcastically to the 'intellectuals'. His view of those who remained in his old party remains uncompromisingly dismissive (see Chapter 2), whilst he argues of the St Andrews deal that 'the cleverest wheeze of all was the wheeze at St Andrews to convert the filling of the First Minister's post to the biggest party…all you have to do is turn up at an election and say, "you might have your problems with us, but it is us or Martin McGuinness. Vote for us to keep Sinn Féin out"'.[25] Operating in isolation in the Assembly, Allister has been a significant presence, instrumental in introducing legislation preventing individuals convicted of substantial prison sentences from working as special advisers to ministers, a measure enacted after Sinn Féin's employment of a former IRA prisoner, Mary McArdle, in such a capacity. Asked, however, what he would have done differently, Allister, whilst insistent that his departure from the DUP was 'right and necessary', ruefully, perhaps jokingly, declared 'Stay at the Bar'.[26]

The Cross-Class Basis of DUP Support

The ascendancy of the DUP reflected a shift from the class-oriented model which had dominated pre-Belfast Agreement intra-unionist electoral contests.

Evans and Duffy's analysis of electoral data in the late 1980s and early 1990s found that Protestants in the lower social classes, the young, the least qualified, the less religious, and those living in areas containing very few Catholics were most likely to support the DUP, with the middle-class salariat much more likely to back the UUP. [27] Their work confirmed the more working-class and secular bases of the DUP's support, which contrasted with the religious fervour of the leadership and members. It also argued that there was a strong left-right element to intra-unionist competition, with left-wing electors, on strictly economic issues, more favourably disposed to the DUP. [28] However, the conflation of 'left' or 'right' labels with constitutional stances, overshadowing those economic issues, can make their application problematic.

The analysis by Evans and Tonge of later electoral and social attitudes surveys, up to 2006, found much had changed amongst the DUP's support base. Whilst the young, not socialized in the UUP's hegemonic era, remained more likely to vote for the DUP, along with the less religious, the DUP's transformation in fortunes has come about via its attraction of middle-class support. [29] Whilst backing for the DUP had risen across all social classes, the steepest ascent was amongst the salariat, where support had risen from not much above 0 in 1989 to over 40 per cent by 2006. [30] Concurrently, the left-right dimension to DUP-UUP electoral competition had markedly diminished. [31]

By the time of the post-St Andrews Agreement Assembly election in 2007, the DUP had assumed the status of a 'catch-all' party within the unionist bloc. Although DUP interviewees often insisted that there remain UUP voters who will never change allegiance, former UUP voters had been attracted in large numbers, as had the Orange vote. At the 2005 General Election, 60 per cent of Orange Order members voted DUP. [32] A century after the Ulster Unionist Council united political and Orange unionism, the Grand Lodge severed the relationship with the UUP, against a backdrop of mass defection to unionism's other political force. Amongst younger (under 35 years old) Orange Order members, the DUP's lead was four-to-one, although amongst those longest socialized in the era of UUP dominance, there was evidence of the resistance to the DUP acknowledged by interviewees. Amongst the Orange brethren aged over 55, the UUP clung onto a lead—although of only 3 per cent. [33] The DUP has been successful in harnessing support among younger Protestants more generally, the most detailed annual survey reporting a near three-to-one lead over the UUP amongst 18–24-year-old Protestants by 2010. [34] Concurrently, the DUP had not merely captured UUP voters; it had turned some into members. Only two-thirds of those belonging to the DUP have always voted for the party. Twenty-eight per cent used to vote UUP, but switched to the DUP, and 5 per cent voted for another party (not the UUP), but changed allegiance.

Vote Transfers and Unionist Electoral Unity

The substantial body of former UUP members in the ranks of the DUP is more likely than other members to support electoral alliances between their old and new parties to maximize the chances of unionist candidates, but the difference is not marked. Such alliances command strong support throughout the DUP, with 82 per cent in favour. Only 12 per cent of DUP members think their party is too positive towards other unionist parties, most being content with current attitudes towards those rivals.

Notwithstanding the occasional promotion of Unionist unity candidates and a feeling that the UUP has been 'seen off', the DUP's senior representatives remain critical of their biggest unionist rival. According to Nigel Dodds:

> The UUP are asking, 'Where can we get some traction with the public?' They have tried getting into bed with loyalist paramilitaries. They have tried getting into bed with the Tories. 'Let's try this sort of coalition between all the discontented, let's get in with UKIP and TUV and Tom, Dick, and Harry'...it won't work. Fundamentally, Ulster politics has come down to, it is Sinn Féin or it is the DUP.[35]

Given the asymmetry of strength, a full-blown DUP-UUP merger would be akin to that of a cat and a canary, even allowing that there remain significant pockets of UUP strength. The most senior of the defectors from the UUP, Jeffrey Donaldson, praised UUP stalwarts but argued that he could 'see the terminal decline of the UUP' some time before he joined the DUP because of its internal divisions, lack of strategic leadership, and its demography, observing:

> There was rarely a meeting I attended where I was not the youngest person. The average age of the Ulster Unionist Council was well in excess of 50, maybe in excess of 60. I could see the party was going to struggle in five or six years' time unless there was change. The change didn't come. Too many members of the Ulster Unionist Council put their party loyalty before the need to recognize that change was necessary. They are still doing it. The orchestra on the deck is playing a different tune, but the boat is still going down.[36]

As the bitterness of the Belfast-to-St Andrews Agreement era subsided, the obvious question begged was the utility of having separate unionist parties. Episodic talks over unionist unity have been held by senior DUP and UUP officials. Two separate sets of discussions were held in early 2010, prior to that year's general election. One set of talks involved the Conservative Party, which eventually went into that election in an alliance with the UUP, entirely unproductive for either side. The Orange Order, which views itself as the most important conduit for unity, also brokered discussions. In 2012, unionist unity talks were revived without the sanction of the UUP leader at the time, Tom Elliott, with Elliott's successor, Mike Nesbitt, also unaware of the moves.[37]

Most DUP members acknowledge that there are scant differences between their party and the UUP. In a typical response, one MLA, who enjoyed cooperative relations with the UUP in his locality, suggested of the gap between the two parties that 'everyone would agree that has closed in recent years...I still believe the DUP would be much more on the ground, much more focused on community issues',[38] whereas the UUP was seen as aloof, still with the remnants of lofty 'Big House' unionism, struggling to adapt to reduced circumstances. Divisions are history and personality based, rather than amounting to anything of long-term policy significance since power-sharing embedded. The attitude of many DUP members to the UUP is one of indifference, rather than deep antipathy. Asked how they would describe their feelings about the UUP, the largest single category of response from members was that of 'neither like nor dislike', as Table 7.4 shows. In a party where preferences and likes are usually very marked, indifference was an unusual finding.

The UUP is the only party to which a majority of DUP members are likely to offer a lower preference transfer vote, under the Single Transferable Vote system used for all non-Westminster election contests, as Table 7.5 indicates. Given the DUP's vote surpluses and intelligent constituency vote management, transfers to the UUP by DUP supporters have generally been cost-free, bolstering the unionists' overall representation in the Assembly without ever harming the DUP's return of Assembly members and consequent number of ministerial portfolios, under the d'Hondt allocation system.

There is a DUP hardline group of nearly one-quarter of party members likely to give a lower preference vote to the TUV. However, much more important is the fair degree of tactical electoral support for the UUP, in terms of lower preference transfers. The lack of propensity of DUP members to switch across the sectarian divide to the Social Democratic and Labour Party (SDLP) or Sinn Féin is, unsurprisingly, replicated amongst the broader electorate. The remarkable nature of Northern Ireland's consociation is laid bare in Table 7.6, which demonstrates the very low level of cross-community vote transfers from the

Table 7.4 Attitudes of DUP members to other political parties

	(%)				
	Strongly Like	Like	Neither Like nor Dislike	Against	Strongly Against
UUP	10.6	23.2	43.0	17.3	5.9
PUP	0.6	7.3	25.9	23.7	42.5
TUV	0.6	13.5	21.1	24.4	40.4
Alliance	1.7	4.3	29.7	32.3	32.0
SDLP	0.0	1.4	10.7	30.7	57.1
Sinn Féin	0.0	0.3	1.2	11.6	87.0

Table 7.5 DUP members' likelihood of voting for a candidate from another party

	Certain	Very Likely	Fairly Likely	Fairly Unlikely	Very Unlikely	No chance
	(%)					
Ulster Unionist Party	12.7	19.8	39.3	12.1	7.3	8.8
Traditional Unionist Voice	4.2	6.8	13.9	12.5	12.2	50.4
Progressive Unionist Party	2.6	3.8	12.3	19.3	17.8	44.2
Alliance Party	1.2	3.3	9.8	17.2	20.1	48.5
Social Democratic and Labour Party	0.3	0.9	5.5	10.8	22.7	59.8
Sinn Féin	0.3	0.9	0.0	1.2	7.6	90.0

Table 7.6 Lower preference vote transfers from DUP first preference voters, 1998 and 2011 Northern Ireland Assembly elections (as a percentage of votes available for transfer)

Transfer from DUP to	1998	2011
DUP	76.0	73.8
UUP	19.5	18.2
Alliance	3.0	4.4
SDLP	8.8	1.0
Sinn Féin	0.7	0.3

DUP. These have not increased at all since the Belfast Agreement and indicate the size of the electoral chasm across which elite level power-sharing has been built. The leaderships of the DUP and Sinn Féin may dominate power-sharing at Stormont, but below that tier, the mutual antipathy between their respective electorates remains stark.

DUP transfers to the UUP are reciprocated at a similar rate, but the dearth of UUP votes means there are far fewer to distribute and the benefit to the DUP is minimal. Other parties receive scant assistance from first preference DUP voters. The hostility is returned from nationalist voters. The percentage of Sinn Féin first preference voters transferring across to the DUP was a paltry 0.1 per cent at the 2011 Assembly election, amounting to a mere 217 votes (the UUP received an even lower percentage of transfers), and SDLP to DUP transfers amounted to a very modest 2 per cent of those available. The avowed willingness of voters to straddle the divide is slightly higher. Five per cent of unionists say they would be likely to give a lower preference vote to a nationalist candidate and 9 per cent of nationalists say likewise about a unionist candidate, with age significant—younger voters are more likely to straddle the divide[39]—but these figures have yet to be realized in elections. When electoral spring does arrive, the thawing may be rapid, but thus far, the

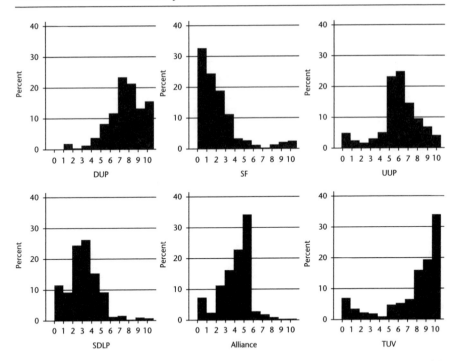

Figure 7.1 DUP members' perceptions of parties on a left-right scale (0 = left, 10 = right)

DUP continues to attract overwhelmingly unionist votes. According to the annual survey of Northern Irish opinion, only 1 per cent of Catholics support the DUP and only 9 per cent of electors with no religion back the party.[40]

Antipathy towards nationalist parties is not merely due to their Irish nationalism. They are also seen as dangerously left-wing. DUP members were asked to place political parties on a left-right scale, where 0 meant left and 10 meant right. The results are shown in Figure 7.1. Sinn Féin is seen as a very left-wing organization, one-third of DUP members placing the party at 0, and the SDLP is seen as a considerably left-of-centre party. DUP members were asked to identify their own position on the same scale, their mean self-positioning at 7.8 aligning very closely to where they placed their party. All parties were seen as to the left of the DUP except the TUV.

As noted earlier, the domination of constitutional issues in Northern Ireland denies left-right the meaning it might (just) still have elsewhere in the UK. For all the DUP's original idea that it would be a party right-wing on constitutional issues and left-wing on social and economic issues, the latter element never really assumed major significance. Left and right still tend to be conflated with pro- or anti-Union robustness. More party members feel closer to the Conservative Party than the other two main British political parties, half of the DUP stating this, with the second largest category, 38 per cent, those who feel close to 'none of them'. Only 7 per cent feel closest to Labour, with another 4 per cent feeling equally close to all three parties, and a mere 1 per cent aligning most to the Liberal Democrats. DUP members are generally not enamoured of the possibility of major British political parties contesting elections in Northern Ireland (the Conservative Party does organize in the province). Only 20 per cent favour this idea, reflecting the DUP's regional autonomist credentials. That said, only 46 per cent oppose the idea, with a sizeable percentage of the membership undecided on the issue. Moreover, age is significant, with younger DUP members more in favour of the idea. Predictably, the possibility of major Irish political parties contesting elections in Northern Ireland, an idea tentatively floated (but little else) by Fianna Fáil a few years ago, meets with short shrift from DUP members, only 2 per cent favouring the prospect and 80 per cent opposing. In terms of attitudes to British political parties, multivariate analysis indicates the significance of key variables and indicates that social class is a significant attitudinal determinant in perceptions of 'mainland' parties. Working-class DUP members are significantly less favourably disposed to the Conservative Party ($p<0.05$), as are those with strong regional identities, i.e. those self-labelling as 'Northern Irish' or 'Ulster' ($p<0.1$). Those self-identifying as right-wing and very religious members are more likely to feel close to the Conservatives ($p<0.01$ and $p<0.05$ respectively).

Could the DUP Attract Support beyond the Sectarian Divide?

If the Catholic population continues to increase in size and vote in ever greater numbers for Sinn Féin, the DUP will need to further increase its vote share amongst Protestants to prevent a Sinn Féin First Minister. Given the modern moderation of Sinn Féin and the ending of conflict, this may come to have little concern for DUP supporters, but that stage has not yet been reached. As further insurance against the prospect, the DUP could embark on a serious effort to broaden its electoral appeal across the divide and attempt to attract support from Catholics. There are several possible routes. Catholics may back individual DUP candidates on the basis of their diligent local constituency work. They may offer support for the DUP based upon particular policies, such as the party's support for educational selection and the retention of grammar schools. Other Catholics may sympathize with the DUP's conservative stances on moral and social issues, such as the party's antipathy towards gay marriage and abortion, as outlined in the previous chapter. Above all, perhaps, the DUP might capitalize on increasing Catholic support for the Union, as they increasingly abandon the old dream of a united Ireland, in favour of the apparent practical benefits of a place in the UK. The DUP leadership is serious about pursuing Catholic votes, but there is not necessarily internal agreement over which of these routes (which are far from mutually exclusive) to that support will be the most accessible and productive.

The number of Roman Catholics within the DUP lies in single figures, a mere 0.6 per cent of the party's membership. Such a miniscule figure is unsurprising, given the party's constitutional position and its previous association with Free Presbyterianism. A party whose previous leader of nearly four decades routinely denounced the leader of the Roman Catholic Church as the 'Anti-Christ' faces an uphill struggle to recruit Catholic members, notwithstanding the considerable personal care and support offered to Catholic constituents by DUP elected representatives. One MLA conceded: 'Dr Paisley was the moderator of the Free Presbyterian Church and obviously, if you are constantly attacking somebody else's faith, then it is very difficult to get them to politically support you. That went on for decades, so twenty years down the line probably isn't long enough for people to get over that.'[41]

Outright sectarian animosity to Catholics is rarely found in the DUP, but hostility to the Roman faith remains unyielding. The (mis)use of the label Catholic irritates some DUP members. One Fermanagh member asserted: 'it really does annoy me. I am a Catholic, but I am not a Roman Catholic . . . I think our politicians need to be more specific, saying Roman Catholic'. Another insisted: 'if you go back to Scripture, the Protestants are actually the true Catholics. They discriminate against the false doctrine of the Roman Catholic Church—that is why they call them the protestors or Protestants.'[42]

There has never been a DUP repudiation of the past, but instead, criticism of the 'myth that was spread around [that] the Roman Catholic community in Northern Ireland had been discriminated against by the Ulster Unionists'.[43] Although this rejection is offered on the basis that *all* non-UUP supporters, including the DUP's, suffered, it is a contention unappealing to older Catholics who lived through the 'Orange state' days. The DUP hopes to connect to a new generation of Catholics who have prospered under the Union.

DUP elected representatives regularly claimed in interviews that lots of Catholics voted for them, but this is not supported by the electoral evidence, either in terms of first preference votes or lower preference vote transfers. The correlation between the proportion of Protestants in a constituency and the combined unionist vote remains extraordinarily strong (r=0.943, p<0.001, in the 2010 General Election, virtually unchanged from 2005), and the strength of the relationship is virtually identical on the nationalist side, in terms of the proportion of Catholics and the combined Sinn Féin and SDLP vote in 2010 (r=0.987, p<0.001).[44]

Yet the virtual absence of backing from the Roman faith has not prevented Peter Robinson making regular pitches at recent DUP annual conferences for Catholics to support the party. Buoyed by successive Northern Ireland Life and Times surveys indicating only minority Catholic support for Irish reunification, Robinson heightened his plea at the 2012 party conference. He dismissed the 'left' and 'far left' policies of the nationalist parties and insisted that, 'as the leader of the party that seeks to represent the whole community, I'm not prepared to write off over forty per cent of our population as out of reach'.[45] Without offering further details as to what this would entail, Robinson nonetheless acknowledged that 'building this new constituency will require as much of an adjustment from us as it will require a leap of faith from those whose votes we seek'.[46]

What could be the 'adjustment' of which Robinson spoke, to repitch the DUP's appeal to Catholics? Robinson acknowledged that Catholics felt culturally Irish, but argued that, for pragmatic economic reasons, they were content to remain within the Union. The shocking collapse of the Celtic Tiger and the subsequent austerity within the Irish Republic had further diminished any case for unity. This assumed that rational choice usurped the emotionalism of national identity, in terms of constitutional preferment. Certainly, Robinson's case for the Union had advanced from it being a necessary defence of Protestant rights into a universal argument. As late as 1995, he had still presented the case for the Union more defensively, as a necessary resistance to the oppression of Protestants, viewed as inevitable in a united Ireland:

> The Protestant community of Northern Ireland will not imbibe the proposition that, on an all-Ireland basis, their 'religious liberties' will be protected. They will remember how, seventy years ago, 10 per cent of the population in the Irish Republic was Protestant, and that the elimination of the Protestant community has been such that now only 2 per cent of the Republic's population are Protestant.[47]

Robinson now offered a more positive and secular set of reasons in defence of the Union, designed to appeal to logic and confident that Catholics are prepared to let the old constitutional question subside. Some DUP members are confident that as the Union diminishes as a point of fracture, the correct policy-oriented pitch can connect to Catholics. Believing, for example, that the party's rigid defence of grammar schools and educational selection is a clear basis of appeal to Catholics, the East Antrim MLA, Sammy Wilson, insisted: 'I know a lot of Catholics who support my views on academic selection and were pleased at my defence of grammar schools, whereas they couldn't find anybody in the SDLP or Sinn Féin.'[48]

For many DUP members, their party does not need to *adjust* to win Catholic backing, but instead, merely needs to stay *steadfast* in its moral and political principles and fill the increasing vacuum created by nationalist parties. On this reasoning, the DUP will eventually win support from Catholics who share the DUP's moral conservatism, opposing gay marriage (supported by

Sinn Féin and the SDLP) and abortion (supported to a very limited extent by Sinn Féin), and are conservative in a different way on policies such as educational selection. As Edwin Poots put it:

for the right-wing middle class Catholic voter who is opposed to abortion, and there are many of them, probably the SDLP can do that. They certainly can't do that when it comes to gay adoption and gay marriage—they have presented a different position. I actually think there is an educated, conservative Catholic vote out there which the DUP is probably best placed to pick up...They want to ensure their kids get a good education, they are supportive of the doctrines of their church. The doctrines of their church largely coincide with the DUP. So conservative Protestantism and conservative Catholicism have an awful lot in common.[49]

There is an assumption amongst DUP members that most Catholics adhere to the social and moral conservatism of their church when, like many in the Protestant community, their faith, or at least adherence to church teaching, may be waning. The Catholic community may be heterogeneous and have a range of views on issues such as gay marriage, making a particular DUP appeal even more problematic. Yet some in the DUP still see potential in a pitch towards Catholic social values. A male Ards councillor, who pointed out that a Roman Catholic signed his election nomination paper, argued that 'most Roman Catholics are conservative and the DUP is a conservative party'.[50] The Lagan Valley MLA, Paul Givan, could see the basis of a 'moral appeal' to Catholics, but was unsure how far it could take the DUP:

How can you vote for Sinn Féin and the SDLP if you are opposed to gay marriage? Sinn Féin certainly, their stance on abortion wouldn't be in line with the Catholic Church. If they could get away with it they would be pro-abortionists, but they know it probably takes them out too far from where their electoral base would be. On those types of issues I think we can appeal to Catholics, but ultimately, how many Catholics actually vote for the DUP?[51]

During the conflict, there were obvious practical barriers to the DUP's canvassing of Catholic votes, even if candidates believed it might be worth testing. These issues have greatly diminished, but not entirely dissipated. According to one MLA, 'there remain some security issues. I'm fortunate in North Antrim, where the only places I wouldn't canvas would be Bellaghy and Dunloy, because there is a slight chance my security would be compromised by doing that.'[52] An East Antrim MLA declared: 'There are mixed areas. We canvass them all. That is not the same for some, where it is much more dangerous to do it.'[53] A Strabane councillor claimed she was 'always told, when going out, certain areas to avoid'.[54] Most areas, other than a small number of hardcore republican districts, might at least be canvassed, but what would they yield? Many DUP representatives are optimistic. In a typical response, a Londonderry (Rural) councillor acknowledged that security in some places 'would be difficult', but insisted that 'when I went to the door at the last election, it wasn't Orange or Green issues. It was, are you are going to be able to solve these issues for me. It is bread and butter issues, rather than what flag you are flying.'[55]

Not all elected representatives believe that winning the Catholics' support is realistic for the party or should necessarily be prioritized. A Carrickfergus councillor acknowledged: 'I don't think there will be an influx of Roman Catholics. Lots of the DUP are in bands and Loyal Orders, so it's not really ideal.'[56] Mid-Ulster MLA Ian McCrea offered a frank assessment: 'I can't see it, if I'm honest... I would be more concerned that in some areas we have disengaged with those who got us to where we are... I think the focus should be on winning back the faith of the people who got us here.'[57] Another sceptic was the South Down MLA, Jim Wells:

It really is a waste of time going into an area where you get the door slammed and you get insulted and you get shouted at. In mixed areas like Newcastle I will do all the doors and you get a polite enough response, but the reality is, when the boxes are opened, I would say, on a very good day, I am getting less than twenty Roman Catholic votes.[58]

A Strabane councillor argued: 'I think anyone in the Roman Catholic community, I can't see them coming out publicly, "I am going to vote DUP". I can't see that happening.'[59] An Enniskillen councillor asserted: 'If Dr Paisley was leader, it [canvassing a nationalist area] probably wouldn't have come up. I haven't—in this area it is too divided. There is no point. You are not getting anywhere.'[60] A Coleraine elected representative argued a traditional constitutional perspective regarding attracting Catholic support: 'I think it is a step beyond because the unionist community are not totally convinced that those within the Roman Catholic community are totally given over to the United Kingdom.'[61]

The DUP's possible appeal across the divide may be tempered by the party's opposition to the separate system of Roman Catholic education. The DUP leader, Peter Robinson, regularly criticized separate education, a critique based partly upon the financial cost of maintaining separate facilities, but whose main thrust is ideological. Robinson has denounced segregation as a 'benign form of apartheid', and argued that, given 'religious segregation at universities would be considered absurd', the same unacceptability applied at the primary and secondary levels. Addressing Castlereagh Council in October 2010, Robinson insisted that Northern Ireland

cannot hope to move beyond our present community divisions while our young people are educated separately... who among us would think it acceptable that a state or nation would educate its young people by the criteria of race, with white schools or black schools? Yet we are prepared to operate a system which selects children almost entirely on the basis of their religion.

As a society and administration, we are not mere onlookers of this: we are participants and continue to fund schools on this basis. And then we are surprised that we continue to have a divided society.[62]

After warming to this theme in a series of leadership speeches to his party conference, Robinson found backing from a powerful external source. The US President, Barack Obama, used a Belfast speech in June 2013 to question the appropriateness of educational segregation. Obama echoed Robinson's lines: 'If Catholics have their schools and buildings and Protestants have theirs—if we can't see ourselves in one another, if fear and resentment are allowed to harden, that encourages division. It discourages co-operation.'[63]

Following Obama's assertions, Robinson reiterated his desire for transformation, but rowed back from the idea that his project demanded the abolition of Catholic schools, at least in the near future:

If you were starting from the beginning, you would have one school system paid for by the state...the gradual process towards integration is where the concept of shared education was born. That largely means you would progressively move towards having classes where education was shared, having campuses where education establishments would be brought together from different backgrounds, having buildings where schools would come together, where you have a Catholic school and a state school wanting to use the same building, they use the same playing field and so forth. I can't help but feel, as time goes on, the two Principals on the one site will say: 'Is there not a bit of saving to be made if the two sixth forms have geography or PE together?' It would be my view that over time we will become much more integrated. It still allows a parental choice, it still allows people to have the old school identities, but hopefully, it will be a process. Quite frankly, you couldn't move from where we are to where we want to be, in terms of the school estate. It just wouldn't work at the present time, so it has to be a gradual process to get us where we want to go to. Geographically, having an integrated school on the Shankill Road? There isn't anyone else to go to it other than Protestants and the same would be in the Falls.[64]

The Catholic hierarchy appeared suspicious of the Robinson and Obama assertions as a closet route to ending Catholic education. The bishops argued that a system of Catholic education disadvantaged no one and allowed grateful Catholic parents to give their offspring a Christian upbringing imbued with the moral fortitude admired by many DUP members. Non-Catholics could be admitted to Catholic schools and facilities were sometimes shared with other schools. Moreover, the claim that division in schooling is the root of evil assumed that Northern Ireland is the only place where Catholics are educated separately, and that this somehow explains Northern Ireland's conflict, which is constitutional, not religious. Catholics are routinely educated separately in England without sectarian problems. DUP proposals for integrated education are seen by Catholic critics, particularly the clergy and Catholic teachers, as unsubtle moves to remove the liberal pluralist right of Catholic parents to educate their children in the faith of their choice. The Catholic Auxiliary Bishop of Down and Connor, Donal McKeown, described the DUP's position of wanting to abolish Catholic schools as 'nakedly sectarian...talking about reconciliation, but ultimately, saying the fault is with the Catholics'.[65] In return, Mervyn Storey, the DUP chair of the Northern Ireland Assembly Education committee, attacked the criticism, arguing that the 'apartheid, in terms of educational provision, cannot continue...the bishops, rather than protecting their own silo, need to come into the twenty-first century'.[66] According to Storey:

> If you allow people to have a degree of autonomy or preference or choice, then that should be proportionate to what they are prepared to pay themselves to have that. I think to give, as has been given to the Catholic Church, an absolute right that you can educate your children in those schools, and by the way, the state will also pay for it. There is a contradiction in doing that and then saying, but we will also, at the same time, advocate shared education.[67]

The DUP MLA also argued that Catholic schools emphasized particular identities beyond the religious:

> If you look at Catholic education, it gives a Catholic child two things. It gives them a Catholic faith-based education, but it also gives them an Irish nationalist identity, which is sometimes overlooked because that Irish ethos is very strong in Catholic schools, so they play the Gaelic games, they have the Irish history, they have the Irish music, they have all of those things.
>
> How do they, in a shared society, actually convince people of a different political view to go to a school in their sector with Irish music, with Irish games, Irish ethos, Irish identity, Irish history, all of that, how does that contribute to being part of the United Kingdom and reaching out to others who have a different view? If you go to a state school, a state school doesn't generally compound that you are British, that you fly the flag, that you are Protestant.[68]

Although some Catholics would back integrated education, others might be wary of the project if it was pushed by the DUP, fearing that it was some sort of sectarian, anti-Catholic project. Denunciations of Catholic systems of education as apartheid are likely to been seen negatively by many Catholic voters, regardless of the merits or otherwise of the DUP argument. Electoral outreach to Catholics will have to be undertaken with sensitivity and concentrate most upon policy logic and the comfortable accommodation of both communities as the northern state finally embeds.

Conclusion

Whilst the rapidity of the UUP's demise provides a salutary warning against complacency, the DUP is seemingly impervious to serious electoral challenge within unionism. Its eclipse of the UUP continues, the party's members are highly active, and the party's support base appears content with the principles agreed at St Andrews in 2006, even if the distrust of Sinn Féin as government partners remains.

The main electoral and political threats to the DUP do not come from any rival force within unionism. The UUP appears in permanent retreat and there is no serious electoral competitor. Instead, the possible difficulties for the DUP lie in the apathy amongst the unionist electorate and changing demography. Barely half of the Protestant population votes in elections. Sinn Féin's mobilization of Catholic voters, compared to the DUP's performance amongst Protestants, is superior, as turnout differentials indicate. Combined with further modest growth in the Catholic population, the status of the DUP as the largest party in the largest bloc cannot be assured in perpetuity. The DUP may of course come to accept 'Deputy First Minister' status for its leader as readily as it eventually accepted Sinn Féin as its main partner in government, but to fend off the prospect, appeals for support across the sectarian divide may need to be converted from regular party conference speech fixtures into serious campaigning. Thus far, the DUP has made no significant progress in attracting Catholic voters or members. The party's task is to decide which one or more of the routes discussed—constitutional, policy-based, or moral—should be pursued to at least begin to attract significant lower preference vote transfers to the party from its hitherto rival ethnic bloc.

Notes

1. Interview with Oliver Gibson MLA, 23 Nov. 2012.
2. Interview with Nigel Dodds MP, 3 July 2013.
3. B. Hayes and I. McAllister (2001) 'Who Voted for Peace? Public Support for the 1998 Northern Ireland Agreement', *Irish Political Studies*, 16/1, 73–93.
4. J. McGarry and B. O'Leary (1995) *Explaining Northern Ireland*, Oxford: Blackwell, 405–6.
5. P. Mitchell, G. Evans, and B. O'Leary (2009) 'Extremist Outbidding in Ethnic Party Systems is Not Inevitable. Tribune Parties in Northern Ireland', *Political Studies*, 57/2, 397–421.
6. P. Mitchell and G. Evans (2009) 'Ethnic Party Competition and the Dynamics of Power Sharing in Northern Ireland', in R. Taylor (ed.), *Consociational Theory: McGarry and O'Leary and the Northern Ireland Conflict*, London: Routledge, 161–2.

7. Interview with Nigel Dodds, 3 July 2013.

8. *Orange Standard*, May 1998, 'NO', 1.

9. P. Mitchell (2001) 'Transcending an Ethnic Party System? The Impact of Consociational Governance on Electoral Dynamics and the Party System', in R. Wilford (ed.), *Aspects of the Belfast Agreement*, Oxford: Oxford University Press, 31.

10. DUP (1998) *Your Best Guarantee for the Future of Northern Ireland. Assembly Election Manifesto*, Belfast: DUP.

11. DUP (2003) *The DUP's Vision for Devolution: Assembly Election Manifesto*, Belfast; DUP.

12. Peter Robinson, cited in *Irish Times*, 'DUP Takes Hard Line on Sinn Féin', 22 Apr. 2005.

13. Ian Paisley, Leader's Speech to DUP Party Conference, 26 Nov. 2005; 'We will Not Accept Terrorists in our Government', *Irish Times*, 28 Nov. 2005.

14. DUP, *Vision for Devolution*, 11.

15. DUP, *Vision for Devolution*, 7.

16. DUP (2007) *Getting it Right: Northern Ireland Assembly Election Manifesto*, Belfast: DUP, 23.

17. J. Tonge and J. Evans (2010) 'Northern Ireland: Unionism Loses More Leaders', in A. Geddes and J. Tonge (eds), *Britain Votes, 2010*, Oxford: Oxford University Press, 158–75.

18. For a consideration of alternative systems, see J. Coakley (2009) 'Implementing Consociation', in R. Taylor (ed.), *Consociational Theory: McGarry and O'Leary and the Northern Ireland Conflict*, London: Routledge, 122–45.

19. Interview with Peter Robinson MLA, DUP leader, Stormont, 25 June 2013. See also Robinson's speech to the Institute of Irish Studies, University of Liverpool, 11 Oct. 2011, <http://www.bbc.co.uk/news/uk-northern-ireland-15281632>, accessed July 2013.

20. David McKittrick (2007) 'No More "Dr No"; Meet the New Ian Paisley', *Independent*, 15 Nov. 2007.

21. Lee Reynolds, 15 Feb. 2008, <http://sluggerotoole.com/2008/02/15/dromore-by-election-a-well-placed-kick-part-1>, accessed July 2013.

22. Interview with Peter Robinson, 25 June 2013.

23. Interview with Peter Robinson, 25 June 2013.

24. Interview with Paul Givan MLA, Lisburn, 11 Jan. 2013.

25. Interview with Jim Allister, TUV MLA for North Antrim, 18 Apr. 2012.

26. Interview with Jim Allister, 18 Apr. 2012.

27. G. Evans and M. Duffy (1997) 'Beyond the Sectarian Divide: The Social Bases and Political Consequences of Nationalist and Unionist Party Competition in Northern Ireland', *British Journal of Political Science*, 27/1, 47–81.

28. Evans and Duffy, 'Beyond the Sectarian Divide'.

29. J. Evans and J. Tonge (2009) 'Social Class and Party Choice in Northern Ireland's Ethnic Blocs', *West European Politics*, 32/5, 1012–30.

30. Evans and Tonge, 'Social Class and Party Choice', 1024.

31. J. Tilley, G. Evans, and C. Mitchell (2008) 'Consociationalism and the Evolution of Political Cleavages in Northern Ireland, 1989–2004', *British Journal of Political Science*, 38/4, 699–717.

32. J. McAuley, J. Tonge, and A. Mycock (2011) *Loyal to the Core: Orangeism and Britishness in Northern Ireland*, Dublin: Irish Academic Press, 144.
33. McAuley et al., *Loyal to the Core*.
34. Northern Ireland Life and Times Survey (2010) available at <http://www.ark.ac.uk/nilt/2010/Political_Attitudes/POLPART2.html>, accessed 30 July 2013.
35. Interview with Nigel Dodds, 3 July 2013.
36. Interview with Jeffrey Donaldson MP, 8 Mar. 2013.
37. BBC Northern Ireland, 'Spotlight', 12 Mar. 2013, <http://www.newsletter.co.uk/news/regional/elliott-i-didn-t-sanction-unionist-merger-talks-1-4889735>, 13 Mar. 2013, accessed July 2013.
38. Interview with East Antrim MLA, Carrickfergus, 8 Jan. 2013.
39. Northern Ireland 2010 General Election Attitudes Survey, available at <http://discover.ukdataservice.ac.uk/catalogue?sn=6553>, accessed 29 July 2013.
40. Northern Ireland Life and Times Survey (2010) *Political Attitudes*, available at <http://www.ark.ac.uk/nilt/2010/Political_Attitudes/POLPART2.html>, accessed July 2013.
41. Interview with Paul Givan, 11 Jan. 2013.
42. DUP Fermanagh focus group members, Enniskillen, 26 Apr. 2013.
43. Interview with William McCrea MP, Ballyclare, 20 Jan. 2013.
44. Tonge and Evans, 'Northern Ireland: Unionism Loses More Leaders', 164–6.
45. Peter Robinson, Leader's Speech to DUP Annual Conference, Belfast, 26 Nov. 2013, available at <http://cain.ulst.ac.uk/issues/politics/docs/dup/pr241112.htm>, accessed July 2013.
46. Peter Robinson, Leader's Speech to DUP Annual Conference, 2013.
47. P. Robinson (1995) *The Union under Fire: United Ireland Framework Revealed*, Belfast: n.publ., 106.
48. Interview with Sammy Wilson MLA, Carrickfergus, 20 Jan. 2013.
49. Interview with Edwin Poots MLA, Lisburn, 10 Jan. 2013.
50. Interview with Ards councillor, 11 Sept. 2012.
51. Interview with Paul Givan, 11 Jan. 2013.
52. Interview with North Antrim MLA, 20 Nov. 2012.
53. Interview with East Antrim MLA, 5 Nov. 2012.
54. Interview with Strabane councillor, 16 Apr. 2013.
55. Interview with Londonderry (Rural) councillor, 26 Mar. 2013.
56. Interview with Carrickfergus councillor, 28 Nov. 2012.
57. Interview with Ian McCrea MLA, Stormont, 9 Jan. 2013.
58. Interview with Jim Wells MLA, Stormont, 9 Jan. 2013.
59. Interview with Strabane councillor, 16 Apr. 2013.
60. Interview with Fermanagh councillor, 15 Mar. 2013.
61. Interview with Coleraine councillor, 10 Oct. 2012.
62. Peter Robinson, Speech to Castlereagh Council, reported at <http://www.belfasttelegraph.co.uk/news/education/peter-robinson-calls-for-end-to-school-segregation-28565048.html>, accessed July 2013.
63. Barack Obama (2013) Speech at Waterfront Hall, Belfast, 17 June 2013, reported at <http://www.washingtontimes.com/news/2013/jun/20/obama-remarks-about-catholic-schools-spark-new-fig/?page=all>, accessed 1 July 2013.

64. Interview with Peter Robinson, 25 June 2013.
65. BBC Radio Ulster, *Sunday Sequence*, 30 June 2013; *The Universe*, 7 July 2013.
66. BBC Northern Ireland, *Sunday Politics*, 30 June 2013.
67. Interview with Mervyn Storey MLA, Stormont, 10 Jan. 2013.
68. Interview with Mervyn Storey, 10 Jan. 2013.

8

Women in the DUP: 'The Backbone of the Party'

> We live in a very rural community, there is a lot of church involvement with our members just because of the way the party is. It is connected largely to the church. You will find in a church-based organization, or faith-based organization, that is what the women do. They make the tea, they stay in the background. They are very good organizers, very good at organizing fund-raising events, things like that. They will let the men stand out at the front and be the face of things, and maybe it is the connection with church...women are raised to be the home-makers, the house-keepers, and all of that.[1]

Tea-makers and Stepford wives have been some of the analogies used to convey the role and position of women in the DUP.[2] Traditionally, men have been the face of unionist politics, whilst women have remained in the background, taking on the roles of party secretaries, treasurers, and fund-raisers. The shortfall of female representatives in the party is often blamed on the reluctance of women to stand for election, as opposed to the existence of any barriers to participating in the formal political arena. The aim of this chapter is to examine the role and opinion of women at various levels of the DUP, to gain their perspectives on whether there is discrimination against women in public life, the position of women in the party, and how they feel female representation could be improved. Evidence is drawn from a battery of questions in the party survey data to quantify the views of party members on issues such as whether a female candidate would lose votes, or whether the party should introduce a fixed proportion of women candidates. Drawing upon in-depth interviews with elected DUP representatives and the party leadership, the chapter also examines the supply and demand of female candidates within the DUP, the opportunities for female participation, and the selection processes within the party. Whilst being described as the 'backbone of the party' and participating at the membership level, few women in the DUP enter representative politics.

Women and Politics in Northern Ireland

The dearth of female political representation in Northern Ireland is evident. The interactions between constitutional politics, religion, and conservative societal values have produced a distinctive political culture in Northern Ireland where the cleavages of nationality and religion have tended to eclipse a cross-cutting gender cleavage. As a result, politics has been centred on communal loyalties, providing little space for alternative agendas. Murtagh describes how, in Northern Ireland, formal politics represents the segregation of society to such an exaggerated extent that 'one's stance on the constitutional question constitutes the central axis around which all political affairs revolve'.[3] In Northern Ireland, alternative interests such as women's rights have generally been seen as subordinate to, or even in conflict with, the national interest.[4] Within unionist politics, the security of the Union is given priority as a political issue, where feminism has been considered a rival force to the constitutional position, subsequently making feminism something of 'a dirty word within unionism...women are unionists first and women second'.[5]

Whilst communal division has eclipsed other societal cleavages, such as gender, the conflict in Northern Ireland has also reinforced gender stereotypes. On both sides of the communal divide, different roles and responsibilities were gender-specific, where 'men engage in a political and military struggle for the nation and women are mobilised to help secure the homeland'.[6] For Ward, traditionally, men and women occupy separate spheres within unionism. The male role is expected to be in active defence of their country, whilst female participation in public and civic life is more passive and described as an extension of their private household responsibilities, remaining relatively invisible in the 'background of politics "doing their bit"'.[7] Throughout the Troubles, the political space occupied by men and women in Northern Ireland remained highly gendered. The roles of women were those of 'help-mate of the active man', fund-raising, canvassing, and making the tea.[8]

More so than nationalism, gendered national symbolism within unionism has been described by commentators as lacking in positive female imagery.[9] When asked why gender stereotypes appeared more prevalent in unionism than nationalism, DUP MP David Simpson reflected on the traditional responsibilities of men and women:

> If you go back, not even 30 years ago, go back 20 years ago or less, within the Ulster Unionist Party, there was hardly even a female councillor because it was seen as it

was the man's thing within unionism to do. Traditionally, within unionism, even in the family, it is the man's job...Especially over 30 years of the Troubles, the ladies were looking after the families and all of that and it was difficult for them, and the men were the ones who were seen to be going out and taking all the risks, I think that may be part of it as well.[10]

Exploring the gender imbalance within unionist politics led Cochrane to claim that the only women of any significance that came to the fore in the DUP were those connected by blood or marriage to famous relatives, citing Iris Robinson and Rhonda Paisley as obvious examples.[11] Rhonda Paisley, daughter of the former party leader, was Lady Mayoress of Belfast and a Belfast City councillor during the late 1980s and early 1990s. She has been described as personifying the culture clash within the DUP between old and new, where her 'social attitudes may have seemed too modern, her lipstick too red, and her skirts too short for some of those of a more traditional bent within the party'.[12] Writing in 1992, at the same time as announcing that she did not intend to defend her seat on Belfast City Council, Rhonda Paisley observed how a persistent feature existed within unionist organizations, where female members had to subjugate their interests and needs as women for the greater constitutional issue:

I accept that many women are happy to be involved on the fringes of Unionist politics, but so are many men...Women and the challenge of feminist issues are a threat to the overwhelming majority of men in unionist ranks. However, when the same are eager candidates to get their backsides on to the green leather seats of the 'mother' of parliaments, they are sickeningly keen to get the women's vote on polling day.[13]

Rhonda Paisley was seen as symbolizing the difference between the 'new women' in the party and the matronly 'Stepford wives' figures with basic education and limited careerism.[14]

The strong association between unionism and Protestantism applies an additional layer to the analysis of gender roles within unionist organizations. For Galligan and Knight, the conservative agenda emerging from unionism has been reinforced by 'male-supremacist religious codes', where religious teachings have 'reinforced the subjugation of women to men. Protestant clerics emphasised male authority in the home.'[15] Ian Paisley echoed this message, stating that, 'The Lord Jesus Christ certainly elevated women and where the Christian message is heard, women will be elevated, but the Bible states clearly that man is the head of the woman and Christ is the head of the man.'[16]

The connection between conservatism and Protestant unionism is typified in the publication of *Ulster Home Cooking*, a cookbook put together by the 'Lady Members and friends of the Londonderry DUP' in the mid-1990s.

The cookbook is described on the first page as having been prepared by 'Ulster-women for Ulster-women'[17] and includes familiar recipes for jams and cakes, as well as helpful cleaning tips. Towards the back of the publication, there is also a collection of light-hearted recipes, humorously describing 'How to Cook a Good Husband' and instructions of how to bake a 'Bible Cake'—directing its readers to include 1 pinch Leviticus, ½lb Jeremiah, and 'bake in a moderate oven'.[18] From the party's creation in 1971 until the turn of the century, it is difficult to find any DUP documentation that addresses the issue of female representation or policies aimed at the concerns of women in the party. Whilst *Ulster Home Cooking* may not have been representative of all females in the party during the mid-1990s, its existence as one of the few documents available from this period is quite revealing of the traditional association between unionism, domesticity, Protestantism, and women in the DUP.

The number of women in political life in Northern Ireland has increased considerably in the past decade, yet women remain significantly under-represented as councillors and at the Assembly level. The dominance of the sectarian divide pushed aside concerns for gender equality, where the rights of the woman were seen, at best, secondary to the national struggle.[19] The position of women in the DUP needs to be set in a socio-political context. In contrast to the rest of the UK, feminism in Northern Ireland has been slow to emerge, the constitutional issue and political violence eclipsed concerns for gender equality in political and public life.

Putting Female Representation on the Political Agenda

The decades of Stormont rule, followed by direct rule during the Troubles, left Northern Ireland behind the modest advancements in gender equality that were occurring in other parts of Britain during the same period. The eventual devolution of powers from Westminster to Stormont in 1998 has been described as a juncture, presenting an opportunity for women to mobilize and to engage in gender-inclusive and transformative politics.[20] With the transition towards peace, the hope was that women's concerns might be placed at the heart of new agendas. It is suggested that issues of gender have been neglected in accounts of political transformation and constitutional change.[21] For example, Hayes and McAllister argue that, whilst anti-discrimination measures were included in the Belfast Agreement, gender issues have been accorded a secondary status at best, despite the number of female elected representatives increasing at both the Assembly and the local level.[22] Although the peace process provided the opportunity to increase female political participation, Gray and Neill are critical of the fact that this opportunity has not been taken. Instead, gender equality 'has continued to be regarded as quite distinct from and less of a priority than equality' between communities.[23]

Making a judgement on the basis of DUP manifestos during the 1990s, Wilford suggests that during this period the party appeared to regress, in terms of its policies on gender equality. In 1992, the party's manifesto included a brief statement on women's issues and called for the creation of a Ministry for Women, which would be given the responsibility of promoting female socio-economic issues. Whilst not necessarily representing major policy initiatives, such policies would at least have provided an institutional focus for the advancement of women. Yet the DUP rowed back from this position and by 1997, the party's manifesto was based exclusively on the constitutional issue.[24]

In 1996, a small group of women active in academia, community groups, and other civic associations formed a new political party, the Northern Ireland Women's Coalition (NIWC). The NIWC campaigned on a platform highlighting the lack of access to political and public life for women, whilst espousing equality, inclusion, and human rights as its three main principles.[25] In 1996, the NIWC contested the election for delegates to the Northern Ireland forum, the 110-seat multi-party negotiating body that would produce the Belfast Agreement.[26] As the ninth largest party, the NIWC won two seats in the forum and in 1998, two members were successfully elected to the Northern Ireland Assembly. The party's mandate declined in the following years, losing both Assembly seats in 2003, and it eventually disbanded in 2006. Research investigating reasons behind the decline of the NIWC points towards institutional obstacles and factors, such as size and geographical distribution, which meant that the party was disadvantaged by the voting system.[27]

The party itself may not have proven its longevity or versatility, but the NIWC is given credit by some for having put gender politics on the agenda for the first time in Northern Ireland and, as a result, forced political competitors in the Assembly to be reactive and address this platform.[28] The NIWC itself claims that one of its greatest achievements was the promotion of women and women's issues within other parties in Northern Ireland.[29] The DUP, along with the Ulster Unionist Party (UUP) and the Social Democratic and Labour Party (SDLP), only began to produce documentation on women's issues after the NIWC was formed. Released by the DUP in 1998, the document *Women's Issues* does not, however, suggest any changes to party policy and does not mention female political participation and representation. Instead, it distinctly discusses the role of women as voters:

> Those of us who seek election depend on the votes of the women in our respective areas. Let us make sure that we are meeting their needs and dealing with the difficulties they face day-to-day... Women of Ulster deserve our very best on their behalf.[30]

Both the SDLP and Sinn Féin adopted internal gender quotas and were considered to be far more receptive to gender equality than their unionist counterparts in the UUP and DUP.[31]

In 2001, for the Westminster and District Council elections, the DUP made reference to needing 'real and meaningful equality for women and ethnic minorities', but any further mention of gender equality within politics or wider society has subsequently been omitted from the party's election manifestos.[32] In the 2011 Northern Ireland Assembly election, Sinn Féin, the SDLP, the Alliance Party of Northern Ireland (APNI), the UUP, and the Green Party all, in varying detail, referred to the need to encourage female participation and equality within their election manifestos. The two parties that did not refer to such issues were the DUP and the Traditional Unionist Voice (TUV), both focusing on communal equality, rather than gender.

Women in the DUP

The following section focuses on the views and opinions of both activists and representatives in the DUP. Drawing on the survey of party members and in-depth interviews with DUP councillors, MPs, and MLAs, obstacles to female representation and ways in which to close the gender deficit will be explored.

Activists

Communal division and political violence have dominated politics in Northern Ireland. According to Hinds, this meant 'political participation' for women has traditionally been very narrow and largely situated in the civic sphere, beyond the formal political realm.[33] Female engagement with politics tended to be at a local level through voluntary associations, churches, community groups, and women's organizations. Women's activism in the informal sector often simultaneously reinforced gender norms and enhanced Protestant unionist identity.[34] Gray and Neil note that 'there continues to be a huge gap between women's involvement in grassroots and voluntary organisations, and their participation in mainstream politics and in positions of decision-making in Northern Ireland'.[35] The deputy leader of the DUP, Nigel Dodds, expressed how there is still reluctance amongst women in unionism to make the transition from civil society to formal politics:

> I go to public meetings, what strikes me about public meetings and residents' meetings and interaction with community groups, in Belfast, I don't know what it is like rural-wise, but in Belfast, overwhelmingly, those people who are at those

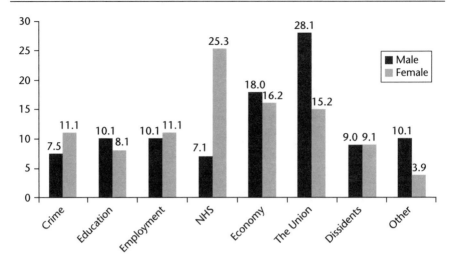

Figure 8.1 DUP members' views on the single most important political issue (%)

meetings and taking part are women…they will be the ones who turn up to all the meetings and be most vociferous. It will be 'we want you men to do this, or we will back you men'. If you said to them, what about you coming forward? 'Oh, no, no, no'. There is that element, now that needs to be broken through, but there is a bit of that in Northern Ireland society.[36]

The number of female members in the DUP has been reported in previous studies at around 60 per cent of the overall membership.[37] However, this is not supported by our detailed membership survey, which shows that female membership is below one-third.[38] The proportion of men and women joining the party has not significantly varied over time, but what has altered is the reason given by women for joining the party. The party's defence of the union was much more likely to be chosen by women who joined before the Belfast Agreement, compared to both men pre- or post-1998 and to women who have joined since 1998. Figure 8.1 shows the importance of issues to male and female party members.

Whilst defence of the Union signified an important reason for women joining the party pre-1998, it is not ranked so highly as a key political concern for females in the party today. There are significant gender differences when members were asked what the single most important political issue was for them. Male respondents were almost twice more likely to mention Northern Ireland's place in the Union as the most important ($p<0.001$). Amongst females in the party, priority was given to more 'bread and butter' issues, such as the health service and the economy.

The membership survey also asked several questions specifically regarding women in the party and public life, exploring if any significant gender difference existed in relation to female political involvement, gender

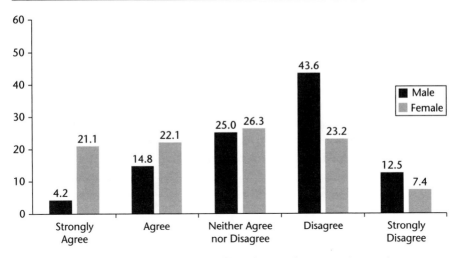

Figure 8.2 DUP members' views on whether there is discrimination against women in public life (%)

discrimination in public life, and attitudes to improving female political representation. Members were asked to grade their answers on a five-point scale (1 = strongly disagree, 5 = strongly disagree). Overall, attitudes towards male hegemony in political and public life are stronger within the female members of the party. Figure 8.2 shows the responses for male and female members.

The most significant difference between male and female members was in their perceptions of gender discrimination in public life. Disagreement with the statement regarding discrimination against women is significantly higher amongst male members of the party (see Table 8.1). Whilst 56 per cent of male members denied that discrimination against women existed in public life, only 31 per cent of females in the DUP thought likewise. Older male members of the party came out more strongly against this statement, but overall, there was no significant generational difference.

Table 8.1 The significance of age and gender in DUP members' perception of gender discrimination

	Politics would improve if more women were elected	Women are better placed than men to represent women's interest	Discrimination against women in public life	Women candidates will lose votes	DUP should have a fixed proportion of women candidates
Male	−0.835***	−1.134***	−1.139***	0.378	−0.902***
	(0.231)	(0.229)	(0.234)	(0.236)	(0.228)
Age	−0.002	0.005	0.002	0.017***	0.008
	(0.00587)	(0.00571)	(0.00589)	(0.00615)	(0.00574)

Standard errors in parentheses

*** p<0.01, ** p<0.05, * p<0.1

Figures 8.3 and 8.4 indicate significant male–female differences. Male members of the DUP are less supportive than female members of the idea that more women would improve politics (Figure 8.3). There is a greater desire amongst female DUP members to see more women in the formal political arena. Fifty-four per cent of female party members either agree or strongly agree with the statement that 'Politics in Northern Ireland would improve if more women were elected', whilst only one in eight females disagree or strongly disagree. Yet only one-third of male members concur with the proposition that increased female electoral representation will bolster politics.

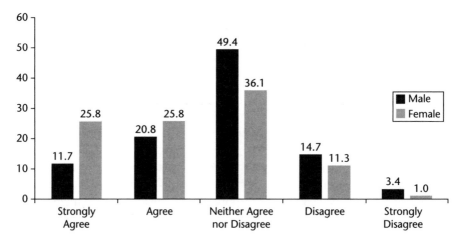

Figure 8.3 DUP members' views on whether 'Politics in Northern Ireland would improve if there were more women elected' (%)

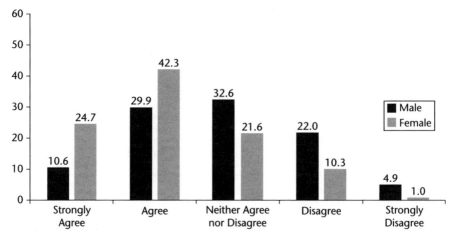

Figure 8.4 DUP members' views on whether 'Women are better placed than men to represent women's interests in politics' (%)

Female party members also overwhelmingly agree that women are better placed than men to represent women's interest in politics (Figure 8.4), 67 per cent agreeing/strongly agreeing and only 11 per cent disagreeing/strongly disagreeing with this statement. Clearly, female members of the party want more women in politics, whilst male members are generally happy with the status quo, an observation that has also been made across other parties in Northern Ireland.[39]

It has been a significantly slower progression for women to make the transition into formal politics within unionism than their nationalist counterparts. Unionist parties are notably more 'bottom heavy' than Sinn Féin, the SDLP, and the APNI in terms of female involvement.[40] Despite female under-representation, especially at elected and salaried positions within unionism, Ward suggests that an examination of the activities, roles, and motivations of these female members shows that unionist women do more than the stereotype that they 'just make tea and buns' allows.[41] In a focus group of female DUP members and councillors, several insisted that, by fulfilling the responsibilities of leaflet dropping, attending meetings, organizing, making tea, and fund-raising, women were the 'backbone of the party'.[42]

It is evident that the roles played by female party members go beyond the gender stereotype of the submissive home-maker. The roles of treasurer, secretary, and organizer are vital to the everyday functioning of the DUP. However, the contribution of female members 'in the background' means that their role within the party does not necessarily outwardly challenge the status quo. A female councillor questioned how the male-dominated sphere of formal politics continues to shape gendered expectations:

> The last figures that I was looking at, fifty-three per cent of the voters in this area are women. There is a vote there. Do they not have faith in their fellow females to hold those types of posts? Are they structured and dominated by a male environment and see that as that type of persona for that job?[43]

Whilst the activity of women behind the scenes in the DUP should not be understated, a reluctance to stand as candidates means that men largely remain the face of unionism.

Local Government

There is a low level of elected female representation evident across the tiers of government in Northern Ireland, despite some progress. In 1993, only 12 per cent of the 582 councillors were women.[44] As a percentage of overall seats won, the Alliance Party had the most women elected at the local level (25 per cent), followed by the SDLP (15 per cent), and Sinn Féin (14 per cent), with the UUP total not far behind (12 per cent). With females only making up 8 per cent of its councillors, the DUP trailed all its political rivals in terms of gender imbalance.[45] By 2005, the number of women in local politics had almost doubled since 1993, with 20 per cent of councillors being female. As a percentage of overall seats won, the Alliance Party still had the most female councillors (33 per cent), with Sinn Féin (25 per cent) and the SDLP (26 per cent) being closely ranked. The DUP (19 per cent) and UUP (13 per cent) still presented the lowest representation of females in local government.[46] In the 2011 local government elections, female representation climbed again, to reach an overall figure of 24 per cent.

The DUP is starting to make progress in terms of female political representation in local elections. In 2011, there were female DUP candidates standing in forty-six of the ninety-four District Electoral Areas (DEAs) that the party contested (two areas had an all-women candidate list[47]), an improvement on the figure of female candidatures in thirty-three districts in 2005. Out of the 175 DUP councillors that won seats in 2011, 22 per cent were women, just slightly below the overall Northern Ireland percentage. Thirty-three female councillors were elected in 2005, rising to thirty-eight in 2011, whilst women candidates also increased over the same period from thirty-three to fifty-one.

Local government in Northern Ireland is described by Galligan and Wilford as not only representing 'a key site for the development of women's political careers, but one that remains largely unexploited'.[48] Being a councillor is considered a valuable learning experience, where most political careers begin, at the local level, and this serves as a launch pad to higher office. The percentage of elected females is gradually increasing with each election in Northern Ireland, with women now making up almost 24 per cent of councillors; this still remains below the 31 per cent average across the UK.[49]

The Northern Ireland Assembly

Northern Ireland was once described as being virtually without female political representation.[50] In the twelve general elections to the fifty-two-seat regional parliament from 1921 until 1969, only thirty-seven of 1,008 candidates were women.[51] During the same period, there were never more than four women elected representatives during any one parliamentary term, and only one ever became a minister.[52] In highlighting the lack of progress over these years, Wilford points out that, at the final election in 1969, the proportion of female candidates dwindled to 2 per cent, the same level as the first election almost fifty years before; in effect, Stormont was a male near-monopoly.[53] Home rule did nothing to advance women's role in the formal political sphere.

Today, female representation in Northern Ireland, whilst improved from the era of Unionist majoritarian devolved government, remains low. As Table 8.2 shows, it is far below that of other devolved institutions in the United Kingdom. In the 2011 devolved Parliament and Assembly elections, women's representation in Wales and Scotland reached 45 and 37 per cent respectively, whilst in Northern Ireland only 19 per cent of those elected were women. The Northern Irish Assembly is thus 'rooted to the bottom of the gender league table'.[54]

Table 8.2 Female representation in devolved parliaments and assemblies, 1998–2011 (%)

	1998/99	2003	2007	2011	Average
Northern Ireland Assembly	13	17	17	19	17
Scottish Parliament	37	40	33	37	37
National Assembly for Wales	40	50	47	43	45

Some evidence of progress is nonetheless discernible in unionist female representation. As Table 8.3 shows, the number of women candidates being fielded in Assembly elections increased considerably from 1998 to 2011. Whilst the percentage of female candidates from the DUP and UUP improved markedly during this period, there remains a significant gap in gender representation between the two unionist parties and Sinn Féin, the SDLP, and the Alliance Party.

Table 8.3 Election of female candidates from five main parties in Northern Ireland, 2011 Assembly election

	Seats won	Females elected	Female representatives elected by party as % of total elected	Female candidates fielded by party (%)	Female candidates successful out of total female candidates (%)
DUP	38 (+18)	5 (+4)	13 (+8)	16 (+4)	71 (+46)
UUP	16 (−12)	5 (+3)	13 (+6)	11 (+3)	67 (+17)
APNI	8 (+2)	2 (+1)	25 (+8)	32 (+5)	29 (+12)
SDLP	14 (−14)	3 (–)	21 (+8)	14 (+1)	75 (+25)
Sinn Féin	29 (+11)	8 (+3)	28 (–)	31 (+9)	73 (+10)

Figures in brackets show change from 1998.

Across all parties in Northern Ireland, the numbers of female candidates, along with their success rates, have improved markedly. As demonstrated in Table 8.3, the DUP has shown the greatest progress in getting women candidates elected, as female success rates have increased by 46 per cent since the 1998 Assembly election. What is also striking from Table 8.3 is the high

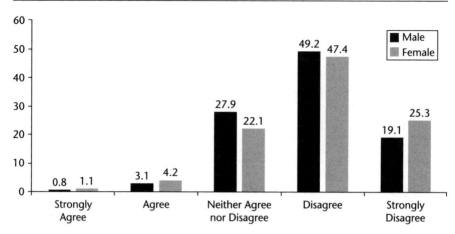

Figure 8.5 DUP members' views on whether 'A woman candidate will lose votes' (%)

percentage success rates of women unionist and nationalist candidates, over 70 per cent of whom were successful. The DUP has far fewer female representatives than Sinn Féin, but has a percentage success rate with those candidates almost the equal of its nationalist rival. Thus, the table at least suggests that the party is fielding women in winnable seats, rather than just fielding token women to appease demands for gender equality in Stormont. The success of women indicates that DUP members are correct in substantially dismissing the proposition that 'a woman candidate will lose votes'. Figure 8.5 shows how this fear is rejected in similar percentages by male and female members.

There is one caveat to the solidity of the dismissal of the proposition that a woman candidate would forfeit party electoral support. Of the five questions regarding gender in the membership survey, age proved an insignificant variable in four. However, agreement with the statement that gender determines the electoral success of a candidate is significantly higher among older members of the DUP. In the 2011 Assembly elections, across all parties it was statistically advantageous to be a woman, the percentage of women elected to the Assembly higher than the percentage chance for males.

Questioned on his awareness of the gender deficit in the Assembly when selecting candidates, the DUP leader, Peter Robinson, insisted:

> Yes, very aware of it. Indeed, we changed our selection system to try and help ... In the Assembly we would have liked to have got to the stage where there would be a pretty even show, but it will be a long time before we get to that.[55]

Under Robinson's leadership, the DUP has begun to take a more proactive approach in selecting female candidates. In 2009, the party constitution and rules introduced a provision on gender for its internal structures. The rules stated that 'throughout the Party there should be a representative character to every group and committee formed by its members…unless there are extenuating circumstances, it is not expected that any association would nominate representatives from one gender only'.[56]

Furthermore, changes introduced to the selection process of candidates suggest that there is an active promotion of women in the party. The party selection procedure is primarily carried out on a localized basis. However, at the Assembly level, there is greater scope for central party involvement. In a constituency where the DUP is contesting more than one seat, the party's Central Executive Committee is able to select one candidate. After local selection through the party's Constituency Associations for the 2011 Assembly elections, only two women had been selected, the remaining incumbents, Michelle McIlveen and Arlene Foster. The three other female MLAs that were subsequently elected, Paula Bradley, Pam Brown, and Brenda Hale, were selected centrally by the DUP at the party officer level.

Women in Westminster and Europe

From 1921–69, only three women from Northern Ireland were elected to Westminster, Patricia Ford in 1953 and Patricia McLaughlin in 1955, both from the UUP, and Bernadette Devlin, a nationalist Unity candidate, in 1969. The DUP's arrival in 1971 did not change things, as the party struggled to achieve substantial Westminster representation. In 2001, the DUP achieved the election of their first female MP in the House of Commons. Iris Robinson was elected MP for Strangford and retained her seat until stepping down in January 2010. At the Westminster elections that followed, in May 2010, there were two vacancies, but males were selected to run in both. Elsewhere, the DUP's decision to support unionist unity meant a female candidate in Fermanagh and South Tyrone stood down. In North Down, the party endorsed the sitting Independent MP Lady Sylvia Herman. Of the eight DUP representatives in the House of Commons, none are female. Deputy leader and MP for North Belfast, Nigel Dodds, stated how the lack of female representation in Westminster is an issue for the party:

> Yes, it is an issue that we are aware of all of the time in terms of party issues and in terms of selecting. Diane, obviously, is our MEP. Two out of the three MEPs in Northern Ireland are female. You are right, in Westminster it is a source of great regret to us that there are no female MPs, and that is a source of regret. It is my view that that issue needs to be addressed at all levels of the party…It is not as easy in Northern Ireland at the Westminster level. It is much easier at the Assembly level.[57]

In April 2006, Eileen Paisley became one of the first three members of the DUP to be created a life peer in the House of Lords. In Europe, the DUP saw the election of its first female MEP, Diane Dodds, in the 2009 election.

Understanding the Gender Imbalance

In order to explore the barriers to female participation, there is a need to examine the supply- and demand-side factors inhibiting equal gender representation. Supply-side explanations of political representation suggest that a party's electoral candidates reflect the supply of applicants wishing to enter politics. Factors influencing the supply of candidates include constraints on resources (such as time, money, and family commitments) and motivational factors (ambition, self-confidence).[58] Supply-side explanations suggest that the low level of female politicians is a result of the 'endemic reluctance' on behalf of women seeking a career in politics.[59] Demand-side explanations of political representation involve structural and systemic barriers involving discrimination through party selection procedures and institutional procedures (such as the voting system).

In exploring the gender deficit in Northern Irish politics, much of the scholarly focus has been upon party culture.[60] However, there is a need to also reflect upon the significance of institutional barriers that may be out of the party's control. For example, can the gender deficit in Northern Ireland be attributed to inherent systemic obstacles such as the voting system? The Single Transferable Vote (PR-STV) has proven popular in Northern Ireland for facilitating ethnic representation. Some argue that it has also encouraged parties to moderate their agendas in order to appeal to the median voter and attract lower preference votes within and across communities.[61] In the Northern Irish Assembly elections there are eighteen, six-seat constituencies, with no limit on the number of candidates a party can field. At Westminster elections, parties can only field one candidate in each constituency. Therefore, with PR-STV, focus is on district size, rather than the seat-vote proportionality that comes with First Past the Post (FPTP) for Westminster elections. With multi-member constituencies in Assembly contests, party selectors are more willing to nominate new candidates and potentially more able to do so without having to displace an incumbent.[62] Therefore, PR-STV is considered friendlier to women candidates than First Past the Post (FPTP) and other single seat systems, but less beneficial than certain elements of list proportional representation.[63] Alternative forms of PR, such the Additional Member System (AMS) used in the Welsh Assembly and Scottish Parliament elections, are considered more encouraging to gender equality than PR-STV. If women are not elected as constituency representatives, the regional list system operated under AMS comes into play on second votes in order to encourage proportionality in the devolved institutions. Therefore, the regional list system almost guarantees elected positions for female candidates if they are high enough up the party list. Of course, the aspiration for gender parity rests upon the assumption that parties will be willing to place their female candidates high up their regional 'top-up' lists. In terms of female representation in the Northern Irish Assembly, it is suggested that PR-STV lies somewhere in the 'mid-range' of gender facilitation rankings.

Research suggests that lack of gender diversity is not a result of the voting system, but stems from attitudinal issues within some parties, which 'might at worst seem antediluvian and at best be seen as a legacy of male dominance—rather than as a product of systemic failings associated with STV'.[64] It would be misleading to consider the impact of structural obstacles in isolation from its broader context; a party list system is described as a necessary, but certainly not sufficient, condition for high levels of female representation.[65] For conservative party cultures, it is far more likely that the socio-cultural context is to blame for the under-representation of women than electoral system failings. Thus, within the Northern Irish Assembly, the issue is largely one of party candidate supply, rather than systemic inadequacy. Some of the blame for the shortfall of women in elected positions has been attributed to the prejudices of local party selection committees. For example, Matthews places responsibility for candidate selection with the political parties themselves, who 'exercise virtually unrivalled control over legislative recruitment. Through their role as "gatekeepers", they determine not only the volume of candidates, but also the identity of those standing for election'.[66] Party selection of candidates represents a valuable opportunity to increase elected female representation, a point that is acknowledged by the DUP leadership. When asked whether gender balance within the party is something the party is aware of when selecting candidates, Nigel Dodds responded with the following:

> This issue needs to be addressed at all levels of the party. We wrote into the rules a special provision. We wrote that in selection, the party should have regard to the issue of gender balance and try and increase the number of women in politics...I am very, very keen to promote the number of women in politics. They do have an enormous contribution to make and the electorate do want to see more women in politics. Even men, they like the idea of much more balance.[67]

Selecting female candidates centrally demonstrates a willingness by the party to engage in a proactive approach in promoting the representation of women. However, party rules insist that it is not at the expense of the merit principle.

The 'merit principle' is crucial here, as it weighs heavily against the idea of a quota system to bolster women's representation. Figure 8.6 indicates considerable opposition to the use of a fixed quota of women candidates.

Even when individuals expressed a desire to increase the number of female elected representatives within the party, antipathy existed towards positive discrimination measures. Whilst women are more supportive than men for the party to have a fixed proportion of women candidates (four times as

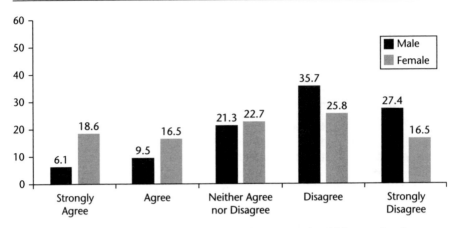

Figure 8.6 DUP members' views on whether their party should have a fixed proportion of women candidates (%)

many men are against than in support), the majority of female members are still against a quota system. Age is insignificant in determining support for introducing such a policy into the party. Opposition to quotas is not confined to the sphere of women's representation (religious quotas for policing recruitment attracted huge opprobrium amongst members). Moreover, the significant (if lesser) extent of hostility to positive discrimination amongst women themselves indicates that this is not a simple problem of misogyny requiring remedial treatment. Nonetheless, the resistance to quotas means that attitudinal change may be required in processes of candidate selection if gender parity is to be achieved.

None of the elected representatives interviewed outwardly supported the use of quotas. Male and female party representatives were keen to stress that selection should be carried out on the basis of merit. At the council level, opposition to positive discrimination measures was expressed in reference to tokenism and 'seeing women coming in and standing as candidates just because they are women'.[68] A male councillor from Coleraine asserted:

> There is no point just having a token woman. If they get selected on merit, then they should be supported, irrespective of whether they are male or female. But I would be supportive of more women candidates, yes.[69]

Such opinions were reiterated by male representatives of the DUP, arguing the need to 'pick someone because they are best for the job'.[70] Merit is promoted as the determining factor in terms of selection: 'I would rather have people selected purely on merit; I don't care whether male or female.'[71] All female elected representatives interviewed reflected their male colleagues' view that quotas do not provide a viable mechanism to improve the gender imbalance within the party. Female councillors and MLAs stressed the importance of the merit principle on the basis that quotas would undervalue their ability to fulfil their position:

> I'm not one for quotas. This idea that women need to get special privileges to get seats is not right. If you are good enough, you will get selected and people will vote for you. There is a gender imbalance across the parties. I don't believe in quotas. I think that if you want something, work hard and get it. It shouldn't matter that you are a woman. I would hate it if I was sitting there thinking that I got chosen just because I was a woman.[72]

Even whilst accepting that the gender imbalance within the party is something that needs to be addressed, there remains an objection to quotas. MLA Paula Bradley's assessment was representative of other female MLAs:

> I don't agree with it [quotas]—absolutely not. I don't think it's right. But we need to do something. I just don't know what the answer is. Any job being done there could be done by a woman. And any job a woman does, a man can do. I believe completely in gender equality. But I don't think a woman should be there just because the law dictates it. I think that would be very wrong.[73]

In another typical aside, one female councillor emphasized: 'if people were treating me different, I would be saying don't bother, I am here on my own right, I am elected in my own right'.[74] In terms of party policy on gender representation, preference is given to informal mechanisms, such as the party working internally to promote female candidates and centrally at party officer level.

According to Ward, the DUP has moved on from a 'gender reinforcement stance', a position which reiterates the separate roles occupied by unionist men and women through a sexual division of labour.[75] Instead, the party now seems to be in a balance between a 'gender neutral' and 'gender recognition' stance. A 'gender neutral' position recognizes gender as a factor in party deliberations, but 'emphasises the principles of merit as a method of selecting candidates'.[76] In party policy terms, a gender neutral position means that men and women are not viewed as having 'specific gendered-based needs arising from their different social functions'.[77] In developing strategies to promote equality of opportunity through central selection and encouraging individual women to stand, there is an indication that the party is trying to create a more 'level playing field'.[78] Equality of outcome through quotas was not supported by any elected representative in interviews across the party.

At the DUP 2013 annual conference, a new initiative was unveiled to help address the under-representation of women in unionism. The 1928 Committee and Association, named after the year women were granted the vote on an equal basis, aims to take proactive steps in developing programmes to attract more female members to the party, whilst building the skills of those who are already members.[79]

In launching the initiative, MLA and chairperson of the 1928 Committee and Association, Michelle McIlveen, stated: 'In the DUP, we recognise and reward talent and ability regardless of gender. However, this party also recognises that there is an under-representation of women within frontline unionism.'[80] The formation of the association acknowledges the shortfall of women across all levels of the party, but does not indicate a departure from the merit principle as the basis of selection, aiming rather to address the supply-side explanations of why too few women choose to engage with political roles and elected office. The association is a positive step towards encouraging female participation in the party and unionist politics. However, reference at the launch to a quote from Margaret Thatcher stating that 'Any woman who understands the problems of running a home will be nearer to understanding the problems of running a country',[81] suggests that separate gender roles are still strongly identified within the party.

Research indicates that structural barriers, such as incumbency, as opposed to gender, best explain candidate success rates.[82] Incumbency can be considered as presenting structural as well as motivational obstacles to female representation. Given that the vast majority of DUP elected incumbents are males, it may be a particularly acute problem within the party.[83] Senior male elected representatives may believe that they have built a substantial personal, as well as political, following in their constituency. They are also difficult to remove, even if the party is desirous for such representatives to step aside. DUP Chief Whip and MLA Peter Weir suggested high retention rates presented the main obstacle in improving female representation:

> I think the only barrier, in the broadest sense, is a certain level of incumbency because one thing within the party as a whole—there is at least a residue of sort of more of a sense of family within the DUP, compared to other parties...Councillor Bloggs, who has been there for twenty-five years, maybe isn't the world's greatest councillor, but there's almost a feeling that we can't deselect him.[84]

Despite the female success rate improving in the last decade, it will take some time for women to reap the incumbency benefits available to male representatives of the DUP, and the party leader acknowledges the distance to travel:

> It is not always easy to get the combination of people who are capable of winning votes at the same time as having them in the right areas and being willing to stand. There are generational problems and whenever you have a party and people have seats, it is very easy to return the existing member, let him stand again. So that means that there are very few new opportunities for women to come into it.[85]

There is also evidence that incumbency presents a supply-side barrier to female participation. Several women interviewed expressed reluctance to compete for a seat held by a man. Two female MLAs acknowledged the difficulty, notwithstanding their own personal triumphs in having secured candidature and election:

> We stand back and let out male colleagues . . . especially if you're running for selection and that seat is already occupied by a man. We tend to go, and I think I speak for most women, 'Actually, I'm not going to go up against him, cause he's the one who's already there doing the job'. I did that as well, for years. And I know from speaking to other women and speaking at many women's events, that they are keen on changing that.[86]
>
> That's a huge barrier. Women don't want to be aggressively fighting for a seat. I've done it. I've decided not to put myself forward because I didn't want to spoil it for my male friend.[87]

Individual factors, such as self-confidence and motivation, also influence the supply of women entering politics. Wilford suggests that women are more sensitive to their own limits than their male counterparts and therefore need more encouragement to put themselves forward to stand, arguing that 'it seems exceptional for women, irrespective of party, to consider themselves eligible for candidature'.[88] Other research also suggests that women often display inhibitions about the appropriateness of their qualifications.[89] As a result, women do not generally consider putting themselves forward until approached to do so. This point was reflected in several interviews with female representatives who were encouraged to stand. In a not untypical response, one woman MLA recalled: 'Then he [colleague] actually said, "Why don't you put your name forward for being a councillor?", and I said, "I don't know. I don't think that I would be able to do it."'[90] Some female representatives were keen to stress that it was indeed male colleagues who encouraged them to stand: 'I've never had any barriers within the DUP. In the last election, I was asked to stand . . . men were pushing me to go into that role,' declared one councillor.[91] Antipathy towards positive discrimination within the party means exhortation has been a key strategy in getting women to stand for election.[92] The encouragement given to women was described as an important factor in deciding to stand throughout all levels of the party. MLA Pam Brown described her experience: 'It was men and women who encouraged me to go forward. If it had been left to me, I probably wouldn't have done it. It did take a lot of encouragement from other people for me to give it a go.'[93]

In exploring the effects of gender on the supply of candidates, Norris and Lovenduski suggest that, due to the division of labour, segregation in the labour market, and traditional patterns of socialization, 'we would expect many women to have lower resources of time and money and lower levels of political ambition and confidence'.[94] Other research also points to supply-side factors, such as lifestyle constraints and a lack of volition, in explaining the shortage of female candidates putting themselves forward for elected positions.[95]

Responsibility for the dearth of female political representatives within unionist politics has been placed with embedded social norms. The division of labour in unionism replicates the traditional conservative attitudes towards women's roles in society. When asked whether it is difficult for women to be involved in politics, Arlene Foster emphasized the attachment of traditional stereotypes regarding domestic responsibilities to women:

> Inevitably, I get asked the question of my children. 'What about your children'? And what is really frustrating is that you never ask that of any of my male colleagues and that's just the reality. Women are still primary carers for children and therefore there are always questions, do you feel guilty, which I was asked about as well. Do you feel guilty going to work...So yeah, I think Northern Ireland is a very conservative society.[96]

Domestic responsibilities are cited elsewhere as having an influence on female political participation and are not necessarily issues specific to women in the DUP. However, the conservative family values that exist within unionism exacerbate the restriction placed on female participation in the formal political sphere. A female councillor referred to these restrictions when responding as to why it is difficult to get more women to stand in the party, 'Men go out to work and would be working quite a lot. I don't think it is really the done thing for women to be out of the house every night.'[97] Several women also referenced the comparative freedom of their male counterparts in being relieved from domestic duties traditionally considered the woman's responsibility. One female MLA observed:

> I think men get it easier...Men can go and get a job without having to think about who's going to look after the kids or do the washing or ironing or cooking...I don't think men have the same guilt that women have. When women go out, it usually falls on them to get a babysitter.[98]

Expressing a feeling of guilt about the time away from their children was evident across all levels of the party. Organizational constraints, such as long hours, the scheduling of meetings, and the unpredictable nature of politics, were commonly noted by female representatives as a challenge to their participation in politics:

> It is very difficult. I feel guilty. Yesterday, I got my child to the bus in the morning at quarter to eight and I was going to a meeting then at half five and wasn't back till ten o'clock...she was in her bed. I didn't see her all day and you feel guilty at times...it is hard to juggle work and home life.[99]

Even amongst younger representatives who did not have children, these factors clearly featured in their considerations of whether they wished to stay in
politics and pursue election to higher office:

> I don't think it will ever become family friendly. Obviously, I am sure [named
> councillor] will be looking to have a family in the future and I would be as well.
> I would probably be questioning how politics fits into my family life. For me, that
> would be my priority.[100]

The sexual division of labour continues to be an obstacle for women entering politics, as well as advancing to a higher level of politics. Traditional
gender roles of women as wives and mothers remain evident in the party,
where responsibility for the domestic setting is still very much placed with a
woman. When asked whether there were obstacles to women being selected
as candidates, a female DUP councillor commented:

> We can be truthful about this. There is no problem with women getting selected
> to stand, but there is an element of councillors in here that think that a women's
> place is at home, and will remind you of that every so often as well—'What are
> you doing here? You should be at home washing the dishes'... Wearing trousers
> is a problem with some of them, but I wear what I think, and my family is happy
> enough with what I wear, and I just say 'if my husband's happy enough, why
> should it bother you?' But it took me a long time to be able to stand up to them.

This discussion expresses a resistance to fit into the gender stereotype of a
woman staying at home, fulfilling her domestic role by 'washing the dishes'.
However, there is an indication that, in challenging this stereotype, with her
husband's being content with what she wears, the male and female gender
roles remain unbroken. When asked why there existed a reluctance of women
in the DUP to move into formal politics, Peter Robinson suggested that the
influence of the church remained influential in shaping the role of women
in society:

> I think the old Ulster farmer's wife and all the rest of it, whose job is at home and
> let the men do that kind of work, that is far too prevalent in the thinking, espe-
> cially within Christian circles, it has to be said. In churches, the women have to
> stay in their place.[101]

Supply and demand explanations of female under-representation have to be
set in their socio-political context. Religion and conservative social values
have been highly influential in determining gendered responsibilities and
provided the setting in which politics have evolved in Northern Ireland.

Whilst the socio-political context is a key factor, some explanations of
female participation are not necessarily specific to unionist women in
Northern Ireland and bear a striking resemblance to the explanations of

female under-representation elsewhere in the United Kingdom.[102] It has been claimed that politics is an environment that supports patriarchy and deters female involvement.[103] Whilst this may be an endemic characteristic of politics beyond Northern Ireland, Galligan argues that this culture of masculinity within politics, which disproportionately deters women, has been enhanced in the region by its troubled history.[104] Several interviewees, both male and female, referred to the lack of respect sometimes afforded to female representatives, especially at the local level. One female councillor referred to her experience, claiming: 'I think politics itself still doesn't lend itself very well to women. It is still very male dominated. You do go into a meeting and they will look towards the man in the row, instead of looking towards the woman.'[105] Whilst denying the presence of any barriers to female participation within the DUP, there is a contradiction in that some women expressed being treated differently because of their gender. A councillor described her experience as the first woman to be elected in her district:

> And they can be hurtful, very, very hurtful. You saw me, when I joined the Council, going out of here and going home in tears—many a night. Till I had to threaten that I was going to take legal action and get a solicitor to look at it. My family were rippin'. They were going to tear strips off people. 'Why are you sticking that?' But I said, I was voted in. [It was] jealously more than anything else—because I beat them at the poll. I topped the poll and have done every year since and they can't heck it—because they've been in here for years.[106]

Whilst no representatives, male or female, accept there are rigid and forbidding barriers to female participation in the party, there is an embedded masculinized culture in politics that the DUP has not escaped. A male MLA described the presence of such culture within the DUP, conceding: 'Party membership tends to be a much older, more conservative type of individual. There are those who don't like women in any powerful position, same as any political party.'[107] This factor may not be a barrier in itself to female participation, but certainly makes politics a less attractive option for women in the party and discourages younger females from believing that politics is a viable future career option.

Obstacles to female participation have been attributed to attitudinal reluctance amongst women in the DUP, rather than the lack of opportunity offered by the party. Blame was attached to the personal choice of women not to pursue a political career, rather than any discrimination by the party towards female candidates. Thus, it was claimed by two MLAs that:

> Of course there's opportunity...I can say that I have not felt any obstacle other than my own obstacles as a female. I think that's the biggest problem. I think females don't put themselves forward.[108]

If there are any barriers they are self-imposed...I certainly don't feel any discrimination or barriers within the party...It is a male-dominated industry.[109]

Whilst a consensus is evident that the party could do more to attract females,
responsibility for achieving political gender equality was placed with the
women themselves, one woman MLA insisting: 'I think we just need a mas-
sive amount of encouragement. Plus, women kind of need to grow balls and
stand up for themselves. But it's difficult.'[110] Focus is placed on women adapt-
ing to fit into a male-dominated environment, as opposed to making politics
an attractive career option for future female generations.

When asking 'what can be done to attract more females?', the response was
often that women will attract more women, with the high-profile roles of
senior figures, such as Arlene Foster and Diane Dodds, serving as inspiration
to other females;

> I suppose women attract women...I think, ultimately, it will be young females that
> will inspire other young females to say, hold on, I can do what they do...I would
> say it is personal and would say that Arlene is probably the champion of women,
> then Diane follows. So Diane and her, I would hold in very high regard.[111]

Arlene Foster, MLA for Fermanagh South Tyrone, is one of four women in the
executive. Serving as Minister for Enterprise, Trade, and Investment at the
time of this study, she took on the role of acting First Minister on behalf of
Peter Robinson in early 2010. As noted in a previous chapter, Foster's popularity is such that when she moved from the UUP to the DUP in early 2004,
she brought support with her. A DUP member in her constituency who made
the transition at the same time declared: 'Wherever Arlene goes, I follow'.[112]
When in the UUP, Arlene Foster openly spoke of how the 'party should
develop skills and give confidence to women in order to play a full and active
role in the party'.[113] When asked whether she was conscious of her role as a
woman in politics, to provide an example, the response was as follows:

> I am conscious of it. Even last night, there were two girls in the audience who came
> up and wanted to have their photograph taken with me, so you are conscious of
> it yeah...We have quite a few ladies coming up, but it's just to encourage them to
> go that step further. I would say that the party membership has some very good,
> strong women, and it is just getting them to move a bit further up the ladder.[114]

The significance of having a woman DUP MEP was emphasized by a female
MLA: 'We have Diane Dodds as MEP. If you're a Councillor at the local level,
you can see opportunities right the way up to Europe.'[115] The starkest problem, in terms of the visibility of women for the DUP, is at Westminster, where
the party is bereft of female representation. However, with three new female
MLAs benefiting from central selection and entering the Assembly in 2011,
there are a growing number of females representing the party in Stormont.

213

Across Northern Ireland, there are also DUP mayors and councillors who have the potential to provide encouragement, at the local level, to a new generation of women that politics is a viable career option.

Conclusion

DUP women remain seriously under-represented on councils and in the Assembly, whilst the party has no women in the House of Commons. Far more men than women belong to the party, although the imbalance is greater at the elected representative level. Various explanations, such as supply (family commitments, self-confidence) and demand (party selection procedures, voting system), help to explain the constraints on women entering politics. Whilst relevant, these factors provide the basis for exploring the gender deficit in politics beyond Northern Ireland and are not necessarily specific to the female members of the DUP. However, the cultural context in Northern Ireland has exacerbated female under-representation. Communal division, religion, and conservative social values have provided the setting in which unionist politics has evolved. There existed a clear sexual division of labour, where men were expected to act in defence of their country, whilst female responsibilities were an extension of their domestic role. Specific policies on women were absent from election manifestos and women were generally allocated supportive roles; men were very much the face of the DUP.

Today, the DUP primarily encourages a 'gender neutral' position, with emphasis on merit as a method of selection. Preference is given to this approach by men and women across the party, as opposed to the implementation of quotas. It is unclear whether reliance upon merit is sufficient to cure internal residual reluctance to field women, caused by the supply or demand factors and internal patriarchal attitudes, as outlined in this chapter and clearly evidenced in the statistics. It is difficult to accept that across the party there is a scarcity of women of adequate calibre to stand for election. Women have always been active within the DUP, but standing for election has been a relatively uncommon activity. The recognition by the DUP of the problem and clear desire for more women candidates, provided they are not selected by quota, has begun to yield results at the Assembly and local level. The question begged is whether progress can be maintained. Movement towards the encouragement of female candidates through central selection suggests that the party is being proactive in promoting the opportunities for women as electoral representatives in the party. Such an approach indicates recognition by the party leadership that more is needed than a vague reliance on merit to address the gender deficit, an approach implying that, for several decades, women DUP members somehow lacked quality.

Notes

1. Female DUP focus group, Fermanagh, 27 Apr. 2013.
2. See F. Cochrane (2001) *Unionist Politics and the Politics of Unionism since the Anglo-Irish Agreement*, Cork: Cork University Press; R. Ward (2004). '"It's Not Just Tea and Buns": Women and Pro-Union Politics in Northern Ireland', *British Journal of Politics and International Relations*, 6, 494–506.
3. C. Murtagh (2008) 'A Transient Transition: The Cultural and Institutional Obstacles Impeding the Northern Ireland Women's Coalition in its Progression from Informal to Formal Politics', *Irish Political Studies*, 23/1, 31.
4. R. Sales (1997) 'Gender and Protestantism in Northern Ireland', in P. Shirlow and M. McGovern (eds), *Who are 'the People?' Unionism, Protestantism, and Loyalism in Northern Ireland*, London: Pluto, 140.
5. R. Ward (2004) 'Gender Issues and the Representation of Women in Northern Ireland', *Irish Political Studies*, 19/2, 14.
6. L. Racioppi and K. O'Sullivan See (2001) '"This we will Maintain": Gender Ethno-Nationalism and the Politics of Unionism in Northern Ireland', *Nations and Nationalisms*, 7, 190.
7. R. Ward (2002) 'Invisible Women: The Political Roles of Unionist and Loyalist Women in Contemporary Northern Ireland', *Parliamentary Affairs*, 55/1, 67–78.
8. Y. Galligan and K. Knight (2011) 'Attitudes towards Women in Politics: Gender, Generation and Party Identification in Ireland', *Parliamentary Affairs*, 64/4: 585–611.
9. Sales, 'Gender and Protestantism', 140; R. Ward, (2006) *Women, Unionism, and Loyalism in Northern Ireland: From 'Tea-Makers' to Political Actors*, Dublin: Irish Academic Press.
10. Interview with David Simpson MP, Westminster, 3 July 2013.
11. Cochrane, *Unionist Politics*, 47.
12. Cochrane, *Unionist Politics*, 48.
13. R. Paisley (1992) 'Feminism, Unionism, and "The Brotherhood"', *Irish Reporter*, 8, in M. O'Dowd, S. Kilfeather, A. Bourke, M. Luddy, M. MacCurtain, G. Meaney, M. Ni Dhonnchadha, and C. Wills (eds) (2002) *The Field Day Anthropology of Irish Writing: Irish Women's Writing*, iv/5, Cork: Cork University Press, 1515–16.
14. Cochrane, *Unionist Politics*, 48.
15. Galligan and Knight, 'Attitudes towards Women in Politics', 587.
16. I. Paisley (1993) *Protestant Telegraph*, 8 Nov.
17. Londonderry DUP (1994) *Ulster Home Cooking*, Londonderry: DUP; emphasis in the original.
18. Londonderry DUP, *Ulster Home Cooking*.
19. M. Ward (1983) *Unmanageable Revolutionaries: Women and Irish Nationalism*, London: Pluto.
20. Racioppi and O'Sullivan See, 'This we will Maintain', 7.
21. A. Brown, T. Donaghy, F. MacKay, and E. Meehan (2002) 'Women and Constitutional Change in Scotland and Northern Ireland', *Parliamentary Affairs*, 55/1, 71.

22. B. Hayes and I. McAllister (2012) 'Gender and Consociational Power-Sharing in Northern Ireland', *International Political Science Review*, 34/2, 131.

23. A. Gray and G. Neill (2011) 'Creating a Shared Society in Northern Ireland: Why We Need to Focus on Gender Equality', *Youth and Society*, 43/2, 480.

24. R. Wilford (1999) 'Women and Politics', in P. Mitchell and R. Wilford (eds), *Politics in Northern Ireland*, Oxford: Westview Press, 210.

25. Northern Ireland Women's Coalition (1996) *Northern Ireland Women's Coalition: Constitution, 1996–2000*, Belfast: NIWC, in O'Dowd et al. (eds), *Field Day Anthropology of Irish Writing*, 431–40.

26. The NIWC won 1.03% of the vote under party-list proportional representation, but obtained two places in the forum as one of the top ten parties in terms of percentage vote.

27. C. Murtagh (2008) 'A Transient Transition: The Cultural and Institutional Obstacles Impeding the Northern Ireland Women's Coalition in its Progression from Informal to Formal Politics', *Irish Political Studies*, 23/1, 21–40.

28. See K. Cowell-Meyers (2011). 'A Collarette on a Donkey: The Northern Ireland Women's Coalition and the Limitations of Contagion Theory', *Political Studies*, 59/2, 411–31.

29. K. Fearon (2002). *Northern Ireland Women's Coalition: Institutionalizing a Political Voice and Ensuring Representation*, available at <http://www.cr.org/sites/cr.org/files/Accord%2013_16Northern%20Ireland%20women%27s%20coalition_2002_ENG.pdf>, accessed July 2013.

30. DUP (1998) *Women's Issues*, Belfast: DUP.

31. Galligan and Knight, 'Attitudes towards Women in Politics', 589.

32. DUP (2001) *Leadership to Put Things Right, Parliamentary and District Council Election Manifesto*, Belfast: DUP, 8.

33. B. Hinds (1999) 'Women Working for Peace in Northern Ireland', in Y. Galligan, E. Ward, and R. Wilford (eds), *Contesting Politics: Women in Ireland, North and South*, Oxford: Westview, 113.

34. Racioppi and O'Sullivan See, 'This we will Maintain', 98.

35. Gray and Neill, 'Creating a Shared Society in Northern Ireland', 470.

36. Interview with Nigel Dodds MP, Westminster, 3 July 2013.

37. Ward, 'Unionist and Loyalist Women in Contemporary Northern Ireland', 171.

38. Personal email correspondence with the DUP Membership Secretary, 18 July 2013.

39. Galligan and Knight, 'Attitudes towards Women in Politics', 585–611; R. L. Miller, R. Wilford, and F. Donoghue (1996) *Women and Political Participation in Northern Ireland*, Aldershot: Avebury.

40. Ward, 'Gender Issues and the Representation of Women in Northern Ireland', 6.

41. Ward, 'It's Not Just Tea and Buns', 496.

42. Female DUP focus group, Fermanagh, 27 Apr. 2013.

43. Interview with female councillor, County Londonderry, 15 Apr. 2013.

44. G. Lucy (1994) *Northern Ireland Local Government Election Results, 1993*, Lurgan: Ulster Society, 171.

45. R. Sales (1997) *Women Divided: Gender, Religion, and Politics in Northern Ireland*, London: Routledge, 170–1.
46. Cowell-Meyers, 'Collarette on a Donkey', 420.
47. Personal email correspondence with the DUP Membership Secretary, 18 July 2013.
48. Y. Galligan and R. Wilford (1999) 'Women's Political Representation in Ireland', in Y. Galligan et al., *Contesting Politics*, 136.
49. Department of Finance and Personnel (2012) *Women in Northern Ireland*, Belfast: Northern Ireland Statistics and Research Agency, 22. Across all parties in England, female councillors make up 31%.
50. A. Brown, T. Donaghy, F. MacKay, and E. Meehan (2002) 'Women and Constitutional Change in Scotland and Northern Ireland', *Parliamentary Affairs*, 55/1, 71–84.
51. Racioppi and O'Sullivan See, 'This we will Maintain', 190.
52. G. McCoy (2000), 'Women, Community, and Politics in Northern Ireland', in C. Roulston and C. Davies (eds), *Gender, Democracy, and Inclusion in Northern Ireland*, Basingstoke: Palgrave, 3–12.
53. See Miller et al., *Women and Political Participation in Northern Ireland*.
54. N. Matthews (2012) 'Gendered Candidate Selection and the Representation of Women in Northern Ireland', *Parliamentary Affairs*, 67/1, 1–30.
55. Interview with Peter Robinson MLA, DUP Leader, Stormont, 25 June 2013.
56. DUP (2009) *Constitution and Rules*, Belfast: DUP.
57. Interview with Nigel Dodds, 3 July 2013.
58. See P. Norris and J. Lovenduski (1993). '"If Only More Candidates Came Forward": Supply-Side Explanations of Candidate Selection in Britain', *British Journal of Political Science*, 23/3: 380–1.
59. Matthews, 'Gendered Candidate Selection', 1–30.
60. See Ward, 'It's Not Just Tea and Buns', 494–506; Wilford, 'Women and Politics', 195–219; Matthews, 'Gendered Candidate Selection', 1–30.
61. See J. Evans and J. Tonge (2009) 'Social Class and Party Choice in Northern Ireland's Ethnic Blocs', *West European Politics*, 32/5, 1012–30.
62. P. Norris (2004), *Electoral Engineering: Voting Rules and Political Behaviour*, Cambridge: Cambridge University Press.
63. C. McGing (2013) '*A Preference for Gender? PR-STV and Women's Representation in the Northern Ireland Assembly*', paper prepared for European Consortium on Politics and Gender Conference, Maynooth: National University of Ireland, 6.
64. House of Lords and House of Commons Joint Committee (2012) *Draft House of Lords Reform Bill: Report Session 2010–12*, 3, HL Paper 284-1, HC 1313-1 196. London: The Stationery Office.
65. P. Norris and J. Lovenduski (1995) *Political Recruitment: Gander, Race, and Class in the British Parliament*, Cambridge: Cambridge University Press.
66. Matthews, 'Gendered Candidate Selection', 3.
67. Interview with Nigel Dodds, 3 July 2013.
68. Interview with male councillor, Belfast, 24 Sept. 2012.
69. Interview with male councillor, Coleraine, 5 Oct. 2012.

70. Interview with Jim Shannon MP, Strangford, 3 Oct. 2012.
71. Interview with Alistair Ross MLA, East Antrim, 5 Nov. 2012.
72. Interview with female councillor, Tyrone, 27 Nov. 2012.
73. Interview with Paula Bradley MLA, Newtownabbey, 20 Sept. 2012.
74. Interview with female councillor, Armagh, 5 Nov. 2012.
75. Ward, 'Gender Issues and the Representation of Women in Northern Ireland', 10.
76. Wilford, 'Women and Politics', 195–219.
77. Y. Galligan and R. Wilford (1999) 'Gender and Party Politics in the Republic of Ireland', in Galligan et al., *Contesting Politics*, 150.
78. Ward, 'Gender Issues and the Representation of Women in Northern Ireland', 1–20.
79. DUP (2013) *My Party: My Future*, DUP annual conference programme, Belfast: DUP.
80. Michelle McIlveen MLA, launch of the DUP 1928 committee at the DUP Annual Conference, 23 Nov. 2013, Belfast.
81. The original Thatcher quotation has various source attributions. See e.g. <http://www.bbc.co.uk/news/uk-politics-10377842>, accessed 25 Nov. 2013.
82. McGing, 'A Preference for Gender?', 13.
83. See L. A. Schwindt-Bayer (2005) 'The Incumbency Disadvantage and Women's Election to Legislative Office', *Electoral Studies*, 24/2, 227–44; R. Y. Hazan and G. Rahat (2010) *Democracy within Parties: Candidate Selection Methods and their Political Consequences*, Oxford: Oxford University Press.
84. Interview with Peter Weir MLA, North Down, 27 Feb. 2013.
85. Interview with Peter Robinson, 25 June 2013.
86. Interview with Paula Bradley, 20 Sept. 2012.
87. Interview with Pam Brown MLA, Belfast, 2 Oct. 2012.
88. R. Wilford (1993). 'In their own Voices: Women Councillors in Northern Ireland', *Public Administration*, 71/3, 344.
89. J. Lovenduski and P. Norris, *Gender and Party Politics*, London: Sage.
90. Interview with male MLA, 9 Jan. 2013.
91. Interview with female councillor, County Down, 19 Sept. 2012.
92. Ward, 'It's Not Just Tea and Buns', 494–506; Miller et al., *Women and Political Participation*.
93. Interview with Pam Brown, 2 Oct. 2012.
94. See Norris and Lovenduski, 'If Only More Candidates Came Forward', 390.
95. S. Bristow (1980) 'Women Councillors: An Explanation of the Under-Representation of Women in Local Government', *Local Government Studies*, 6/3, 73–90; J. Hills (1983) 'Life-Style Constraints on Formal Political Participation: Why So Few Women Local Councillors in Britain?', *Electoral Studies*, 2/1, 39–52.
96. Interview with Arlene Foster MLA, Fermanagh, 24 Jan. 2013.
97. Interview with female councillor, Antrim, 28 Feb. 2013.
98. Interview with Pam Brown, 2 Oct. 2012.
99. Interview with female councillor, Tyrone, 16 Apr. 2013.
100. Interview with female councillor, Antrim, 28 Feb. 2013.
101. Interview with Peter Robinson, 25 June 2013.

102. Matthews, 'Gendered Candidate Selection', 3.
103. See Norris and Lovenduski, *Political Recruitment*; Ward, 'It's Not Just Tea and Buns', 494–506.
104. Y. Galligan (2006) 'Women in Northern Ireland's Politics: Feminising an "Armed Patriarchy"', in M. Sawer, M. Tremblay, and L. Trimble (eds), *Representing Women in Parliament*, London: Routledge, 204–20.
105. Interview with female councillor, Armagh, 5 Nov. 2012.
106. Interview with female councillor, Antrim, 4 Oct. 2012.
107. Interview with Alistair Ross, 5 Nov. 2012.
108. Interview with Paula Bradley, 20 Sept. 2012.
109. Interview with Brenda Hale MLA, Lagan Valley, 11 Jan. 2013.
110. Interview with Pam Brown, 2 Oct. 2012.
111. Interview with female councillor, Armagh, 5 Nov. 2012.
112. Fermanagh focus group, 26 Apr. 2013.
113. A. Foster (1998) Transcript of Speech to the UUP Conference, cited in Ward, 'It's Not Just Tea and Buns', 501.
114. Interview with Arlene Foster, 24 Jan. 2013.
115. Interview with Brenda Hale, 11 Jan. 2013.

Conclusion: From Never to Possibly to Yes to What Next?

The DUP's political journey has been extraordinary. Transformed from a ramshackle, leader-dominated, religiously driven party, based upon seemingly perpetual opposition to fiendish plots to betray 'Ulster', the modern DUP looks much more like a 'normal' political party. In an era when there is much commentary on the decline of parties, the DUP has expanded, albeit from a very small size, and continues to attract strong partisan loyalty. Although their party has radically altered, there remain plenty of internal witnesses to the party's long journey. Almost one-quarter of current members joined the party during the 1970s and 1980s and one in eight have been involved from the first three years. These stalwarts, original Paisleyites and often members of the Free Presbyterian Church, could scarcely have envisaged the denouement to the party's fourth decade: power-sharing with the republican 'enemy', with the DUP and Sinn Féin dominating the government of Northern Ireland. Long-standing members were joined in the late 1990s and early 2000s by a large tranche of Unionists disaffected with the leadership of the UUP and its handling of the Belfast Agreement. More than one-quarter of the DUP's current membership joined between 1998 and 2005, many from the UUP. Robust, but also pragmatic, they desired strong unionist leadership which, if incapable of reversing the 'concessions' of the Belfast Agreement, would make republicans offer all future compromises first, rather than unionists.

The moves towards a deal began soon after the Belfast Agreement and gathered pace with the arrival of young and ambitious political refugees from the UUP. Outright opposition to the deal, particularly vocal on the mainly irreversible issues of prisoner releases and policing changes, was subtly displaced by movement towards a replacement deal which quietly accepted the constitutional provisions of the 1998 version. This acceptance surely indicated how incorrect had been the DUP claims of a constitutional sell-out of the Union under the Belfast Agreement, although it certainly represented a potential hollowing out of Northern Ireland's Britishness. Equally however, the DUP had a sympathetic audience to the contention that republican ambiguities and evasions following the 1998 deal—on the IRA, decommissioning, and support for policing—could not be sustained and that the DUP would exercise leadership to ensure these 'great wrongs' would end. The DUP was true to its word. Even though the inexorable direction of republican travel under Adams and McGuinness meant that the DUP's desires would have been realized at some point anyway, there is little question that Paisley and Robinson hurried Sinn Féin towards the finishing line marked 'constitutional politics', whilst marginalizing the internal 'refusenik' opposition which could potentially have coalesced around Jim Allister.

In so doing, the DUP's political leaders were assisted by a small cluster of political advisers who brought clarity to negotiations, in sharp contrast to the confusion evident within the UUP. The roles of Timothy Johnston and Richard Bullick, as advisers to Paisley and Robinson respectively, were important in bringing a forensic approach to the renegotiation of the Belfast Agreement, removing its ambiguities and ending the obfuscations which had resulted. Johnston and Bullick, alongside a small number of senior DUP elected representatives, helped develop the party's transition from the politics of outright opposition to a position which fused principles with pragmatism. Like their political masters, these advisers did not wish to see the newly born electoral dominance of the DUP wasted amid the impotence of perpetual Westminster direct rule, abetted by Dublin. From the party's electoral success in the 2003 Assembly elections onwards, the DUP direction of travel was firmly headed towards a revised power-sharing arrangement which would be obliged to accept Sinn Féin as coalition partners, but on terms which required full republican immersion in constitutional waters.

The DUP then had to worry about its internal constituency. A party that opposed power-sharing and categorically rejected sharing political spoils with republicans had to justify why it was taking exactly that course. The DUP defended its partnership with Sinn Féin at the head of the Northern Ireland Executive on the grounds that a much worse fate would have befallen unionists had direct rule been extended. Yet, for all the dire warnings and justifications offered by the DUP, there remains 'no evidence that "Plan B" would have been anything close to joint sovereignty between Dublin or London, or the end of the Union'. Indeed, there was no 'Plan B', as joint sovereignty was 'never discussed' between the two governments.[1] At worst, bolstered partnership arrangements between London and Dublin would have given the latter increased influence. This would not have altered the position on the moral concerns of some DUP members (on issues such as abortion or gay marriage) and would not have shifted the constitutional position. A 'Mark Two' Anglo-Irish Agreement might eventually have resulted, shifting the Irish Republic's role from the consultative towards the executive in certain areas—a move towards joint authority, but this was way down the track and had not been formulated in any meaningful sense. The DUP's position as lead party, with most MLAs and as the provider of the First Minister; the exit of the Provisional IRA; the shift by Sinn Féin on policing; and the removal of the salaries of MLAs were all much bigger incentives for the DUP to do the deal than a non-specific and barely credible threat of shared authority—a position which the Irish Republic's government, on the available evidence, has never really coveted. Having failed to adequately prepare its base for the shock move, the DUP's support rallied after a brief wobble. The context of 2007–9 was very different to that of 1998–2002, when the UUP leadership sold the deal. Sinn Féin now supported policing; there was no Provisional IRA and the institutions of government were stable, thus DUP support recovered.

A Changed Party

The DUP is a much-changed party from its original Paisleyite creation. The founder, leader, and dominant figure for most of the party's history may have departed slightly earlier than he might have preferred, but what matters more is the subsequent direction of travel of the party. Paisley's criticisms of his mode of exit and of senior party figures, expressed several years later,[2] allowed the DUP to move even more quickly from those aspects of its past from which distance was now sought. A focus upon leadership personalities is entirely understandable given the party's history, but what truly matters is the broader state of the DUP. How quickly has it adjusted to being a party of government? Has it recruited a new form of member? What does the modern DUP member want their party to represent and articulate?

The first thing to note is that there are more of those members. The party continues to grow, 2008 to 2012 seeing further expansion, to add to the influx of the Belfast to St Andrews Agreements period. The lack of previous data on the DUP means that we cannot say how many members quit the party in disgust at it entering government with Sinn Féin, but it seems improbable that those exercising the exit option amounted to anything close to the number of entrants.

Examined superficially, the portrait of the average DUP member revealed in our membership survey may not startle. He (and it is much more probably a 'he') is a middle-aged, married with children, socially conservative, right-wing, church-going Protestant, either sympathetic to, or belonging to, the Orange Order; whose primary concern is the Union; who will never give even a lower preference vote to any non-unionist party and is still begrudging some aspects of the peace process, such as changes to policing. However, the overall picture masks important shifts. The new, post-1998 type of DUP member is rather different from the older version: still Protestant of course and quite likely to be Orange, but unlikely to be Free Presbyterian (only one in seven post-1998 members have been from that church) and less overtly religiously driven, but certainly religiously influenced.

Within the DUP's senior ranks lie talented former UUP members, most comfortable within the order, discipline, and grasp of power offered by the DUP. Fundamentalist Paisleyism has been replaced by pragmatic 'Robinsonism', based upon political details rather than political-religious rhetoric. The party's members, new and old, tend to practise their Christian faith and are happy for their party to be religiously influenced, making the notion of a 'secular' DUP rather fanciful. They do not hanker, however, for a return to the days when it was denominationally dominated by the Free Presbyterian Church, a skewing seen as off-putting to DUP membership for many. In the same manner that the DUP has become a communal catch-all party in social-class terms, so the party leadership aims for it be a natural repository for all categories of Protestant. More recent years have also seen the leadership offer encouragement to Catholics to join the party, but have hardly been knocked down in the rush; double figures have yet to be reached. Appeals for Catholics to join have been based upon the apparent unionism of many—so why not join a strong unionist party, with lesser pitches based upon social conservatism or support for selective education from which middle-class Catholics have benefited. The DUP is still confronted by the obvious legacy issue, however: the vitriolic denunciations of Catholicism by the party's former leader. Undoubted individual generosity towards Catholics from that leader and from the party's elected representatives may not offer sufficient recompense. A communal, largely single-religion future for the DUP seems far more likely and the party may suffer the (somewhat meaningless) label of 'sectarian' for decades.

The party remains small and with a serious gender imbalance, but for the DUP it is a case of quality, not quantity or quotas. The party has a very high-level activist base and its members are enthusiastic about their party and leadership to an extent which may be the envy of the hierarchy of other British political parties. Crucially, some of that enthusiasm extends to the current political disposition. DUP members have adapted reasonably comfortably to devolved power-sharing. The majority support devolution and similar favour is also found for the requirement for cross-community consent and even for executive ministries being shared between the DUP and Sinn Féin. Most members concur that political deadlock has been broken. This represents remarkable acquiescence given that many members were socialized politically in an era of unyielding opposition to the undemocratic nature of power-sharing and the claimed perpetual evil and cunning of republicans.

Whilst some new recruits may have joined the party for less ideological reasons than was once the case, to ride on the wave of success (members have a high rate of becoming elected representatives), the tasks confronting the party are not glamorous. The DUP jointly heads an executive with little fiscal clout, presiding over an economy still easily the most public sector dependent in the UK. Meanwhile there remain contentious issues of parades, flags, symbols, and the past. Technically, flags and symbols are devolved issues, notwithstanding the provision of the Flags (Northern Ireland) Order 2000, but they have often been seen as beyond executive control. The failure to reach cross-party agreement during the Haass talks of 2013 indicates that the ability of the DUP—influenced by strong modern Orange leanings—to shape a cultural consensus may be very limited.

Incentivising unionists to join (or even turn out to support) the DUP will not be easy, in a largely post-conflict Northern Ireland in which the constitutional question, if not finally resolved, has been parked. The DUP will need to oscillate between positive visions for the future—a strong economy and good education and public services—and cruder 'Stop Sinn Féin' messages.

The Remnants of Older Discourses

The 'Stop Sinn Féin' messages will be the modern outworking of the older discourse of fear evident within the DUP. In terms of attitudes to contemporary political institutions, it is noticeable that, whilst most receive support, despite the need to deal daily with Sinn Féin within them, North–South bodies are still not endorsed by DUP members. Older discourses of fear and caution are still evident. Given Northern Ireland's new era, the extent to which dissident republican violence is seen as a major threat may surprise and it is evident that a sizeable number of DUP members are not convinced by the 'end-of-(violent)-history' messages offered by either the Belfast or St Andrews Agreements. The reforms of policing are seen as risky and unnecessary and few see republican challenges to Northern Ireland—constitutional or otherwise—as concluded.

The dilution of Britishness is a continuing fear of members, even with their party being pre-eminent in government. Bitter disputes over the removal of the Union Flag from Belfast City Hall and over the routes of Orange Order parades have exposed the political impotence of the DUP in highly sensitive arenas. Members want nothing to do with a recasting of their Britishness towards a more neutral 'Northern Irish' identity, which has very few takers within the party. Many unionists are proud to say that they are from Northern Ireland, but not that they are Northern Irish. Most reject any form of Irish in their identity and the political outworking of that is the wholesale rejection of all-island institutions, however unthreatening to British identity or UK sovereignty.

The form of Protestant Britishness chosen by DUP members may of course be largely unrecognizable to their fellow British citizens. Its exaggerated regional sense derives from the historically contested status of Northern Ireland. The constitutional securities offered by successive political agreements have impacted upon DUP members and few believe that a united Ireland is imminent, or even likely in the longer term, but there is still a perception that republicans have not accepted this state of affairs. The particularistic form of identity is accompanied by religiously conditioned views probably closer to those found in the Britain of the mid-twentieth century, not the first part of the twenty-first. Some survey evidence suggests that only a minority of Britons now belong to a religion, whilst only one-third believe homosexuality is wrong and a majority support abortion rights.[3] These views are starkly at odds with what is found amongst the DUP membership, although those members are themselves products (albeit particularly 'robust' examples) of the more religiously conservative culture found in Northern Ireland.

The Future DUP

Given the continuing fears and insecurities of DUP members, the TUV might have offered a significant alternative repository. After all, most DUP members feel that nationalists benefited 'a lot more than unionists' from the peace process. That a significant outflanking of the DUP has not occurred reflects the leadership capacities within the DUP to steer their party, in contrast to the immediate post-Agreement chaos of the UUP. It also derives from the desire for power, however constrained, of the large number of elected members of the party and from the changing nature of the DUP, now more pragmatic and less fundamental. The DUP's dominance over rivals is also recognition of the lack of political alternatives to what is currently on offer.

The hegemonic position of the DUP within unionist politics is unlikely to be seriously challenged by the UUP, TUV, PUP, NI21, or any other unionist grouping in the near future. However, the party does face significant challenges on several fronts. It needs to galvanize an apathetic unionist electorate, barely half of which now votes at elections, into turning out for the unionist cause. High rates of unionist abstention may lead to Sinn Féin becoming the largest party in Northern Ireland, one which would concentrate minds on a DUP-UUP merger, although nationalist turnout is also now plummeting. While not an electoral problem, the disaffection evident amongst sections of the loyalist working class over issues of flags and parades will not easily be dealt with by the DUP, which as the main unionist party of government is now seen as part of an ill-defined 'establishment'. Many of the party's elected representatives tried to ride simultaneously the protest and 'respect for law' horses, empathizing with the protesters, but there are limits to what the DUP can possibly achieve on their behalf.

The DUP also needs to ensure that the commitment of recent joiners recruited on a rising tide is as great as those who stood by the party in its wilderness years. Many members acknowledge and endorse the changes they have seen within the party. One recently elected MLA spoke of how 'he was glad to see the back of the "reputation of blood and thunder" and the receptiveness to "new ideas"'.[4] These new ideas include a very different depiction of what the DUP's defence of the Union—and Northern Ireland's place within it—entails. One senior adviser put it as follows:

> Winning doesn't mean having fifty-two per cent of the people wanting to stay in the UK and them all being Protestants and having a single party government...the real victory is not to defeat people, but to persuade. The very fact that nationalists and Catholics now have a say in government is actually part of the success of Northern Ireland and part of the reason that support for Northern Ireland's position in the UK is so strong.[5]

Given the DUP's earlier history of support for majoritarian government, some may see this as chutzpah, but to future generations that is irrelevant. To sustain its victory, the DUP needs to undertake progressive work within and beyond what the former UUP leader David Trimble, wrongly dismissed as a 'Lundy', called a 'pluralist parliament for a pluralist people'[6] and engage in outreach to communities well beyond the party's comfort zone. The base foundations for that work have begun with a recasting of the DUP as a modern, professional, and outward-looking party, rather than the religious sect of old, but the journey is of the long-distance variety.

Notes

1. D. Gordon (2009) *The Fall of the House of Paisley*, Dublin: Gill & Macmillan.
2. BBC Northern Ireland, *Paisley: From Genesis to Revelation*, interview with Eamonn Mallie, 20 Jan. 2014.
3. National Centre for Social Research (2013) *British Social Attitudes: Findings*, Summary at <http://www.natcen.ac.uk/series/british-social-attitudes/25-years-of-bsa>, accessed Oct. 2013.
4. Interview with MLA, 9 Nov. 2012.
5. Interview with senior DUP adviser, 8 Feb. 2013.
6. Cited in D. Godson (2004) *Himself Alone: David Trimble and the Ordeal of Unionism*, London: HarperCollins, 381.

List of Interviewees and Focus Groups

Number	Name	Councillor/MLA/MP	Constituency/Council
1	Peter Martin	Councillor	North Down
2	William Walker	Councillor	Strangford
3	Robert Adair	Councillor	Strangford
4	Thomas Hogg	Councillor	Newtownabbey
5	Eddie Thompson	Councillor	Newtownards
6	John Hussey	Councillor	Belfast
7	James Tinsley	Councillor	Lisburn
8	Hazel Gamble	Councillor	Banbridge
9	William Leatham	Councillor and Mayor	Lisburn
10	Paula Bradley	Councillor	Newtownabbey
11	Alan Leslie	Councillor	North Down
12	Guy Spence	Councillor	Belfast
13	Victor Robinson	Councillor	Newtownabbey
14	Tom Haire	Councillor	Belfast
15	Pam Brown	MLA and Councillor	South Antrim
16	Jim Shannon	MP	Strangford
17	Mark Fielding	Councillor	Coleraine
18	John Finlay	Councillor	Ballymoney
19	Ian Stevenson	Councillor	Ballymoney
20	James Nicholl	Councillor	Ballymena
21	Beth Adger	Councillor	Ballymena
22	Maurice Bradley	Councillor	Coleraine
23	Sam Cole	Councillor	Coleraine
24	Christopher Stalford	Councillor	Belfast
25	Maurice Mills	Councillor	Coleraine
26	Billy Henry	Councillor	Ballymena
27	Lee Reynolds	Councillor	Belfast
28	Trevor Cummings	Councillor	Ards
29	Stephen Moutray	MLA	Craigavon
30	Drew Niblock	Councillor	Larne
31	Carla Lockhart	Councillor and Mayor	Craigavon
32	Darryn Causby	Councillor	Craigavon
33	Gladys McCullough	Councillor	Craigavon
34	Robert Smith	Councillor	Craigavon
35	Mark Baxter	Councillor	Craigavon
36	Sydney Anderson	MLA and Councillor	Craigavon

(*Continued*)

List of Interviewees and Focus Groups

Number	Name	Councillor/MLA/MP	Constituency/Council
37	Alistair Ross	MLA	East Antrim
38	Simon Hamilton	MLA	Strangford
39	Peter Weir	MLA	North Down
40	Jonathan Bell	MLA	Strangford
41	Thomas Buchanan	MLA	Omagh
42	Errol Thompson	Councillor	Omagh
43	Charlie Chittick	Councillor	Omagh
44	William Irwin	MLA	Newry and Armagh
45	David McIlveen	MLA	Antrim
46	Oliver Gibson	Councillor	Ballymena
48	Alan Graham	Councillor	North Down
49	Kim Ashton	Councillor	Dungannon
50	Charlie Johnston	Councillor	Carrickfergus
51	Paul Frew	MLA	Ballymena
52	Gareth McKee	Councillor	Belfast
53	Uel Martin	Councillor	Lisburn
54	Allan Ewart	Councillor	Lisburn
55	Andrew Ewing	Councillor	Lisburn
56	Roy Young	Councillor	Lisburn
57	Alex Easton	MLA	North Down
58	Ian McCrea	MLA and Councillor	Cookstown
59	Adrian McQuillan	MLA and Councillor	Coleraine
60	Gordon Dunne	MLA	North Down
61	Robin Newton	MLA	Castlereagh
62	William Humphrey	MLA	Belfast
63	Arlene Foster	MLA and Minister	Fermanagh
64	Anon	Stormont	Belfast
65	Jeffrey Donaldson	MP	Lagan Valley
67	William McCrea	MP	South Antrim
68	Gregory Campbell	MP	East Londonderry
69	Simon Hamilton	MLA	Strangford
70	Paul Girvan	MLA	South Antrim
71	Lord Maurice Morrow	MLA/DUP Chair	Fermanagh & South Tyrone
72	Jim Wells	MLA	South Down
73	Ian McCrea	MLA	Mid-Ulster
74	Gavin Robinson	Belfast Lord Mayor	Belfast
75	Gary Middleton	Councillor	Londonderry (Rural)
76	Gareth Robinson	Former Councillor	Castlereagh (East)
77	Billy Ashe	Mayor of Carrickfergus	Carrickfergus
78	Sharon Skillen	Councillor	Castlereagh (East)
79	Tommy Jeffers	Councillor	Castlereagh (East)
80	Nelson McCausland	MLA	Belfast (North)
81	Michelle McIlveen	MLA	Strangford
82	Paul Robinson	Councillor	Fermanagh (Erne East)

(*Continued*)

Number	Name	Councillor/MLA/MP	Constituency/Council
83	Cyril Brownlee	Councillor	Fermanagh (Enniskillen)
84	Bert Johnston	Councillor	Fermanagh (Erne North)
85	Alison Brimstone	Councillor	Fermanagh (Enniskillen)
86	Edwin Poots	MLA	Lagan Valley
87	Jim Allister	MLA/TUV Leader	North Antrim
88	Allan Bresland	Councillor	Strabane (Glenelly)
89	April Garfield-Kidd	Councillor	Londonderry
90	John Donnell	Councillor	Strabane (Glenelly)
91	Rhonda Hamilton	Councillor	Strabane (Glenelly)
92	Thomas Kerrigan	Councillor	Stranbane (Derg)
93	Sammy Wilson	MLA	East Antrim
94	Peter Robinson	MLA/DUP Leader	Belfast East
95	David Simpson	MP	Upper Bann
96	Nigel Dodds	MP/DUP Deputy Leader	Belfast (North)
97	Jimmy Spratt	MLA	Belfast (South)
98	Sammy Douglas	MLA	Belfast (East)
99	Jonathan Craig	MLA	Lagan Valley
100	Brenda Hale	MLA	Lisburn
101	Trevor Clarke	MLA	South Antrim
102	Paul Givan	MLA	Lagan Valley
103	William Hay	MLA	Foyle
104	David Hilditch	MLA	East Antrim
105	Mervyn Storey	MLA	North Antrim

List of Interviewees and Focus Groups

Focus Groups	Participants
Student Focus Group	David Brooks
	Philip Brett
	Ruth Maxwell
North Belfast Focus Group	John Fitzsimmons
	Philip Brett
	Brian Kingston, Councillor
	Naomi Thompson, Councillor
Fermanagh Focus Group	Jack Thompson
	Maurice Pogue
	Henry Mayne
	Austin Campbell
	Jeremy A. Campbell
	Andrew Wilson
	Paul Robinson, Councillor
Female Focus Group	Angela Robinson
	Alison Brimstone, Councillor
	Carla Lockhart, Councillor
	Sharon Skillen, Councillor
	Diannah Gott
	Carol Johnston
	Naomi Givan
	Gwen Egerton
Ballymena Focus Group	Andrew Burke
	Bill Kennedy, Councillor
	David Herd
	Samuel Thompson
	Linda Finlay
	Marian Stevenson
	Ian Stevension, Councillor
	Jason Atkinson, Councillor

Index

Index

Index

Paisley, Ian (*Cont.*)
Stormont, to 13, 84
Westminster, to 84
equality agenda 23
European elections 164
evangelicalism 11, 15, 31, 83–5, 87–8
First Minister, as 10, 37–8, 50, 51–4, 70, 85,
88–9, 96, 110, 123–4, 136, 141, 222
Free Presbyterian Church 7, 10, 70, 81,
140–2, 144
ideal type, Paisley as 84
IRA 12–13
Ireland 11–12, 59–60
launch of DUP 13
leader, as
DUP 1, 7, 18, 29, 31, 39, 51, 70–3, 110,
123–8, 140–1, 149, 183
First Minister, as 10, 37–8, 50, 51–4, 110
Free Presbyterian Church 7, 52, 70, 85,
88–9, 96, 123–4, 136, 141, 222
standing down 52, 54, 102, 110, 123–4,
128, 141, 222
Martyrs Memorial Church, removal as
minister from 141
new Paisleyism 123
Orange Order 149
Paisleyism 2, 11–16, 31, 39, 81–9, 102, 123,
133–7, 220, 223
parades 151
quasi-paramilitary elements, associations
with 12–13, 137
rhetoric/oratory 11–13, 52, 66, 84–5, 123,
125, 134, 136, 223
Robinsonism 223
'Save Ulster from Sodomy' campaign 153
Sinn Féin 1, 103, 169–70
St Andrews Agreement 2006 1, 39–46,
49–52, 101, 110, 123, 169–70, 172
standing down
DUP leader, as 54, 102, 110, 123–4, 128, 140–1
First Minister, as 52, 54, 110
leader of church, as 52, 123–4, 141, 222
Ulster Constitution Defence Committee
(UCDC) 84
Union, defence of the 1, 89, 120
UUP 84
violence 12–13
women 192
Paisley Jr, Ian 52, 114–15, 154–5
Paisley: Religion and Politics. **Bruce,**
Steve 2
Paisley, Rhonda 192
parades 120–1, 224–5
culture 151
Haass talks 152, 154
Orange Order 6, 151–2, 224
Parades Commission 151–2

working class 225
paramilitary activities, cessation of *see*
also **decommissioning**
Blair necessities formula 35
electoral politics 165
Independent Monitoring Commission 26,
36
pretence of ceasefire 91
St Andrews Agreement 2006 39, 41, 45, 47,
61, 100, 224
Ulster, threats to 6
patriarchy 212, 214
Patten, Chris 24–5, 68, 92, 94
Patterson, Henry 69
peace walls 148
personal advancement 72–3
Phillips, Jonathan 36, 42
Pledge of Office 50
police service and police reform
50/50 recruitment 60, 68, 93–4
accountability 94
age 93–4
Belfast Agreement 1998 22–7, 29, 31, 36–8,
68, 92–4, 220–1, 224
demographic attitudes 76
devolution 36–7, 52–5, 92
dissident republican threat, perceptions
of 96–8
Human Rights Commission, establishment
of 22
Independent Commission on Policing for
NI 24–5, 68, 92, 94
IRA 38, 95
Ministerial Pledge of Office 50
NI Policing Board 24
Orange Order 68, 94–5
Patten Report 24–5
Police Service of NI 6, 24, 61, 68–9, 92–3
quotas 60, 68, 93–4
religious background 24–5, 68
RUC, change from 24, 31, 68–9, 92–3, 127
security discourse 92–5
Seven Principles of DUP 26
Sinn Féin 6, 24–5, 36, 38, 52, 61, 68, 94–5,
170, 220–1
St Andrews Agreement 2006 52–3, 61, 95, 100
political discourses 82–104
altered discourses 100–4
British identity 75, 113
change 100–4
culture 83
demographic basis of DUP 74–6
dominant discourses 82–3
economic issues 4, 65, 75–6, 174, 178
existing beliefs, reinforcing or
changing 82–3
Free Presbyterian Church 133–7